What shall we tell
the children?

JOHN WREN-LEWIS

What shall we tell
the children?

Constable London

First published in 1971 by
Constable & Company Ltd
10 Orange Street, London WC 2H 7EG

Copyright © 1971 by John Wren-Lewis

ISBN 0 09 456050 1

Set in Monotype Garamond
Printed in Great Britain by
Ebenezer Baylis and Son Limited
The Trinity Press, Worcester, and London

Contents

Acknowledgements

I should like to thank the following publishers for permission to quote from recent books: S.C.M. Press, London, for *Honest to God* by Bishop John A. T. Robinson; Faber & Faber Ltd, London, and Harcourt Brace Jovanovich, Inc., New York, for *The Family Reunion* by T. S. Eliot; William Collins Sons & Co. Ltd, London, and Pantheon Books, Inc., New York, for *Memories, Dreams, Reflections* by C. G. Jung; Rider & Company, London, for *The Quiet Mind* by John E. Coleman.

Dear God,

    Are you real? Some people don't
not believe it. If you are you better do
something quick.

               Harriet Ann

                        from *Children's Letters to God*, compiled
                        by Eric Marshall and Stuart Hample

1: What this book is about

What shall we tell the children about religion? The question is a vexed one for parents and teachers all over the world today. The much-discussed issue of school religion in Britain only spotlights a far more widespread problem: the problem of living in a world where, for the first time in human history, the general climate of educated opinion has lost the religious assumptions that have hitherto been almost universal.

In this situation straightforward religious teaching of the traditional type is impossible, even for those who are still devoutly religious. Children detect at once any note of uncertainty in the voice of those who teach them, even if it is uncertainty disguised as defiant convic-tion. My own elder son was moved to declare himself an atheist at the age of twelve mainly because he was given religious instruction by a very convinced Christian teacher, whose desire to hold her convic-tions against the general unbelief of modern society was so great that the boy felt at once that something was being put over on him. Even in the protected atmosphere of a religious home-and-school combina-tion the uncertainty and scepticism of the general educated public will seep through, both in the assumptions on which books are written in almost all other fields of interest, and in the tendency of would-be teachers of religion, whether parents or professionals, to protest just a little too much. And once a child detects uncertainty concealed, his confidence in his elders is undermined – a consequence which can sometimes do grave harm to his whole development, and will certainly preclude the growth of the conviction his mentors are trying to give him.

Yet, on the other hand, not even the most convinced atheist can seriously maintain that teaching about religion should be completely abandoned. A child brought up in total ignorance of religion would be unable to make any sense of most of the world's history, social customs, legal traditions or artistic productions – and he would also find considerable difficulty in coping with the fact that religious ideas and practices continue to hold a grip on vast numbers of people, often in very crude forms. Some friends of mine who tried to bring up their little boy without 'contaminating his mind with religious nonsense' had to deal during his first weeks at school not just with puzzlement, but with quite serious emotional disturbance following his encounter with a Roman Catholic boy who told him there was a God who would kill you if you 'did a sin'. It was no use merely assuring him that this was nonsense, for his confidence in his parents' ability to understand the world had been shattered and, moreover, deep-rooted irrational fantasies had been activated in his mind, which were impervious to purely rational argument.

The same kind of shock can afflict children of enlightened agnostic parents when they encounter references to hell in literature for the first time, or hear in history lessons of war, bloodshed and torture having taken place in the name of religion. On the other hand, it may well be the parents who experience a shock, at finding religious fantasies springing up spontaneously from their own children whom they thought they had protected from corruption by superstition. A very famous atheist scientist of my acquaintance, and his almost equally famous wife of like persuasion, were ironically amused to hear their five-year-old son, who had been very carefully told nothing about religion, explain that it did not matter that his favourite teddy bear had been forgotten when they went on holiday, because, 'he can see me and hear me everywhere I go, and help me to be good'. And even in Communist countries, where there is actually atheistic indoctrination in schools, it seems impossible to exorcise religious ideas completely: there seems to be no lack of vigorous young men coming forward for the barely-tolerated priesthood, and the young atheist intellectuals begin to flirt with religious notions as soon as censorship is relaxed.

It would seem that the whole problem of religion in education needs to be looked at much more deeply than is commonly done, either by educators or evangelists, and this involves nothing less than trying to understand the unprecedented transition through which humanity's beliefs about life are currently passing. The common habit is for evangelists and religiously-minded teachers to think of this transition simply as a widespread defection of the human race from truth and spiritual values, which they have to resist as best they can, while atheists tend to take the equally *simpliste* view that we are witnessing the all-too-slow dawn of enlightenment in a world hitherto submerged by superstitious ignorance; but neither of these assumptions comes anywhere near to doing justice to the real human facts of our situation. As I shall try to show in detail in due course, each of these views is blind to the fact that there is truth and vital human value in the opposite view. An even less satisfactory position, however, is the milk-and-water agnosticism with which many people have tried to dodge the problem. This establishes a totally unreal kind of neutrality and tolerance by ignoring *all* the vital human facts associated with belief and unbelief. It is utterly fatuous to tell children 'People used to believe in all sorts of gods, and in heaven and hell after death, but now many people don't, and we can never know anyhow.' In these terms it is impossible to see how anyone could ever have slaved to build pyramids or copy Bibles, ever have gone to war, ever have castrated themselves or tortured others, ever have inflicted or suffered martyrdom, in the name of religion; it is not even really possible to understand what it means to fight passionately against religion in the name of science or free thought, when the issue is reduced to such banal terms as these.

Mankind's changing attitude to religion is a vitally important thing, affecting every part of human life, and it needs to be understood in its full psychological depth. It needs to be understood not only by teachers and parents who have to try to say something to children about religion, *but also by the children themselves,* for they will have to live in a world where this change is one of the dominant factors in their whole cultural situation. It is sometimes said, for example by representatives of the British 'Establishment' who wish to justify the current law making Christian instruction the general rule, that it is wrong to impose the burden of uncertainty on children until they are nearing school-leaving age, but the fact is that it cannot be avoided today, whether it is desirable in theory to avoid it or not. It is far better that even the youngest children should be made aware of the world's uncertainty, than that they should become uncertain of their parents' or teachers' honesty through being presented with a conviction that cannot, in the nature of things today, be unruffled. When a subject is open to doubt, the only safe way of presenting it even to children is to bring the doubt into the open and seek to understand it. And on this particular issue, doubt and uncertainty is precisely what children need to understand in order to cope with the world they will face as they grow up.

The purpose of this book is to show just how children may be brought to understand the change that is taking place in humanity's beliefs about life, and how, on the basis of this understanding, parents or teachers of any religion or none can help their young charges to see something of the inner meaning of all the various alternatives of belief or unbelief open to them. It is an approach which should make it possible for schoolteachers in Britain to use the compulsory periods of religious instruction to positive advantage, irrespective of their own personal convictions – not suppressing these convictions in any way, but declaring them openly as their own choices amongst the alternative possibilities that have been displayed. It is often said that an objective approach of this kind is impossible, because there can be no real neutral ground between belief and unbelief. But my conviction is that neutral ground can be found simply by penetrating below the surface of most of our ordinary approaches, and starting from the elementary facts of personal experience, in terms of which belief and unbelief alike have meaning.

Because the book is written for adults and not for children themselves I have written it in adult language, trying to take account of relevant trends in contemporary thought wherever possible, while avoiding the use of specialised philosophical, theological or psychological terminology and argument except in cases where its meaning can be made clear in more ordinary language. Thus, for example, I have throughout kept in view the fact that in the modern world it is increasingly difficult, if not impossible, to talk of religious issues in terms of any one religion alone. I fully realise that a Sunday-school teacher talking to seven-year-olds will not have much occasion in the ordinary way to take account of contemporary propaganda in favour of Buddhism or other eastern styles of mystical religion, but it would be fatal for him to be unaware of the fact that his young charges will be bound to encounter this influence, however inarticulately, before many more years have gone by, if only by hearing of the latest pop star's adoption of some *guru*. (Indeed, with the current rate of immigration from non-Christian countries, growing numbers of children are likely to come into contact with other religions even at the earliest ages, so perhaps a Sunday-school teacher needs to consider revising his teaching to take account of these changed conditions, and the basic approach of this book may be of some use in helping him to work out how to do so.) Again, I have throughout assumed at least a basic smattering of knowledge of traditional Christian and Biblical ideas, although at least some teachers I know tell me they have to deal with children who have never heard of Christ except as a swear-word. I suspect them of some exaggeration, but even if it is true it does not alter the fact that they will need a standpoint from which to start saying anything about Christ, and I have tried to provide the kind of basis which will make it possible to see why 'Christ' *is* a swear-word.

At the same time, this is not a technical book, but a book written at speed to meet a growing and urgent need, which is my own personal need as a parent, as much as anyone else's. This is why I have tried to

4

avoid elaborate technical terminology or argument, and have been deliberately impressionistic rather than exhaustive in my accounts of the historical development of our present situation. For example, I make a number of references to one or two of the best-known names in the early days of the so-called 'conflict between science and religion' without mentioning other figures who would certainly need to be mentioned in a full scholarly account, because such scholarship would be quite out of place in a book like this, and the better-known names serve quite adequately to illustrate my points. On the other hand there are other points in the book where I give considerable prominence to lesser-known figures, who I believe had things to say of particular importance to my theme (such as the French thinker Auguste Comte) to the neglect of much better-known names who would certainly have to be mentioned in a technical philosophical treatise (such as the British sceptical philosophers Locke and Hume). This is quite deliberate, since I am not writing a philosophical treatise and it would be altogether inappropriate to overburden a book like this with detail of this sort. For those who wish to follow up special issues of this kind I have provided at the end of the book a critical reading list relevant to each chapter, but even this is limited for the most part to books capable of being appreciated by non-specialists.

I see no reason why older children should not be able to use this book directly, for it is to a considerable extent based on discussions I have had over the past ten years with sixth formers in Britain and, to a lesser degree, with their European and North American equivalents. I cannot claim any expertise as a teacher, however, and am only an amateur parent, so I have not attempted to work out any detailed lessons for younger children. I have given hints of lines of approach where I have thought them appropriate, but my main task has been to create a general understanding for adults and then leave them to work out their detailed lessons for their own circumstances, probably better than I could ever do.

The structure of the book should be obvious from the table of contents. Chapters Two to Seven represent a general diagnosis of the situation we face today in understanding religion. Chapter Eight, which is as long as the rest of the book put together, is an outline course of religious discussion based on this diagnosis, giving practical guidance both to teachers and parents about how they may pursue understanding of some of the major religious issues of our time either amongst themselves or in actual encounter with older children. Any reader who finds the discussion of Chapters Two to Seven hard going at any point might like to skip them and go straight to Chapter Eight to see how my ideas work out in practical terms, and then come back to the earlier chapters to see how I have arrived at various major conclusions. Chapter Nine sums up the whole argument by putting forward such practical suggestions as I have to make – strictly as a non-professional – about issues like talking to younger children, how to deal with controversial problems like that of psychedelic drugs, and what future we may envisage for school assemblies and other forms of religious worship.

2: Coming to terms with a haunted world

All questions of belief and doubt, in relation to religion or anything else, arise from the fact that human beings have imagination. Other species may have rudiments of it too, but the characteristic of human kind is that we *never* merely react to what is around us with straight-forward biological responses. Our most mundane perceptions of scenes or situations, people or things, are shot through with images of other scenes, other perspectives, other situations, other persons or other relationships with the same person, other things or other aspects of the same thing. Each of us lives in a world haunted by images and impressions that do not come directly out of what we have perceived, and this is what makes it possible for us to conceive of gods or demons, heavens or hells, miracles or morals. It is also, however, the basis of all art, all science, indeed all thought of any kind – and equally of day-dreaming, hallucination, self-deception and insanity. Issues of belief and doubt arise from the fact that the possibility of delusion is a neces-sary concomitant of being human.

If it were possible to discipline the inner life of imagination in such a way that its contents always corresponded directly to the immediate (or remembered) facts of ordinary common experience, the result would be a purely animal life shorn of all distinctively human charac-teristics. On the other hand, a life lived entirely without proper reference to the facts of ordinary common experience is an insane life. The question is, what is 'proper reference'? In childhood the issue is often blurred, but as the child grows up into society he learns, usually without being aware that he is doing so, certain criteria by which he is expected to distinguish sane, creative uses of imagination from meaningless fantasy. Every society expects its members to know generally (although not usually articulately) how to tell contents of the inner world that 'mean something' from those that are 'wholly

B

subjective'. The significant thing about our society today is that, for the first time in history, humanity has begun to change its mind in a fundamental way about this basic psychological question. The changes that have been overtaking mankind's attitude to religion during the past two or three centuries spring from this, but so also do most of the other social problems that face us today.

The traditional assumption, which we all still make for much of our lives, is that imagination is valuable insofar as it enables us to understand features of the world that in common experience are hidden from us – concealed meanings in situations, underlying structures in things, realms of being unperceived in the ordinary course of events. In other words, it is assumed that the images, ideas and impressions of the inner life must correspond to *something* in the universe outside us if they are not to lead us into delusion or insanity, so that those which are not derived directly from the ordinary world of common experience must be delusions *unless* they correspond to realities which in some way or other exist beyond the world of common experience. For example, since our perceptions of the point of a needle can pass over into images of atomic particles dancing in it or of angels dancing on it, the traditional assumption is that we shall be sane and capable of creative action with needles if we settle for the image that corresponds to the true underlying reality, but insane and deluded if we spend any time imagining needles in ways which have no relation to their real underlying nature. Again, a stroke of ill fortune can be imagined as pure chance, or as a subtle evil influence exerted by an enemy, or as a lesson imposed by a higher power wishing to teach us patience or humility, and probably in many other ways: the traditional assumption is that our response to such ill fortune will be sane if it corresponds to the truth, deluded otherwise. Yet again, a human relationship can be conceived as anything between a contract and an invisible spiritual bond: the traditional assumption is that our conduct will be sensible or disastrous according to whether what we imagine is correct or not. And we can imagine death as entry into an undiscovered country (heaven or hell, or a new incarnation), or as absorption into the Universal Consciousness, or as merely ceasing upon the midnight: the traditional assumption is that if one of these ideas is true, then conduct based on any other is likely to be madness.

This traditional view of the business of human living implies that the cardinal need in everyone's life is to arrive at some truly authoritative understanding of what the realities behind the scenes of common experience are like, either by trying to work out logically what the realities behind the scenes must be like in order to produce the phenomena we actually experience in the common-or-garden world, or else by intuiting that some particular group of images represent a direct vision or revelation of the underlying realities. These two approaches have been regarded as complementary in most human societies, and indeed in both cases the fundamental appeal is to the authority of wisdom – on the one hand, the wisdom of those who can tell a genuine logical deduction from a fallacy, on the other, the wisdom of those who in some way or other convey conviction of genuine insight.

This view of life is so deeply ingrained in all the world's educational systems, formal and informal, primitive and sophisticated, that most of us go through life without appreciating that there is any alternative; disagreements about belief are interpreted and discussed as if they were all disagreements about whose insight is correct or, more commonly, about the relative claims of revelation and reason. The most important doubts and disagreements of our modern world, however, are much more fundamental than this. They arise from the fact that the last three centuries have seen the steady growth and spread of an entirely new approach to the whole business of distinguishing meaningful uses of imagination from delusory ones. Some parts of the world have not yet been much affected by this revolution, but everyone in the industrialized world employs the new approach for some parts of his life, even people rooted in conservative traditions. Very few of us, on the other hand, realise when we are doing so, or appreciate just why there is a clash with traditional habits of thought even when we feel the clash. In fact, the new approach has not yet been much articulated even in the natural sciences where it has had its greatest influence, although its existence has been recognised in that field, and a name coined to describe it: the experimental method.

In popular discussion the experimental method is commonly equated, often by its most vociferous advocates, with appeal to reason as against revelation (or intuition), but it is really something utterly different from either. Its crucial feature is that *any* idea, whether arrived at by intuition or by logic, should be subjected to rigorous experimental test. This means being prepared to abandon an idea, however logical or authoritative, if it fails to stand up to experimental test, and, even more important, it means constructing new experiments deliberately designed to expose ideas – new and established alike – to the possibility of being refuted by failing the test of practical application. Such a procedure would have seemed quite insane in any of the great civilisations of the past; it would have seemed like asking for trouble, going out of the way to make difficulties for yourself in a world which is already quite difficult enough. The point is very nicely made in a story told by the anthropologist Evans-Pritchard about the pre-scientific thought of the Azande tribe concerning the operation of the oracle

9

which they believed to govern all life. The oracle was consulted by feeding a poisonous plant in a ritual manner to specially-prepared fowl: if the fowl died the omen was unfavourable, if not, favourable. Evans-Pritchard asked the Azande chiefs what their reaction would be if the same question were addressed twice to the oracle and received contradictory answers, to which the chiefs replied that only a white man would be such a fool as to waste good oracle-poison in so prodigal a fashion. Pressed, they explained that of course it would simply mean that a slip had been made in the ritual, or perhaps that a hostile tribe was interfering.

I have found that this story commonly evokes laughter, but at some time in our lives we all take this attitude towards some of our beliefs, and it is a perfectly rational attitude so long as the basic assumption is made that the purpose of our thinking is to arrive at a firm truth about the nature of things so that life may be lived on the basis of reality rather than illusion. On this assumption it is natural to hold on to any belief that is regarded as authoritatively established and interpret the facts of life in terms of it, explaining discrepancies in the same kind of way as the Azande chiefs did. The belief may possibly be shattered if life throws up too many discrepancies – if, in Aristotle's famous phrase, it too obviously fails 'to save the phenomena' – but if so the result is a conversion to new beliefs, accompanied by something of an upheaval in habits of living: not the kind of thing that can be contemplated as a common occurrence, and certainly not something to be actively sought. The experimental method implies that an utterly different assumption is being made about the purpose of thinking, although so far not many people, even scientists, have consciously articulated the fact. It implies that the products of the imagination are being judged, not by whether they correspond to something that exists, but in terms of the practical actions they suggest and the viability of those actions: in other words, imagination and perception are no longer being considered in analogous terms. The experimental method implies an entirely new way of coming to terms with our haunted world. It implies seeing it as haunted, not by images of possible or actual realities hidden behind the scenes, but rather by images of ways in which things might change, or be made to change, in the future.

On this view, the important thing about any ideas we may have on the subject of needles is not whether they are 'true' in the sense of corresponding to unperceived facts about needles, but whether they enable us to do something new and interesting with needles. If ideas of atoms and electrons in the point of a needle are preferred to ideas of angels dancing on it, it is not because we have some authoritative reason for thinking that atoms and electrons exist while angels do not, but simply because the one idea is found in practice to lead to new and unexpected uses of metal (for example, electrical uses), while the other has – so far – no such practical application. In the same way, the view of life implied by the experimental method means that any ideas we might form about strokes of ill-fortune, human relationships or death are to be judged in terms of their practical value for living rather than as descriptions of what the world is 'really like' behind the scenes, and modern doubts about traditional religious views on these matters arise, not from the conviction that there are authoritative grounds for believing that the religious views are false, but because these views seem uninteresting and meaningless in that they do not seem to be of a kind which can be experimentally verified in practical action.

Because only a few people have yet succeeded in articulating their doubts in this way, the issue is commonly confused by being treated as if it *were* a matter of which beliefs are held to be 'true' and which 'false', and in particular this confusion has shown itself in the continual discussions that have taken place over the past three centuries about whether or not the progress of science was undermining religious belief. Significantly, the first major figure in history to be involved in a 'conflict between science and religion' was also one of the first great pioneers of the experimental method, the sixteenth-century Italian astronomer/physicist Galileo Galilei, but it is commonly assumed, in popular and scholarly thought alike, that his clash with the Inquisition was a straightforward conflict of beliefs about whether the sun was a planet of the earth, as had been traditionally supposed, or vice versa, with little relation to his experiments on sliding weights down inclined planes. Yet the truth is that the Pope had already authorised Copernicus's sun-centred astronomical theories as a basis for calculating calendar revisions, and within a generation of Galileo's time the great majority of intelligent ecclesiastics had agreed, with the general support of scientists, that belief in a Divine Mover could not really be supposed to depend upon any particular theory about the precise shape of planetary orbits, or indeed on any specific view of the physical heavens. Indeed, scientists as well as theologians were prepared to argue that the vistas of cosmic regularity opened up by new astronomy gave more grounds than ever for believing in a Divine Mover, but this had no success whatever in preventing the spread of a feeling of conflict between science and religion throughout Europe, affecting all classes of the population – a feeling which grew apace during the following centuries.

Seeking to explain this curious phenomenon – which, as I shall show later, has been repeated at every major phase of the history of the so-called 'conflict of science and religion' – some writers have stated that the conflict occurred because the Galilean view undermined religion psychologically, since once the earth could no longer be thought of as the centre of the universe, people inevitably doubted whether humanity could possibly have the significance implied by Christianity. This, however, is a pure misunderstanding, based on inadequate knowledge of traditional religious cosmology, and it was never thought to be the issue at the time. On the contrary, in mediaeval Christian thought the centre of the universe was held to be a place of special *in*significance – the lowest place, farthest removed from God, who was supposed to dwell in the outermost spheres beyond the fixed stars. Man was held to have been relegated to the surface of the earth because his fall had condemned him to near-destruction: the only lower place in the mediaeval Christian universe was hell itself, which was supposed to be at the earth's centre.

The real cause of the conflict which Galileo precipitated was not the content of his astronomical theories at all, but the basis on which he put them forward. He suggested that the debate between the heliocentric and the geocentric views of the solar system could be settled by looking through a telescope at the moons of Jupiter, and to us today, with the benefit of hindsight, the story that people refused to look down his telescope is apt to seem almost incredible. By mankind's traditional standards, however, to which most of us still adhere for much of our lives, it would be Galileo's proposal which would seem absurd to the point of perversity, just as Evans-Pritchard's views seemed perverse to the Azande chiefs. How could the sight of a few specks of light through pieces of glass possibly cast doubt on the reasoning of generations of the most authoritative scholars? If people had been meant to look at the heavens through pieces of glass, God would have provided us with pieces of glass in front of our eyes from birth; any conclusion drawn from such artificial means of observation would seem likely to have curiosity value at best, and to be capable of misleading people gravely if taken too seriously. In fact, Galileo's use of the telescope, which we today would tend to think of as pure observation, would seem from the traditional point of view to be just as much an experiment – i.e., the creation of an artificial situation -- as his laboratory experiments on the rates at which bodies slide down inclined planes. His willingness to set such artificial operations at the centre of his scientific work betrayed that he had implicitly abandoned the whole traditional approach to natural science as a source of clues to the hidden meaning of things, in favour of a fundamental concern with how human action might change things.

Although no one at the time (not even Galileo himself) was in a position to articulate this explicitly, the Inquisition quite correctly sensed that the spread of such an attitude to life could undermine people's willingness to accept traditional authority on any subject. Once people cease to be primarily interested in realities which are supposed to lie behind the scenes of common experience, they will inevitably begin to lose interest in what authority has to say about the nature of such realities. So Galileo was threatened with torture and persuaded to recant, but the revolutionary attitude for which he stood was already spreading like wildfire all over Europe, producing its effects in social upheavals of many different kinds. It was the birth of a situation which the world had never seen before, but which today dominates the human scene throughout the world – a situation in which life is shot through with the most radical of all kinds of conflict, conflict about what constitutes a sane approach to life.

This is the situation which we have to try to understand, so that we can convey something of that understanding to our children. In recent years this task has been made a great deal easier because the situation has been given a new and illuminatingly simple name – the 'two cultures' situation. The term derives from C. P. Snow, in his now classic lecture on *The Two Cultures and the Scientific Revolution*, but all too few of those who quote Snow have yet appreciated the full breadth and depth of his analysis. Many people, including many who bandy the expression about most frequently, still suppose it to refer merely to a relatively minor defect of the British educational system, the inability of 'arts' and 'science' faculties in British universities to understand each other's terminology. The whole point of Snow's analysis of this specific problem, however, was to show it as a symptom of a much deeper division in our society between two different 'ways of responding to life' (Snow's rather elegant definition of the anthropologist's word 'culture') – one, a very traditional way of responding to life exemplified by (but by no means restricted to) the ethos of classical Greek and Roman civilisation, the other a relatively new arrival on the human scene, a way of responding to life exemplified by the 'scientific revolution' of the sixteenth and seventeenth centuries and the subsequent development of industrial civilisation. Perhaps even Snow himself did not fully appreciate the breadth or the depth of the conflict, and there may be many detailed points on which his analysis of it can be faulted, but he must nevertheless be ranked as a major prophetic figure of our time for having identified and named a most important (perhaps the most important) phenomenon of recent history. The conflict between the two cultures is now going on all over the world, affecting every aspect of human life, and to some extent it goes on inside almost every one of us, for there must be very few people indeed in the modern world (except perhaps in very remote underdeveloped territories) who do not partake to some degree of both attitudes to life. And the most distinctive of all symptoms of the conflict is the fact that the unprecedented surge forward of science and technology over the past two hundred years or so has been accompanied by the first major decline in popular allegiance to religion that the human race has ever seen.

3: Cultures in conflict

Some of the most powerful attempts that have yet been made to articulate the conflict of basic attitudes which began in the sixteenth century were made at that very time, and in England. While Galileo recanted before the Inquisition, his English contemporary, Francis Bacon, Lord Verulam, wrote a number of books quietly urging that a revolution in science should be consciously planned by the deliberate foundation of institutions for the practice of 'experimental philosophy', and he suggested that these should seek patronage from the Establishment, in the person of the English Crown, precisely because they would inevitably find themselves revolutionising the whole of society. Meanwhile William Shakespeare, who as far as we can tell was utterly uninterested in matters of science (one of the strongest reasons for believing that he was *not* a mere front-man for Bacon), was pouring out plays which analysed the impact of the new outlook on morality, social life and religion with an accuracy which has rarely been equalled since.

The fears which probably led the Inquisition to condemn Galileo, and which have since disturbed people again and again as they have faced the rise of the new outlook, have never been better expressed than in the famous speech which Shakespeare put into the mouth of his character Ulysses in the play *Troilus and Cressida*. Society must be rooted, Ulysses asserts, in a revelation of the hidden plan underlying the construction of the universe, since human beings are thereby enabled to know their proper places in relation to one another by fitting into the plan, and the authority of those who rule in society can be seen as part of the same Grand Scheme whereby the lion rules over the beasts of the forest, the eagle over the birds of the air, gold over the minerals of the earth and the sun over the other planets:

15

> The heavens themselves, the planets, and this centre,
> Observe degree, priority, and place,
> Insisture, course, proportion, season, form,
> Office, and custom, in all line of order.
> And therefore is the glorious planet Sol
> In noble eminence enthroned and sphered
> Amidst the other; whose med'cinable eye
> Corrects the ill aspects of planets evil,
> And posts like the commandment of a king,
> Sans check, to good and bad.

Should man ever lose this sense of a universal plan, Ulysses goes on to
say, society will break up into chaos, and even the order of nature itself
will be threatened:

> . . . O when degree is shaked,
> Which is the ladder to all high designs,
> The enterprise is sick. How could communities,
> Degrees in schools, and brotherhoods in cities,
> Peaceful commerce from dividable shores,
> The primogenity and due of birth,
> Prerogative of age, crowns, sceptres, laurels,
> But by degree stand in authentic place?
> Take but degree away, untune that string,
> And hark what discord follows. Each thing meets
> In mere oppugnancy. The bounded waters
> Should lift their bosoms higher than the shores,
> And make a sop of all this solid globe.
> Strength should be lord of imbecility,
> And the rude son should strike his father dead.
> Force should be right, or rather right and wrong,
> Between whose endless jar justice resides,
> Should lose their names, and so should justice too.
> Then every thing includes itself in power,
> Power into will, will into appetite,
> And appetite, an universal wolf,
> So doubly seconded with will and power,
> Must make perforce an universal prey,
> And last eat up himself.

It is impossible to tell whether Shakespeare took this view of the
matter himself. Undoubtedly many of the characters in his other plays
who are critical of the traditional view of things are villains – most

notably, perhaps, Edmund in *King Lear*, with his dismissal of the traditional outlook as 'excellent foppery o' the world', which he uses as an excuse for murder and war. On other occasions, however, the traditional social schemes of 'degree' are themselves shown to be cloaks for the very vices they purport to control – witness, in *Julius Caesar* 'The fault, dear Brutus, lies not in our stars but in ourselves', and the ending of *Lear*, where the King sees the need to justify his rule in terms of concrete good done to his subjects, even to the point 'where distribution should undo excess'. All we can say for certain is that Shakespeare gave superb expression both to the new social and moral attitudes emerging in his day and to the anxieties they aroused amongst people who still held the traditional outlook, and he did the same for the changes that were taking place in the role of the arts in society, in relation to his own art of drama.

It has long been recognised that the advice he made Hamlet give the Players contains a good deal of sound theatrical wisdom derived from his own stage experience: what is not so widely recognised, largely because of the changing use of language, is that this famous speech also contains a description of the traditional philosophy of drama. The appeal to tradition is deliberately emphasised: Hamlet refers to the purpose of playing 'whose end, both at the first and now, was and is to hold, as 'twere, the mirror up to nature'. But this is no mere assertion that a play should 'be like life': Shakespeare was certainly not presenting an apology for stage naturalism in advance of his time. His mirror was, in fact, not an ordinary looking-glass at all, but one that would be capable of showing 'the very age and body of the time, his form and pressure' – an expression which loses its force today, when we are wont to speak in a naturalistic sense of 'the pressure of events', but which in Elizabethan times would have been seen at once to have had a direct occult reference. 'Pressure' in Elizabethan usage meant 'impression', the impression of the sealing-ring upon the wax, so that the nearest modern term would be 'signature'. The mirror was to show the *signature* of the time – the reference being to the ancient magico-religious doctrine that all things and all events have their own particular signatures, or secret names, by which their inner occult essences may be grasped, understood and perhaps even controlled. Hamlet's reference was in fact to the well-known magical use of mirrors whereby they are supposed to reflect, not the ordinary situation, but the hidden spiritual forces controlling the situation – the force of scorn, the force of virtue, or whatever, and behind these the *astrological* forces determined by the age of the time and its position in the invisible 'long body' of history. Drama was supposed, in other words, to make the audience aware of the hidden spiritual significance of some situation in which they themselves participated. That was why Greek drama could serve as a ritual of social significance, and equally it was why Hamlet could expect his play to catch the conscience of the King.

Shakespeare articulated this traditional philosophy against the background of a recognition that growing numbers of people in his own audiences would no longer be seeing either life or drama in that light; at the close of one of his very last plays the character Prospero, into whom, many scholars believe, Shakespeare projected something of himself, is made deliberately to renounce the role of magician and conjurer of occult powers:

> . . . But this rough magic
> I here abjure . . .
> . . . I'll break my staff,
> Bury it certain fathoms in the earth,
> And deeper than did ever plummet sound
> I'll drown my book.

Not until our own century has there been such clear articulation of the way in which mankind's newly-developing outlook necessarily changes the role of the arts.

Until quite recently, for example, it was widely assumed that perspective began to be commonly used in post-Renaissance painting simply because this was the first point in history at which artists understood how to draw in perspective – although scholars knew perfectly well that mediaeval architects understood perspective well enough to narrow streets in order to make them seem longer, and there is evidence of similar understanding in Greek paintings and Egyptian carvings. The truth is now being grasped that artists prior to the Renaissance were simply not interested in the question of perspective for most of the time, because their concern was precisely to bring out the fact that objects in the ordinary world of experience should be seen first and foremost as symbols of realities behind the veil rather than as self-sufficient solid entities. Painters would depict justice, chastity, greed, and so on as personal beings in combat, not merely because they wanted a nice allegory for representing abstractions to the simple-minded, but because these qualities were believed to be produced by the indwelling in people's souls of real quasi-personal beings in the occult world. Similarly modern criticism has shown that poets traditionally used metaphor, not merely as a stronger variant of simile, but because they were trying to show their public a real occult identity between two different things. A king could be described as a lion because the same archetypal leonine power in the universe was believed to govern both the animal and the man in their performance of their different functions. With the decline of this whole outlook in the period since the Renaissance, the traditional symbolic function of art has necessarily seemed to be undermined in precisely the same way as moral authority in society has seemed to be undermined, and the modern critics who have analysed the situation have frequently spoken in terms of a 'dissociation of sensibility', a 'disinherited mind'. Shakespeare, on the other hand, may well have taken a more optimistic view. There is surely a hopeful rather than a despairing note struck when, at the very end of *The Tempest*, Prospero turns the conventional speech to the audience into a statement of the dramatist's new role as one who speaks simply for himself:

> Now my charms are all o'erthrown,
> And what strength I have's mine own.

In the centuries that have followed Shakespeare's death, the new outlook has spread to such an extent that it is no longer merely a disturbing trend of unrest amongst a minority, but has begun to affect the 'public philosophy' in most countries throughout the westernised world, and its spread has commonly been associated with optimistic feeling. Probably the most important factor in bringing this about has been the enormous achievements which have followed the adoption of the new outlook in the scientific field, not only advances in knowledge but, even more important for general public opinion, applications of science in industry. These have changed the whole character of practical human life more in the last three hundred years than it had ever changed before in the entire course of human history. The fact that these changes have occurred is itself a sign of the new outlook even apart from the fact that they sprang from the experimental revolution in science; for deliberate attempts to change the physical conditions of life or established habits of living and working would seem like dangerous blasphemy to people taking the traditional attitude to the world, in which the ordinary course of nature is assumed to be the manifestation of some hidden divine plan. Indeed, the industrial revolution, which in its first stages was to a considerable degree independent of the scientific revolution, *did* to begin with seem like dangerous blasphemy to a great many people in all classes of the community, and the feeling is far from dead today, even in the industrialised societies: in fact in the second half of the twentieth century it has undergone a considerable revival with the widespread concern about pollution. Apprehension about industrialisation is never just a matter of resistance to particular unpleasant consequences such as overcrowding in cities or atmospheric pollution, which are, after all, just as apparent to industrialisers and technologists as to anyone else, and in sheerly practical terms have simply to be seen as problems to be solved, weighing up the gains of industrialisation against the unpleasantnesses of pre-industrial communities. When such problems lead to worries about the propriety of industrialisation *as such*, as they often do, it is because of a conviction, deep-rooted in all the world's traditions, that the practical business of human life should properly be a kind of ritual in which human beings cultivate nature along the general lines of nature's own underlying Grand Design. The industrial revolution, and the subsequent technological application of new scientific knowledge, has been possible only because increasing numbers of people in western society came, whether they knew it explicitly or not, to regard work as a matter of achieving practical changes rather than as a ritual with value in itself, and to regard nature as raw material for human action rather than as the manifestation of any kind of Grand Design: good results and bad alike would have been impossible unless people had taken this new way of looking at the world.

Very few people did know it explicitly, of course, and one of the paradoxes of the past three centuries has been that scientists have been amongst the last people to grasp the implications of what was happening, even though it was in their field that the new outlook on life found its most consistent expression (in the general acceptance of the experimental method as the central discipline). The great scientific pioneers who founded the Royal Society in England, a generation after the time of Galileo and Bacon, came very close to formulating the essential point by giving an unusual twist to the language of the established religion. They asserted (following Bacon) that the knowledge mankind should now be interested in seeking, the knowledge of 'experimental philosophy' as contrasted with traditional 'scholastic philosophy', was the kind of knowledge which would enable human beings to fulfil the promise of the Book of Genesis and exercise dominion over nature. In subsequent generations, however, this clarity of recognition of the essentially practical character of scientific knowledge tended to be lost, even by scientists directly concerned with discoveries that were applied in technology. The generality of the scientific community has tended, right up to our own times, to interpret its findings in traditional terms, as discoveries about hidden realities (atoms, chemical bonds, electrical forces, gravitational fields and the like) underlying the phenomena of the world of ordinary experience. Today, it is gradually beginning to dawn on the more philosophically-minded scientists that this cannot be a correct way of looking at the matter. In modern physics, progress is impossible if it is assumed that the aim is to describe real entities underlying experience, since the formulae which work in practice would be mutually contradictory if they *were* descriptions: thus matter would have to be described as composed of waves and at the same time of particles which can move from one place to another without passing through the space in between. This kind of thing makes sense only if scientific concepts are consciously recognised to be what scientific philosophers call 'operational constructs', practical formulae for enabling human beings to imagine new (and usually more complicated) experimental actions, and not descriptions at all – and this, far from being a peculiar limitation of modern physics, is actually implied wherever science is based on the experimental method. Atoms, chemical bonds, electrical forces, gravitational fields and the rest are all, in experimental science, tools of the imagination for securing hitherto unsuspected forms of practical action rather than realities supposed to underlie the ordinary world of experience. This has shown through clearly in the actual behaviour of scientists even when they have failed to recognise it: over the past three centuries science has progressed to a degree undreamt of by scholars of earlier ages, precisely because scientists have been willing to discard (or radically modify) theories in a way which would have been quite impossible had those theories really been felt to be descriptions of the ultimate nature of reality.

Some contemporary scientists have resisted this description of their theories as 'operational constructs' on the ground that it demeans science from being a search for truth to being a mere handmaid of industry and commerce, but this is to continue to judge the matter from the point of view of traditional assumptions about the proper use of imagination. To take the modern experimental approach really seriously it is necessary to consider that 'truth' *means* 'truth of creative action', and hence that there is nothing undignified, second-rate or even secondary about the search for new potentialities of creative action – if the term 'search for truth' means anything at all, it means just this. Only if we start from the assumption that the business of imagination is to reveal hidden structures and meanings rather than practical potentialities does it seem that every successful formula for practical action must rest on, or at very least imply, some truth about the ultimate structure of things. The use of experiment as the ultimate criterion of judgement implies that the world is *simply what we know it to be in the practical business of meeting it, handling it, and doing things in it* – not so much a thing, a system, a reality, an order, as an opportunity, a potentiality for creative action. A modern scientific theory, such as electronic theory of matter, gives new knowledge of the world, not in the scientific papers in which the theory is described, but in the experience of new things, like transistor radios, laser beams, computers, etc. (or, at an earlier stage, new laboratory experiments) which become part of the world when the theory is put into practice – and to say this is not to degrade science, if the experimental point of view is taken really seriously, since on that understanding no other kind of knowledge is possible or desirable. I do *not* mean by this that we cannot think of anything better than the manufacture of transistor radios or computers: there are other kinds of science besides physical science, and other kinds of experiment apart from scientific experiment. What I *do* mean is that the experimental outlook is always concerned with practical new life, not with abstract truth, and this is implied in the whole structure of modern scientific thinking.

One philosopher of science who succeeded in expressing this revolutionary implication of the experimental method, and in formulating explicitly the impact of the new outlook on social life generally, was the early nineteenth-century French philosopher Auguste Comte, sometimes called the father of the science of sociology. He cast his analysis in the form of a doctrine of social evolution. The habit of explaining the world by reference to supposed powers behind the scenes is a primitive form of thought, he suggested, corresponding to a primitive style of life in which actions are dictated by the supposed disposition of the powers behind the scenes. He held that this must, as the human race evolves, be superseded by the more mature 'positive' outlook which simply seeks correlations between experienced events in order to make practical changes, and judges forms of behaviour experimentally by their results. In his early formulations he claimed to discern a transition stage, which he called 'metaphysical' or 'rational', as contrasted with the 'theological' or 'magical' character of primitive thought and the 'positive' or 'scientific' character of mature thought: in this intermediate stage, he suggested, the primitive multiplicity of powers behind the scenes gives place to more general metaphysical principles, such as the Universal Law of Stoicism, the All-Pervading Consciousness of Hinduism, the One Overriding Good Will of Christianity or the Basic Energy of certain vitalist or quasi-materialist philosophies, and on the social plane people try to live by seeking broad general rules of conduct capable of governing all aspects of life. In his later writings, however, Comte tended more and more to play down this transition phase in order to emphasise the radical contrast between the traditional and the 'positive' attitudes to life, and to persuade people that social progress depended on universal acceptance of the positive outlook.

It is a matter for great regret that the many legitimate doubts cast by subsequent thinkers on Comte's theory as a general account of social evolution should have led to a neglect of its acute psychological insight into the particular social transition through which western civilisation has been passing over the past three hundred years or so. If people had been more aware of it, the 'conflict between science and religion' over the past century might have been a little less like those animals in mediaeval bestiaries which disappeared as soon as anyone tried to get to grips with them. In Comte's own time, for example, and indeed for much of the preceding century, people had long since outgrown the notion that there was any necessary conflict between religious belief and the discoveries of astronomy, but the sense of conflict persisted, and since scientists commonly interpreted their discoveries in terms of the classical human outlook, people sought to identify the conflict as a clash between the various laws emerging from science and the idea of divine purpose. The central issue round which much debate raged was that of miracles. Sceptics urged that whales were now known scientifically to be incapable of swallowing Jonah, that angels with wings contradicted the laws of anatomy and aerodynamics, that the law of conservation of matter forbade the conversion of five loaves and two fishes into a banquet for five thousand, and so on, while diehard ecclesiastics condemned the whole business of science as a demonic exercise in human pride precisely because it led to conclusions like these instead of encouraging a humble acceptance of the Bible's revelation of God's infinite power. No sooner had the conflict been apparently pinned down in these terms, however, than it proceeded to dissolve, just as the conflict about astronomy had done.

All the more intelligent theologians began to realise, with the support of the great majority of scientists, that scientific laws are in themselves merely generalisations about the way things ordinarily happen, and miracles are by definition out of the ordinary, so that science can say nothing one way or the other about them. A scientific training might make a man sceptical of particular miracle stories, but there is no special 'conflict of science and religion' in this, since a legal training, with its emphasis on people's ability to distort evidence, might do so equally well. On the other side of the coin, the assertion that nothing can possibly happen outside the framework of contemporary scientific generalisations is certainly not a scientific assertion – on the contrary, the practice of science should if anything breed scepticism about the finality of any set of current generalisations. More generally, theologians and scientists alike came to recognise that a clash between scientific laws and the idea of divine purpose is a logical absurdity, since it is always possible to see divine or spiritual purpose behind scientific laws: to say that lightning is produced by electrical discharges cannot in itself contradict the belief that it is caused by God or spirits or demons, since anyone interested in that kind of cause will inevitably ask whether or not God or spirits or demons are behind the electrical forces. Comte's achievement was to bring this logical consideration into focus and to ask why some people *should* be interested in that kind of cause, even to the extent of misguidedly resisting science in the name of their beliefs, while other people are utterly unconcerned with this kind of thing once scientific accounts of natural phenomena have become available, and so feel that science renders religion out of date. His answer – that the conflict is between two radically different attitudes to life – failed to catch the public eye, however, and in the half century that followed his writings the public arena was dominated by a new attempt to pin down the elusive conflict between science and religion as a straight conflict of beliefs about 'the way things are' – the great debate about evolution.

This debate began when geologists and others showed that the earth must, on any scientific reckoning, have existed for more than six days before the beginning of human life, but it reached its peak with Darwin's theory about the gradual descent (or ascent) of man from primitive life-forms by natural processes of evolution. This occasioned a wave of religious scepticism on an unprecedented scale, since it was assumed by great numbers of people to prove that the whole idea of divine creation was mere primitive myth. Well before the end of the century, however, there was widespread agreement amongst both theologians and scientists that the Biblical creation story was clearly meant from the first to be symbolic rather than literal (a 'day' before the creation of the sun and moon is clearly not meant to be an ordinary day, and indeed the Bible itself asserts elsewhere that in the sight of God a day might be a thousand years!). There was also widespread agreement that a slow process of evolution spreading over thousands of millions of years could be just as much a divine plan as a six-day series of cosmic conjuring tricks. Once again, that elusive beast, the science-religion conflict, seemed to have vanished, and since then it has been little heard of in the general public arena, yet the sense that science has somehow undermined religion has certainly remained stronger and is more widespread today than it has ever been. For many people today it is something so much taken for granted that they cannot be bothered to argue about it, while those who try to argue about it mostly have a helpless feeling that it is something they cannot quite understand.

This is the situation into which children are plunged as soon as thet start learning about science in school, or reading their first popular science books at home. They become aware not only of a contrasy between the specific things that are said in, for example, the story of creation in the Bible and in the story of the earth's evolution as told by modern astronomers or biologists, but also – without being able to express it – of the radical antagonism between the 'theological' attitude implied in the one kind of statement and the 'positive' attitude implied in the other. Their parents and teachers, however, commonly concern themselves only with the first contrast, with the result that their attempts to help the children understand the situation are unsatisfactory – not just logically unsatisfactory, but practically unhelpful to the children – no matter what particular line they take.

Not many, nowadays, take the line of the Victorian ecclesiastical diehards in urging that the scientific accounts are simply wicked untruths, although it is still within living memory that a young schoolteacher was prosecuted in one of the southern states of the United States for teaching evolution, because the state laws forbade the teaching of anything contrary to the Bible. (This was the famous 'Monkey Trial', one notable feature of which was that the prosecuting counsel was a US Presidential Candidate.) Equally, there are nowadays rather fewer people than there used to be who are prepared to dismiss the Biblical story as just a primitive superstitious way of explaining something which science has now learned to understand more accurately. This view undoubtedly lurks in vague forms at the back of the minds of a large number of the general public, and it can still be heard voiced from time to time by more aggressive humanist parents and schoolteachers, but there is by now a fairly general recognition amongst most thinking people that the Biblical story was never meant to be a scientific statement about how the earth originated, and most schoolteachers are aware of this. The commonest line today, certainly amongst teachers, is that the Biblical story is a moral or spiritual allegory which can be accepted as complementary to scientific accounts of stellar and biological evolution. This notion received a beautiful symbolic portrayal at the end of the Hollywood film based on the 'Monkey Trial', entitled *Inherit the Wind*. This had a fine performance by Spencer Tracy as the counsel who successfully defended the young schoolteacher against the charge of breaking the law of blasphemy by teaching evolution (the defence turning on the point that a 'day' before the creation of sun and moon would be no ordinary day), and at the end came a particularly dramatic shot of Tracy walking out of the deserted courtroom with the Bible and Darwin's *Origin of Species* tucked firmly together under his arm. In one way or another this view of the matter forms the basis of what is taught about 'Genesis and evolution' – and more generally about 'science and religion' – in the vast majority of western schools today, and it leaves a fundamental uncertainty of the worst kind in children's minds, an uncertainty which they cannot properly express.

Those who try to write off the conflict between science and religion in this kind of way may be likened to naturalists concluding that the mysterious beast people have been seeking over the past few centuries is simply non-existent, since all the sightings that have been reported have turned out on close inspection to be merely ripples on the lake surface, not a living creature at all. What they fail to ask is why people so often see ripples, and so they never come to see that there is a colossal creature right under the very boat on which we are all standing. The Victorian ecclesiastical diehards who opposed science outright, and the equally diehard proponents of scientific atheism, knew better than most would-be reconcilers of science and religion, even though they were guilty of faulty logic in trying to define the issue between them: they at least insisted that there was something alive in this particular ocean, even though they failed to identify the beast under the boat and kept arguing about supposed shoals of minnows where there were really only ripples. Comte's analysis points towards the real identity of the elusive animal precisely because it makes us look underneath the surface of ordinary arguments about facts or logic, into the waters of human psychology on which all our arguments necessarily rest. It enables us to see that there is indeed a colossal beast lurking there, but that its name is not really 'conflict between science and religion': it is really a conflict of cultures, of 'ways of responding to life' – on the one hand the traditional attitude which is vitally concerned with what meanings or purposes (if any) lie behind the scenes of ordinary practical life, and on the other hand the 'modern' attitude which simply cannot take such concerns seriously *because it just does not approach ordinary life as a scene.*

It is easy to excuse ordinary teachers and parents from failing to see this, since, as I have said, it is commonly not recognised by scientists themselves, either by those who have discarded religious belief or by those (of whom there are still a great many) who believe their ideas can be reconciled with it. For example, scientists tend to take the experimental method so much for granted in their own particular sphere that they often treat a scientific idea as a simple matter of factual observation, when it is really nothing of the kind. Just as Galileo's observation of Jupiter's moons implied (by taking an artificial observation as the standard of judgement) the revolutionary outlook of the experimental method, in spite of its apparent straightforwardness to us who look at it with the hindsight of three centuries of modern astronomy, so equally did Darwin's theory of evolution, although this is often presented as if it rested purely on logical deduction from simple observed facts. Darwin's particular theory was quite consciously constructed on the basis of the experiments of animal breeders, but in any case the whole business of interpreting fossils is shot through with the assumptions of experimental chemistry and physics. If this had not been so the probability is that no one would ever have thought it presented any challenge to religious belief at all, for everyone would automatically have concluded what the 'reconciling' theologians now conclude at the end of long arguments, namely, that the divine creative process was simply cast on a larger 'day'-scale than had formerly been realised. As it is, less sophisticated people, including children, are wiser in their instincts than the reconcilers are in their logic: like the diehards of the Victorian conflict, they know quite well that there is a radical antagonism somewhere, even though they cannot express it. The great task facing teachers or parents who have to guide children on the subject of religion is to understand this antagonism for themselves so that the children in turn can be brought to understand it in their own terms.

I believe children *can* understand it, without necessarily going into the philosophy of science or the ideas of Comte – even without knowing much about Shakespeare or the industrial revolution (although older children would certainly be able to follow discussions of these matters, and it is my personal conviction that adults are constantly prone to underestimate the ability of even younger children and less academic children to follow quite complex argument if it is presented with sufficient skill and patience). The essential task is not to induce any kind of philosophical thought, but simply to enable children to look around them and see the two contrasting attitudes to life in operation in the way ordinary people behave at different times. On this basis, as I shall now try to show, it is possible to sort out the whole business of 'science and religion', indeed the whole business of 'belief and unbelief', against the background of an articulate consideration of whether the 'modern' or 'positive' outlook is really an advance in sanity in relation to the traditional or 'theological', as Comte believed, or whether it represents a sacrifice of sanity in the name of material progress, as many modern conservative thinkers believe. The result of such a consideration is likely to produce some surprises by cutting across many of our intellectual stereotypes, as may be foreseen by taking note of the fact that Comte himself did *not* conclude that the abandonment of the 'theological' outlook would be the end of religion altogether. He believed, as Bacon had done in a different way before him, that the new outlook would transform religion, just as it was transforming natural science, into something richer and more vital than it had ever been in previous ages.

4: Religion and the occult

Extreme cases sometimes highlight the essential factors in a complex situation, and one of the clearest indications of the way the whole modern world has been affected by a radically new outlook is our attitude to astrology.

A great many people – far more than would be willing to admit it publicly – have a sneaking feeling that 'perhaps there's something in it somewhere', but it *is* a sneaking feeling, it *is* something many people would hesitate to admit, and the whole public philosophy of the western world takes for granted that the continuing interest in astrology in newspapers and magazines is really something of a joke. In almost every civilisation prior to the scientific revolution, on the other hand, astrology was an accepted part of culture for educated and uneducated people alike, and remained so even in Europe for some time after the new astronomy of Galileo and Copernicus had become widely accepted (just as it manages to co-exist with modern astronomical ideas in some parts of the east today). From time to time the authorities of the Christian church condemned astrology, but this very condemnation was an acknowledgement of its intellectual force in Christendom, while the generality of Christians, even the generality of theologians, far from seeing any contradiction between Christianity and astrology, actually used astrological ideas to fill out their basic Christian convictions. They did so at the level of general doctrine, for example, by interpreting the coming of Christ as mankind's transition into a new astrological age, the Age of the Fish, but even more commonly, astrological ideas were used in ordinary life to provide detailed practical guidance for the *minutiae* of everyday existence, in the overall context of Christian laws for behaviour. People have begun to take astrology less seriously only during the past two centuries or so, in parallel with the tendency to take religion less seriously, and in neither case was the change primarily a matter of a direct conflict between specific scientific discoveries and traditional views of the world's workings.

Well after the time of Galileo, it was still widely assumed, even by the majority of scientists, that any new discovery made by scientific investigation could be brought to the service of religious truth on the principle expressed by Milton's Adam in *Paradise Lost*:

> In contemplation of created things
> By steps we may be led to God.

And on precisely the same principle, astronomers commonly pursued their studies of the stars partly, or even wholly, in order to extend the range of facts available for making astrological interpretations of life. The fact that post-Copernican astronomy places the sun rather than the earth at the centre of our planetary system and opens up galactic vistas undreamt of in the ancient world need not in itself have altered anything in principle, for the actual relationship of the earth to the other planets and the heavenly constellations has not in itself altered one jot, and it is this relationship which forms the basis of astrology. Modern serious apologists for astrology, who are by no means uncommon in the west and quite common in parts of the east, are sometimes quite prepared to admit that modern astronomy makes it difficult to think, as many people did in the past, that the stars and planets are exercising some sort of quasi-physical influence on human affairs, but even this view of the matter cannot be said to be in any way *disproved* by modern astronomical discoveries, since if there were to be some influence of this type (for example, through fields of force of a kind not yet scientifically understood), it would necessarily be the appearance of the stars and planets from the earth which governed the form of the influence on the earth, and not any other kind of perspective of the heavens such as astronomers might use for discussing the gravitation of the solar system or the movement of the galaxies. But in any case, the astrological apologists argue, it is quite possible to believe in a correlation between the patterns of the heavenly bodies and the events of human life without necessarily holding that the actual movements of the stars and planets have any significance in themselves at all. It may be, for example, that they merely provide us with an indication of the precise 'universal time' at which significant earthly events occur, and that the astrologer is using astronomical calculations simply to plot the regular cycles of certain hidden psychological forces that govern human affairs. The only thing that is really essential to astrology is the conviction that the astrological tradition through the ages embodies insight into the underlying meaning of events which can help people to find meaning and purpose in their own lives, and this conviction cannot in the nature of the case be invalidated by any discoveries which natural science makes about the detailed workings of the physical world.

This, however, is precisely what makes it hard for most people today to take astrology seriously, at any rate with the parts of their minds that have been formed by the modern experimental or 'positive' outlook. For this outlook, insights are valuable only insofar as they make it possible to do something different from what would have been done otherwise: any notion which is unaffected by what happens in practice is simply uninteresting and meaningless. This is why an experimentally-oriented investigator is prepared to go out of his way to find a crucial practical test which could disprove an idea, however elegant, and if the idea fails to pass the test he is willing, if not actually to abandon it straight away, at least to consider doing so. When an astrologer casts a horoscope, on the other hand, he is not at all prepared to abandon his fundamental interpretation if it fails to agree with what can be subsequently observed concerning the horoscope's subject; like the Azande chiefs to whom I referred in Chapter Two, he merely concludes that other factors which he has not taken into account are obscuring his fundamental truth, or that it holds good at a deeper level than ordinary superficial observation can discern.

Now although many modern Christian apologists would probably be horrified to be likened to astrologers, there can be no doubt that they commonly adopt just this point of view, not only in the many books, articles and sermons which argue that scientific discoveries about the world's detailed workings cannot possibly disprove the truths of religion, but also in more everyday religious contexts. For example, it is a common theme of preachers that natural calamities should not be allowed to shake a believer's faith in the loving care of the Ruler of the Universe, since God's infinite love necessarily shows itself in mysterious ways which our puny understanding cannot comprehend: this is quite explicitly a call for belief in something beyond the bounds of experimental valuation. The same applies to the claim commonly made by spiritual directors (equally by Christian ones and by those from eastern religious traditions) that prayer should be persevered with even if it is not apparently answered either in practical events or even in terms of inner spiritual comfort or illumination, since the inscrutable wisdom of God (or the Universal Consciousness) often knows that it is best for us, at particular stages in our overall spiritual development, to receive no clear answer. It has become something of a fashion in recent years for religious apologists (more commonly the apologists for eastern, mystical styles of religion, but also of quite a few Christians) to claim that religious faith is 'verified experimentally in life', but inasmuch as this is held to be true no matter what actually happens in life, such assertions are of precisely the same logical and psychological form as those of the astrologers, however different in detailed content, and not experimental in the modern scientific sense at all.

It is this logical and psychological form which makes religious statements seem meaningless to great numbers of people today, even to many who find the arguments advanced by religious apologists generally persuasive. The most striking instance of this divorce between the logic used by religious apologists and their ability to carry conviction is the way in which fewer and fewer people are capable of being influenced by evangelistic appeals to fear of hell. From the strictly logical point of view there can be no gainsaying Pascal's argument that even if the chances against hell are billions to one, the pains of hell are so awful that even the billionth billionth chance is not worth taking. But the logic simply has no force at all for very large numbers of people today, because the terms of the argument simply have no meaning for them. It is not only the cruder doctrines of Christianity, however, which suffer in this way. In the past few decades many spokesmen have come forward to claim that if only western man would turn to eastern forms of religion rather than to Christianity, his 'scientific scepticism' would be completely by-passed, since the eastern religions are concerned with generalised spiritual principles rather than with belief in a personal God or personal survival after death, but such claims have always proved hollow as soon as the unfamiliarity of eastern religious or spiritual ideas has worn off. If some non-Christian religions in their home territories are less affected by fundamental scepticism than Christianity has been in the west, it is only to the extent that those territories have as yet not been penetrated much by industrialisation and western scientific ways of thought, and the areas of the world for which this is true are dwindling every day. In terms of the perspective of the modern, positive attitude to life it makes no difference whether the underlying meaning and purpose of things is said to be the soul's progress to heaven or hell or the development of consciousness to perceive higher levels of reality. Both kinds of statement are akin to the statements of the astrologer rather than to experimental statements, so long as they are held to be true irrespective of the way things actually happen in practical life. And in the same way, it makes no difference whether a religion holds that it is a good or a bad thing, in the universal pattern, for believers to be actively concerned in the business of practical life. Some religious apologists make great play of arguing that their particular brand of religion is compatible with the modern scientific outlook because it is 'world-affirming' rather than 'world-denying', but in fact even the most 'world-affirming' religion is still of

31

the astrological rather than the experimental order if it gives the events of practical life significance by virtue of their place in a larger pattern (the Divine Plan, the evolution of world-consciousness or whatever).

What is more, it is not only those who call themselves atheists or agnostics who find statements about underlying meaning and purpose radically unconvincing. The same feeling often assails those who like to count themselves religious believers. For just as great numbers of people who most pride themselves on being modern, sceptical and scientifically-minded nevertheless inherit sufficient of the traditional outlook to be driven from time to time to take sly looks at astrology columns (usually under cover of a joke) and to wonder if there may not after all 'be something in it somewhere', so even the most devout believers are affected by the modern outlook to some degree if they live anywhere within the influence of western civilisation. And insofar as they are affected by it, they find themselves suffering from a fundamental lack of conviction about all statements implying belief in realities behind the scenes. This is why all the world's religious traditions and institutions have been attenuated, over the past two centuries or more, not only by the historically unprecedented phenomenon of people proclaiming themselves, in ever-growing numbers, to be sceptical or indifferent, but also by an equally unprecedented internal erosion by doubt within the ranks of those who sincerely wish to remain faithful. The religious literature of past ages often contains references to the need to convert 'the ungodly' or 'the unenlightened', and to maintain faith in the face of doubt, but close analysis shows that such terms referred to people holding, or finding their minds flirting with, religious beliefs different from those approved of by their society. The unbelief and doubt of the modern world is something much more radical – a sense of utter unreality about all beliefs that have to do with the underlying meaning or purpose of things.

The effect of bringing this fact into consciousness is to force those who call themselves religious believers to look at the roots of their belief in a way which very few have done in the past. If they are not prepared to abandon religion altogether, they must face the question of precisely what it is they wish to hold on to or defend. Do they want deliberately and consciously to defend the traditional outlook, for which astrology can in principle make sense even if, as a matter of belief, they happen to hold it to be a false view of the underlying meaning of things? Or is the core of their religious conviction something altogether different, which could (at least in principle) survive the complete abandonment of beliefs about realities behind the scenes of ordinary experience and perhaps be compatible with the modern, 'positive' outlook? Normally this question is never even raised:

believers and unbelievers alike, in east and west alike, have mostly taken it completely for granted that abandonment of belief in realities beyond the ordinary practical world must of necessity mean abandonment of religion altogether. It is significant, however, that Francis Bacon and the early pioneers of the scientific revolution, who were much clearer about the revolutionary character of the experimental approach than most subsequent thinkers, hinted at quite a different possibility; and Auguste Comte, who articulated the problem of the two contrasting attitudes to the world so clearly, raised quite explicitly the question of whether religion was or was not intrinsically bound up with the 'theological' view of things.

As I have said earlier, the pioneer followers of Francis Bacon knew quite well that his 'experimental philosophy' would change the whole shape of society, but they certainly did not envisage the total disappearance of religion: on the contrary, they actually used the terminology of the Bible to express what they felt to be the essence of the new outlook, saying that man was at long last taking seriously the notion of the Book of Genesis that he was destined to have dominion over nature. Was this merely because they were unable completely to break free from the linguistic habits and social forms of their day, or were they seriously trying to adumbrate the possibility that Biblical faith was at bottom something quite different from the common religion of Christendom which proclaimed a revelation of the supposed divine plan of the world? There is a suggestion of this possibility in Bertolt Brecht's play *Galileo*, although I doubt if it has any real historical authority. A central scene is devoted to a dialogue between the astronomer and a young disciple who accepts his conclusions as scientifically correct but sympathises with the concern of the Inquisition over their impact on religion. After hearing Galileo's vivid account of the possibility of understanding the whole universe by scientific means, the young disciple asks 'But where then is God?'. Galileo makes no verbal reply, but simply taps his heart.

Brecht does not attempt to follow up what this might mean, and as far as the historical Galileo is concerned, all we can say is that he appears to have believed – or at least given lip-service to the idea – that the new experimental science would change Christianity without destroying it. Such professions of faith as he made remained quite conventional, although his tone of voice conveys a quite unconventional lack of interest in theological realities as compared with the practical future of human life. Bacon, on the other hand, had the advantage over Galileo of living within the tradition of the Protestant Reformation, which was rooted in the belief that the historical Christian religion radically distorted the original Biblical faith by muddling it up with ideas of

33

other worlds called Purgatory and Limbo behind the scenes of life, and with beliefs about hidden powers exercised from another world by saints and martyrs. Against the background of this Reformation tradition it was possible for the Baconians to suggest, as Galileo could not have done even had he wished, that their revolutionary new outlook would be capable of benefiting Christianity as well as science, since it was simply a continuation of this process of rescuing true Christianity from the distortions imposed on it by the Church. They did not work out what this might mean in any detail, and they too continued to make conventional statements of belief about God the Creator and heaven after death, but at the practical level they showed a very real earnest of a new approach to Christianity by proclaiming, as a matter of Christian virtue, that there should be charitable toleration of religious differences in the scientific world itself – a marked contrast to the fanaticism of the Christian world around them, in which Christians of different shades of opinion persecuted and fought bitter wars against each other.

Comte, with a perspective of two centuries of the scientific revolution behind him, was more explicit. He believed that mankind's abandonment of the theological outlook, far from spelling the end of religion, would bring about its apotheosis in the worship of humanity. The impulse towards worship and towards moral behaviour, he held, is a vital element in human experience which is in no sense integrally bound up with beliefs about realities behind the scenes of experience: on the contrary, the theological outlook may be considered to have diverted this impulse from its true practical outlet in exactly the same way as it diverted mankind's speculation about nature from its true practical fulfilment in experimental science. Hence he considered that the Reformation had, as it were, thrown out the baby and retained the bathwater: 'While the Protestants . . . have always attacked religion in the name of God, we must discard God, once and for all, in the name of religion,' he wrote in a letter, and he toyed again and again with the fantasy that the Jesuit order might be prepared to do just this. He seriously considered that it might be possible to take over most of the practical religion of Catholic Christianity for 'de-theologised' use as psychological discipline whereby people learned to subdue their selfishness to the service of humanity. Thus where Protestantism had sought to get rid of the cult of saints and the cult of the Virgin Mary as distractions from the proper worship of God, Comte sought to adapt them for non-theological use in focusing the inspiration of great men or of the principle of womanhood. Where the Reformation had turned away from elaborate ceremonial and church ornamentation, Comte told a correspondent that he looked forward to a day, not far hence, when the cathedral of Notre Dame would be transformed into 'the great

Temple of the West' in which 'the statue of Humanity will have as its pedestal the altar of God.'

Whether this was even remotely what the early Baconians had in mind, even in their private thoughts, is very doubtful. True, Bacon himself had suggested, in his book *The New Atlantis*, that in the new age scientists might take over some of the traditional roles of the priesthood (an idea which was taken up directly by Comte's master, Saint-Simon, and so no doubt influenced Comte himself), but the Baconians would have been unlikely to want to describe this as a new kind of religion – the Protestant feeling was too strong in them for that. And for the same reason, they would have been unlikely to acquiesce readily in the notion of a total disappearance of Biblical or Christian faith. Certainly the practical effect of Comte's proposal on the churches of his day was to precipitate the very reaction against the 'positive' outlook which Bacon and his followers had deliberately tried to avoid by attaching themselves to the English Establishment through the quasi-religious institution of the monarchy.

A common theme of preachers and religious writers throughout Europe after Comte became the need to defend the idea of the super-natural as an essential foundation for any religion worthy of the name, while the defence of religion against unbelief became a matter of accusing the 'positive' or 'modern' outlook of being a wilful form of blindness with dangerous consequences for the moral health of society. A few minority movements tried to take up the idea of a 'scientific' or 'non-supernatural' religion, and various 'ethical' or 'humanist' churches were formed, usually linked with the promotion of socialistic reforms of the political structure, but they had little effect on the public imagina-tion generally, and after the hullabaloo about evolution in the second half of the nineteenth century (in most of which, as I have said, Comte's insight into the psychological character of the science-religion conflict was completely ignored) it came to be taken for granted by almost everyone that humanism and the positive viewpoint necessarily meant the total repudiation of religion. Socialistic ideals in particular became linked with militant opposition to religion in the rapidly-spreading Marxist philosophy. After the Marxist revolution in Russia the Com-munist Party there came very close to applying some of Comte's ideas, in creating ceremonies around Lenin's tomb and May Day, but they would have repudiated any suggestion of the term 'religion', and so equally would Hitler when he attempted something very similar to cement people's allegiance to his 'National Socialism' in Germany. At the same time religious apologists in other countries, both from the Christian and from the great eastern religious traditions, were not slow to point out the resemblance between these totalitarian movements and

Comte's 'religion of humanity', and to use the fact to discredit Comte's ideas completely.

So in our contemporary situation the defence of religion is almost universally linked with the defence of the traditional attitude to life as against the positive attitude. (The few isolated figures like Sir Julian Huxley who invoke the idea of a humanistic 'religion without revelation' are mostly regarded, by believers and unbelievers alike, as simply interesting eccentrics, sources of quotations in support of more orthodox religion or humanism.) For most religious apologists the defence of the traditional outlook is still implicit rather than explicit, in that they seek to uphold certain specific theological or mystical beliefs against what they see as the alternative, or much more limited, world view of 'materialistic science', and are then confronted with the frustrating situation that their arguments meet with no effective response of any kind, since people are neither convinced by them nor able to refute them. Insofar as argument about religion takes place at this level, it is argument of that special kind in which people try to allay their own doubts in the process of trying to convince others, and never really succeed in doing either, because the real issue is never brought into the open. (This holds good equally for those who seek to defend religious ideas and for those who make the old-fashioned kinds of attack on them, by claiming that evolution disproves the idea of creation and so on; for just as religious apologists who argue in favour of their beliefs are wrestling with the basic lack of conviction that must, in the modern world, continually assail them, so the atheist or agnostic who argues that modern scientific discoveries 'disprove' religion is engaged in convincing himself that he really is justified in ignoring all ideas of realities beyond the empirical world. That was why Auguste Comte was anxious to dissociate himself from conventional atheism, which he quite correctly saw to be a half-admission of the possibility that the idea of God might be worth taking seriously.)

In the past few decades, however, the frustrations of this situation have begun to drive growing numbers of religious apologists to make their defence of the traditional outlook explicit, and in so doing to be prepared to align themselves with astrology and similar beliefs in principle, even if disagreeing with them in practice. Some, indeed, have gone further and embraced astrology as an embodiment of at least some valid insights into the underlying meaning and purpose of things, on the basis of which the higher religious truths about the salvation or development of the soul in the cosmic plan may take their place. This is perhaps commoner amongst apologists for eastern styles of religion – Hinduism or Buddhism, or modern variants of them such as theosophy – than amongst Christian apologists, but some very distinguished

Christian thinkers have taken a similar view in recent years: T. S. Eliot, for example, made a great deal of use of astrological and similar occult symbolism in his poetic evocations of Christianity, on the ground that these traditions contain truths about the underlying spiritual laws of life which prefigure the great truths revealed by Christ and the Church. More common amongst Christian apologists, however, is the point of view which may be paraphrased by saying that however absurd astrology may be in itself, nevertheless a world where people can consider that astrology *might* have something to say to help them is in the end a saner world than one in which all ideas of underlying purpose are dismissed as meaningless. One of the most trenchant declarations on these lines was the assertion of G. K. Chesterton, in a book written between the two world wars, that the tragedy of modern man is not so much his failure to believe in God as his inability to believe in fairies.

This, then, is the first fundamental position that has to be appreciated and understood in trying to make sense of the religious issues of our world today – the conviction (or belief, or feeling) that the modern outlook, with its total lack of concern with ideas of reality, meaning or purpose underlying the world of ordinary experience, marks a decline in sanity in relation to the traditional outlook, even though the traditional outlook allows of enormous differences of view about the specific nature of the underlying reality, meaning or purpose, and even perhaps leads to violent conflicts between rival views. Some powerful arguments can be put up in favour of this general position, as I shall now try to show, and in recent years many people who have no special religious commitment to uphold have joined in the defence of this position, because they have come to believe that the 'total lack of supernatural or spiritual dimension' in the modern outlook has disastrous effects on culture, on morality, on social stability and on individual mental health. I cannot discuss these arguments fairly, however, without declaring in advance my own conclusion, which I shall do my best to substantiate, that this whole attempt to defend the traditional outlook is profoundly mistaken.

In fact I have reached the point in this book where I have to try to test myself the claim I made at the beginning, that by penetrating below the surface of the problem of understanding religion, it is possible to arrive at a basis from which a teacher or parent can present all the many alternatives of belief and unbelief quite fairly to children, irrespective of his own personal views – not by suppressing his own views in any way, but by declaring them openly, and even defending them, as his particular choice amongst the alternatives. My hope is that the insight I have tried to develop so far is broadly acceptable (with however many reservations on points of detail) as objective 'neutral ground' from which a person of any view may see other views in a perspective that does them reasonable justice, and see his own view as it would appear to others. The questions I have to discuss from here on, however, are questions on which neutrality is impossible: at every stage I shall necessarily have to state my own conclusions, but my hope is that I can now do so in such a way that those who decide to disagree with me at any point can see clearly the implications of doing so. In this way I believe I can help them to see what it is they have to tell the children, even though it is necessarily different from what I should tell them myself.

On the specific question of the defence of the traditional outlook as against the modern or positive outlook, I believe, for reasons which I shall give in due course, that the criticisms which are commonly made against the sanity of the positive outlook are based on misunderstanding – either misunderstanding of the true nature of the positive outlook itself, or misunderstanding of the problems which beset human life today in comparison with past ages, or both. I believe the transition from the traditional to the positive outlook constitutes a real advance in sanity, which is if anything of greater value even than Comte realised, and I hold that the greatest problems of the modern world arise, not from the decline of the traditional outlook, but from mankind's failure, so far, to embrace the new outlook wholeheartedly enough. But I also believe, and shall try to show, that the implications for religion of wholeheartedly embracing the positive outlook are quite different from what most believers, unbelievers and agnostics alike suppose. I believe we still have to consider the line of possibility suggested in their different ways by the Baconians and Comte, even though we cannot seriously accept their attempts to express that possibility. I believe Brecht spoke better than he knew when he made Galileo respond to the question of God by tapping his heart.

5: Which way to sanity?

The belief that our modern world has purchased the material gains of science and technology at the price of spiritual loss is not confined to elderly spokesmen of established religions, nor even to representatives of the Establishment. One of the most remarkable phenomena of recent years has been the spread of this feeling amongst the young of all classes in many western countries, reflected alike in the 'swing away from science' amongst university entrants, which is now recognised to be an international phenomenon, and in the upsurge of mystical interests in the world of pop music. The feeling finds expression in the use of terms like 'superficial', 'external', 'materialist', 'calculating', 'utili-tarian', 'unbalanced', 'frenzied' and 'disintegrated' to describe the ethos of technological civilisation. The attempts to trace back these charac-teristics to the lack of a spiritual or supernatural dimension in the modern 'scientific' outlook have been many and various, but I shall try to summarise the most important.*

The general contention is that it may be all very well for certain limited scientific purposes to set aside all consideration of realities beyond the ordinary world of what can be seen, touched, weighed, measured or subjected to mathematical calculation, but to extend this attitude to life as a whole is either crass superficiality or possibly even a

---

* Since this chapter was written the American writer Theodore Roszak has produced a classic statement of the case in his book *The Making of a Counter-Culture*, which argues that the common theme underlying all the youth protest movements of our time, from the hippies to the 'new left', is a desire to break from the scientific world-view and return to a more traditional way of looking at the world. However, I have not found it necessary to modify my summary of the case against the scientific world-view in the light of his book, since I seem to have anticipated it very closely – indeed in some cases I think I have done more justice to it than he has done. The concluding part of this chapter, stating my case for the defence of the modern outlook, might well have been written as a reply to Roszak.

D

kind of wilful blindness. Quite a few people argue that this may actually be dangerous for the future progress of science itself in the long run, in general because it stultifies the imagination, in particular because it leads to the dogmatic dismissal of such subjects as spiritual healing or extra-sensory perception instead of true scholarly objectivity about them. More commonly, it is argued that the superficiality of the modern outlook is fatal to the arts, for without their traditional *raison d'être* in giving symbolic expression to deeper realities underlying the surface of things, they are reduced either to mere decoration or to violent meaningless protest. Moreover our society's concentration on the kind of calculation and external observation which leads to manipulative control over things cuts off the springs of human creativity, denying that sense of participating in the inner life of things which is of the essence of art. And in this, the argument continues, the plight of the artist in the modern world merely highlights the plight of humanity in general. Deprived of a sense of meaningful involvement in the larger patterns of nature, people more and more find themselves isolated, neurotic and forced to live at an increasingly frenzied pace which brings about mental breakdown on a hitherto unprecedented scale, while the total loss of any sense of underlying meaning and purpose in life as a whole undermines the entire moral basis of society.

In this context, the famous 'degree' speech from Shakespeare's *Troilus and Cressida* to which I referred in Chapter Three is frequently quoted with the contention that events since Shakespeare's death have borne out Ulysses' warnings all too grimly. With the continuing decline of the sense that human life is part of a larger plan, discord has indeed become the rule both in the individual psyche and in society at large: 'Each thing meets in mere oppugnancy' describes both the rat-race of social life and the fragmentation of culture into totally unrelated specialisms. In the absence of a universal moral vision, force has indeed become right, while terms like 'right', 'wrong' and 'justice' have lost their meaning in the welter of propaganda that is put out equally by totalitarian governments and by the advertising industry of private capitalism. Where there is no 'instinctive respect for customary authority' arising from a sense of underlying moral order, power falls to demagogues ('strength should be lord of imbecility'), while increasing numbers of the young, lacking any feeling of the 'prerogative of age, crowns, sceptres, laurels', become violent and delinquent, possibly even to the point where the rude son strikes his father dead. At the same time, the disappearance of all ideas of plan or pattern in the universe as a whole has allowed technology to get quite out of control, leading to ugly urbanisation, polluted atmospheres, dust bowls, silent springs, and the threat of world extermination through starvation or through nuclear or biological warfare, so that we may well be within a hair's breadth of a situation where our own inventions will 'make a sop of all this solid globe'.

One of the most powerful spokesmen for this general line of thought has been the great Swiss analytical psychologist, C. G. Jung, who died in 1961. In many of his writings, from the First World War on, he expressed the conviction that a great deal of the mental ill-health of the modern world is due to the way in which materialist civilisation deprives mankind today of any sense of soul. In his essays on wider cultural and political subjects he frequently spoke of a fatal lack of balance in the modern world in favour of the purely intellectual, external aspects of life, which he warned his readers would lead not only to individual mental impoverishment and neurosis, but also, by reaction, to the upsurge of violent waves of unruly mass emotion of the kind seen in Nazi Germany. One of the most vivid formulations of his view of the modern predicament was his statement, originally made in a lecture delivered in England, that the positive, technological outlook impoverishes man because it deprives him of 'the symbolic life'. We may laugh today, he said, at the tribe of American Indians who solemnly believe that everything they do, waking and sleeping, working and playing, is part of a great ritual which makes the sun rise every morning and proceed on its course across the sky, but really these people are much saner than we are, for their lives have meaning in terms of some kind of overall scheme of things, whereas ours have none. Many people who have no brief for Jung's particular psychological theories feel that his warning has been borne out all too well in the years since the Second World War by the vast increase of mental ill-health throughout western society, and by the even more startling incidence of psychological disturbance in the developing societies as industrialisation uproots people from their traditional ritualised patterns of living.

Jung took his diagnosis seriously enough in his own life to build a lakeside retreat in an old tower near Bollingen where technology was kept right out. 'I have done without electricity, and tend the fireplace and stove myself. Evenings, I light the old lamps,' he wrote in his autobiography *Memories, Dreams, Reflections.* 'There is no running water, and I pump the water from the well. I chop the wood and cook the food. These simple acts make life simple; and how difficult it is to be simple! . . . I live "in modest harmony with nature" . . . At times I feel as if I am spread out over the landscape and inside things, and I am myself living in every tree, in the plashing of the waves, in clouds and the animals that come and go, in the procession of the seasons.' Nevertheless Jung never suggested, as some really aggressive opponents of the modern outlook have done, that we should forego the advances of science completely. On the contrary, he claimed to be entirely scientific himself in the development of his psychology, and in fact his main prescription for enabling modern man to find a soul again was to pursue science to the point where, he believed, it would itself drive beyond the positive outlook. And this is the line taken by most thinkers who are concerned about the modern world in the ways I have been describing. Again, the particular arguments are many and various, but I shall try to summarise them.

To begin with, the argument runs, we now know that the old idea of science as pure, cold logic is a complete myth. The actual business of scientific work – certainly at all the points of major discovery, and often in minor matters too – involves frequent leaps of intuition, very similar, in many respects, to the creative work of artists. Moreover it also involves considerable exercise of personal judgement, and many cases can be found of scientists holding on to a theory from a kind of inner faith when experimental evidence seemed to go against it, only to be vindicated in the end. If science itself uses faith based on intuition in this way, why is the faith of the religious believer or the mystic so ridiculous? And at the same time the actual progress of science in many fields is beginning to expose the total inadequacy of the superficial materialism of the conventional 'scientific' outlook, the argument continues. Modern physics, having made nonsense of the straight-forward nineteenth-century ideas of matter, also forces us to consider the possibility of other dimensions beyond the three of our ordinary experience: in these circumstances is it any longer reasonable to reject out of hand all ideas of other worlds behind the scenes?

Again, it is argued, modern biological science is increasingly exposing an incredible range of organic inter-relationships between all the different parts of nature, and is being more and more forced to see that the life-process has to be considered in terms of purposive organic wholes rather than of elements which merely interact mechanically. In this situation, is it any longer reasonable to reject out of hand the notion that our whole universe may be (in the words of one particularly notable writer in this field, the French Jesuit scientist Pierre Teilhard de Chardin) 'a vast scheme of psychic evolution'? Jung's particular argument along these lines consisted of the claim that psychological science, although still in its infancy, has already begun to find it necessary to outgrow the cruder materialistic concepts both of behaviourism and of Freud, and to recognise that the conscious mind is subject to continual influxes from a much wider psychic realm which appears to be common to all men and possibly even to all nature. In the light of this, he argued, it is surely reasonable to see religious concepts not as abstract

42

metaphysical speculations but as straightforward expressions of the realities of human experience itself, if only we are prepared to take off our materialistic blinkers and recognise that our external experience always implies inner experience. Jung also took a great deal of interest in the odd findings claimed by the 'para-psychologists' or 'psychical researchers' who investigate reports of telepathy, clairvoyance, visions of the future, 'mind-over-matter' and apparent evidence of survival of death. Difficult as it is to apply scientific objectivity in this kind of investigation, Jung held (and a great many other people have independently argued along the same lines), it does now seem as if there is genuine statistical evidence that odd phenomena of this kind do occur, and if they do, surely the bottom is knocked right out of materialism.

It is not my intention here to go into the details of any of these arguments: that would be inappropriate in a book of this kind, and any reader who wishes to do so will need to undertake reading on a scale quite beyond the compass of any single book. My concern is simply to show a general line of argument which is frequently advanced today, and which can be pursued very powerfully in particular cases by thinkers who know their facts and know how to argue; I have tried to make my summaries not only fair but reasonably powerful in order to reflect this fact. I want now to go on to try to show why I believe this general line of argument is mistaken, even though there is a great deal of validity in many of the special arguments which are put forward by those who hold such views.

Specifically, I shall contend that the arguments in support of a return to, or recovery of, the traditional outlook are based on misunderstandings both of the fundamental nature of the scientific outlook and of the nature of the problems faced by the modern world. If the reader decides to reject my contention, then he can take it from me, if he has no time to convince himself by further reading, that the detailed arguments of my opponents are indeed powerful and in many cases unquestionably valid. If on the other hand my contention is accepted, the implication is not that the specific views and arguments of the people I have been describing are necessarily valueless (though perhaps some of them are), *but rather that they point to different conclusions from those which their proponents commonly draw.* In particular, I would contend that many of the arguments I have been rehearsing provide valid grounds for the condemnation, not of the positive outlook itself, but of common misunderstandings of the positive outlook which are often widespread amongst scientists and even more widespread amongst people who like to style themselves 'scientifically minded'. I believe the public philosophy of modern scientific and technological civilisation often is genuinely inadequate to the full depth of human life, and often stultifies human development, especially the development of human creativity, but I shall try to show that the remedy lies, not in abandoning or trying to modify the positive outlook in favour of the traditional outlook, but rather in taking the positive outlook much more seriously than our public philosophy has yet taken it, and rooting out vestiges of the traditional outlook which still survive in the most unexpected places.

The root misunderstanding, I believe, is of the nature of the experimental attitude, and I have tried to anticipate this in my description of that attitude in earlier chapters. The core of the point I want to make is that the experimental attitude is not negative, as those who criticise it always suppose, but positive in an absolutely precise sense. When it ignores the idea of realities (or meaning or purpose) behind the scenes of ordinary experience this is *not* a negative affirmation (conscious or unconscious) that such realities are non-existent or not worth taking seriously, or even that they can be ignored for the particular scientific purposes in hand: it is a positive affirmation (sometimes conscious, but usually unconscious) that the world of ordinary experience is not in any sense a mere scene. Hence it seems to me quite false to describe the experimental outlook as superficial, although of course individual people holding that outlook may very well be superficial, as indeed there have been superficial people in every age. The essential thing about the experimental outlook is that it is concerned with depth and meaning and purpose *in* the world of ordinary experience, and particularly in its potentialities for the future, rather than with trying to attribute depth or meaning or purpose to otherwise shallow experience by invoking other realms 'beyond' or 'behind' it. If anything, therefore, it is the traditional outlook which should be accused of reducing life to superficiality, because it assumes that our own meanings and purposes must of necessity be insignificant in their own right.

This same fundamental point can be put from the subjective side by saying that the experimental outlook breaks with the traditional outlook in that it does not treat imagination and perception in analogous terms: its criterion of sanity is not that the products of the imagination should in some way correspond to something that is there already in the world (and which must therefore be in some way 'behind the scenes' if it is not part of the world of present or remembered experience), but rather that they should be capable of translation into effective action in the world. The philosopher A. N. Whitehead made this vital point about the outlook of modern science in a classic phrase when he said that it is much more important that a scientific theory should be interesting than that it should be true – but once this attitude is adopted anywhere, it is impossible to confine it only to science or any other special area of human activity, because it implies a basic judgement about the nature of sanity. And the essence of that judgement, it seems to me, is an affirmation that the capacity which is distinctively human, the imaginative capacity, is of its fundamental nature creative rather than merely responsive. All conscious creatures live by response to their environment, and since the animal world shows frequent examples of the development of novel behaviour-patterns, it is possible that animals have elements in them of something which might conceivably be called imagination; in man, however, the imaginative faculty dominates responsive behaviour, and this makes man the distinctively creative animal even when judged in strictly biological terms. The point I am now trying to make is that the traditional outlook, by treating imagination as a peculiar kind of perception, minimised the fact of human creativity by, as it were, organising creative departures back into the general behaviour pattern appropriate to response. Accordingly the gradual emergence of the experimental outlook may indeed be described as the most important revolution that has ever overtaken human society, since it amounts in effect to a decision to take man's nature as a creative animal really seriously, as was never done before. This, it seems to me, is the point C. P. Snow was trying to make when he described the new culture as having 'the future in its bones'.

The modern recognition of the role of intuition in science and of the resemblance between scientific innovation and artistic creativity does not in any sense call for a modification of the 'positive' outlook, therefore: it is simply an affirmation of what the positive outlook has always been about. If eighteenth- and nineteenth-century science was, as is often said, 'narrowly rationalistic', this was certainly not because it stuck closely to the 'positive' outlook, but rather because it failed to take that outlook sufficiently seriously: it is the traditional outlook, not the positive, which sets aside imaginative ideas (such as Galileo's idea about the motion of the planets, or Darwin's about the evolution of species) because they fail to conform to what the most logical minds of the day can deduce from what is already accepted.

I rather doubt myself whether real science ever was narrowly rationalistic in this sense, although certain self-styled scientific philosophers may have been. It seems to me a tremendous feat of imagination to have considered, as the early chemists did, treating the materials of common experience as latticeworks of atoms in repeating patterns, or to have thought of atoms having electrical shells which interlock, as did the chemists of the nineteenth century. If ideas like these were preferred to ideas of quasi-spiritual substances such as those conceived by mediaeval alchemy, or to ideas of angels dancing on needle-points, it was not because the more traditional ideas failed to fit the narrow, mechanical dogmas of scientists' minds but simply because no way

45

could be found of giving them practical meaning in experience: *if they had been useful, they would have been used*. Moreover if some 'organic' biologist or some psychical researcher were to come forward today with a modern version of these ancient ideas *in a form which could show how to do things that could not otherwise be done*, he too would find his ideas used. But if such notions ever do become accepted within the framework of science they will automatically cease to be statements about realities underlying the world of ordinary experience, and become instead provisional models suggesting ways of organising new and more subtle forms of behaviour *in* the world of ordinary experience – and vice versa. In other words, so long as they *are* statements about supposed realities underlying ordinary experience, and are *not* provisional models capable of being here today and gone, or radically revised, tomorrow, they are scientifically useless.

If many scientists today are, like me, sceptical of claims made by Teilhardian biologists or Jungian psychologists or para-psychologists, it is not because we are prejudiced by 'the limitations of the positive outlook' in favour of purely materialistic or mechanistic ideas. Some prejudice there may be, as an inevitable (and perhaps even up to a point healthy) reaction in any age to strange new ideas, but there is no great prejudice against ideas of modern physicists, in spite of the fact that they talk about entities which are invisible, intangible and far from straightforwardly mechanical, or about four or five or more dimensions, or about matter which is also energy. The point is that the physicists are in no sense opening the door to the idea of deeper realities underlying experience. They are simply using their ingenuity to go beyond the simpler imaginative models of older science and find ways of making practical use of more *recherché* models, more subtle imaginations, which are judged as useful or useless exactly as the older models were, by their ability to pass the experimental test, and are accordingly never more than provisional, entirely expendable if they fail to pass the test. Our scepticism of the ideas of Teilhardian biology, Jungian psychology and para-psychology arises partly from the fact that we cannot see how they can be built into systematic and experimentally-testable plans for doing things that would not otherwise be possible; and partly from the fact that so many of those who put them forward seem quite openly to want to interpret them as statements about realities behind the scenes of ordinary experience, which would rule them out as useful scientific theories automatically. We suspect, therefore, that if events prove us wrong on the first score, and there does turn out to be something useful for future science in some of these ideas, then they will at that point lose their interest for many of the people who now advocate them, since they will then have the status of provisional, expendable models and provide no grounds whatever for holding on to, or reinstating, the traditional outlook.

I am not trying to deny that there is a real bias towards the use of mechanical and 'materialist' concepts in contemporary science, in the sense that efforts tend to be made to use them in preference to others whenever possible. What I am denying is that this is a necessary consequence of the positive outlook. Insofar as there is any connection between these two things at all, it arises from a perfectly proper desire on the scientists' part to try to link new realms of science with established ones, in the hope that the kinds of imaginative models that have proved so fruitful in suggesting new things to do in the realms of chemistry and physics, will be equally fruitful when extended to biological and psychological questions. Insofar as the bias towards mechanistic and materialistic concepts goes beyond this, it arises, not from the positive outlook, but from the persisting influence of the traditional outlook. When scientists, or more commonly philosophical thinkers who style themselves 'scientific', claim that the whole universe is 'really' nothing but a vast machine, they are, precisely, interpreting the theories of contemporary science in classical terms, taking them as descriptions of what the universe is 'really' like behind the scenes of the ordinary world of loves and hates, hopes and fears, purposes and meanings. Materialistic metaphysics of this kind are every bit as incompatible with the positive outlook as are metaphysics of the more traditional kind which claim that everything is 'really' under the control of astrological forces, or of angels or demons, or is a manifestation of Universal Consciousness. And equally, insofar as the bias towards mechanistic or materialistic concepts in modern thought corresponds to a practical bias in our society towards utilitarian activities rather than towards artistic or humanitarian imagination, this is in no sense an implication of the experimental attitude as such, which is of its essence an affirmation of the creative character of man's inner life: this kind of bias is rooted in the traditional organisation of society as a hierarchy of 'degree' in which manipulative work was assumed to be the ordained and natural lot of the great majority of people.

Whether the bias towards materialism in this sense is any greater in modern industrial civilisation than it was in earlier civilisations is in my view very doubtful. One of the toughest critics of ugly urbanisation and the degradation of craftsmanship in our society, Lewis Mumford, has made the point in his book *The Myth of the Machine* that the origins of mechanisation are to be found, not in the eighteenth century, but in ancient Egypt, when great tasks of engineering were undertaken by, in effect, building a machine out of human beings. He is able to trace the same principle, which he calls the principle of 'the Megamachine', right

47

through into the industrial revolution, so that the arrival of machines powered by steam, petrol and electricity comes to be seen as no more than an incident in an age-old process; at worst this final development intensified what had already been happening for centuries, but at the same time it offered the prospect of setting people free from mechanisation in a way which had never really been possible before without relapse into barbarism, and I would wish to add that this prospect of freedom from mechanisation is now coming within sight of realisation as we learn to develop the more subtle machines of the automation age. Mumford also makes the point that the mechanical organisation of society in Egyptian times and after was made possible because people felt the universe as a whole to be organised in great ordered revolving cycles, exemplified by the unchanging order of the stars and planets in their progress round the earth, and I am inclined to believe that the Grand Designs of the traditional outlook had the effect of making people feel themselves to be cogs in a vast machine far more than most people ever do in modern industrial society, where the work-organisations are seen as purely local, temporary things to which allegiance is given simply as a way of earning money. Ugliness, overcrowding and the stunting of human personality are real enough in the modern world, but we shall not overcome them by looking at earlier societies through rose-coloured spectacles, and that is what I believe is continually done by those who urge the recovery of the traditional outlook.

In particular, I believe the idea that the rise of industrial society and the decline of the traditional outlook has been accompanied by a withering of mankind's artistic imagination is for the most part a myth. The experimental outlook is of its nature an affirmation of the creative character of mankind's inner life, and it was therefore no accident, in my view, that the beginning of the scientific revolution was bound up with the Renaissance and the greatest flowering of the arts ever known in human history. Since then the different arts have had various periods of stagnation and various periods of vigour, but the only way to represent the whole period as one of uniform decline is to start out by assuming dogmatically that art *must* have the traditional outlook in order to be great, and then forcing the facts into the dogma by interpreting all poor artists as typical and all greater ones as somehow exceptions.

It is a complete misunderstanding to say that the positive outlook precludes people from feeling themselves into 'the inner life of things', as Wordsworth called it long before Jung. What it does is to make us think of inwardness as part – a crucially important part – of ordinary experience itself, instead of as a mysterious hidden life which has to be guessed at behind the surface of ordinary experience. The paradigm here is of course the inwardness of people, the autonomy of which is the basic assumption of the positive outlook: approaching life experimentally means taking the creative character of the inner life seriously in others as well as oneself, since experimental validation is always and essentially a communal business, even in the most abstract of sciences. In personal encounter we respond to the inwardness of others all the time, continually validating our intuitions or deductions about each person's inwardness by the way they work out in the practical business of continuing the relationship on its own appropriate level, whether it be a relationship of scientific exchange, business co-operation, war or love. The same principle can hold equally well if the artist, or for that matter the scientist, feels moved to respond to animals or trees or landscapes or inanimate objects in terms of a sense of some kind of inwardness. The positive outlook in no sense requires that such feelings be automatically set aside as false. It requires rather that they should be judged as sane or insane, not by any abstract authoritative view of whether they are correct statements of what lies behind the ordinary experience or not, but by whether they can be worked out in creative action of the appropriate kind (scientific or artistic) so as to achieve something new in the world of ordinary experience – in other words, that they should be seen as interesting rather than believed as in some sense authoritatively true. If the Teilhardian biologists or Jungian psychologists really are on to something scientifically interesting, then their ideas will work out in terms of new know-how in relation to life-processes or mental processes, but that is at present problematical. What is not at all problematical is that artists can and do produce viable enrichments of ordinary life from this kind of response to 'the inner life of things', as much today, when technology has created a whole new range of things, as in any earlier age.

It seems to me that the great artists of earlier ages bore witness to human creativity in spite of, and not because of, their need to work within the authoritative traditions of symbolism characteristic of the traditional outlook. The decline of that outlook deprived the artist of his traditional role in society as an interpreter of the great hidden truths of the world, but it gave him the even more significant role of a visionary who articulates new possibilities of experience in symbolic form – sensuous experience in painting or sculpture, emotional experience in music, social experience in drama, all three in poetry – in terms of which other people can decide how they wish to enrich their own lives, turning to science to provide the know-how. In this role the artist is inevitably from time to time at odds with the established habits of his society, but this is a function of artistic sensibility as such, and was every bit as true of artists in civilisations governed by the classical

49

outlook; their acknowledged role as interpreters of the hidden mysteries of existence did not preclude the possibility that their interpretations would be found uncomfortable by their patrons or their public, and the greater the artist the more frequently, on the whole, this happened, because his creativity disturbed people however devoutly he believed himself to be interpreting commonly-accepted truth. When traditionalist critical theory persuades contemporary artists to attribute their tensions and frustrations with modern society to the fact that they can no longer exercise the traditional artistic role, it seems to me that critical theory is guilty of misleading art from making its full response to the real challenges of our world, and to be flying in the face of the historical facts in doing so.

Fortunately artists of any real ability are capable of giving the lie to critical theories even when they hold them themselves, and I believe we have a superb illustration of this principle in the work of T. S. Eliot. His description of the period of the scientific revolution as 'a dissociation of sensibility', and his contention that the artist must be able to appeal to a symbolic tradition in order to produce really great work, are invoked again and again in support of the view that art has no future unless mankind recovers something of the classical outlook, yet in his own poetry and plays he shows himself capable of appealing to audiences that know scarcely anything of the classical Greek or Christian symbolism he chose to use. He demonstrates impressively that the absence of belief in the truth of a symbolic tradition does not prevent the artist from making telling use of symbolic language, not even of traditional symbolic language if he finds it interesting for articulating a vision: if his creative power is great enough he can make other people interested in his symbols, even though they never come to accept them as 'true'. In art, as in science, the modern mind's emphasis on interest rather than truth implies that the creative nature of the human animal is being taken seriously in the recipients as well as in the initiators of creative activity, which in the case of art means that the audience makes a genuine creative response (as implied by 'This is interesting') instead of a response in which creativity is subordinated to obedience (as implied by 'This is true').

When Eliot used his poetic skills and his Christian or classical Greek symbolism to articulate the trivialisation and dehumanisation of life in contemporary civilisation, he was in reality doing no more and no less than Shakespeare did when he exposed the 'wars and lechery' of classical society in the later acts of *Troilus and Cressida*, or the inhumanities of his own near-contemporary England in his plays about the Wars of the Roses. The dignified moral order and balanced sanity which some modern advocates of the traditional outlook seem to believe existed in earlier civilisations was not what the artists of those days saw. William Blake saw the wings of the angel of art clipped and the human image crucified by Christendom quite as much as by the 'dark Satanic mills' of the industrial revolution, although traditionalist critics tend to remember only the latter. Francis Bacon wrote of the lonely crowd three centuries before David Riesman, and before the industrial revolution had even begun. 'They make a desert and call it peace' was a comment on life in the Roman Empire, two thousand years before the threat of nuclear warfare. Above all, the image of people being driven mad by the pressure of society recurs again and again in the works of the Greek dramatists, of Seneca, of the Wandering Scholars in the Middle Ages, of Spenser and of Shakespeare. In fact the idea that the rise of industrial society and the decline of the traditional outlook has been accompanied by a lowering either of mental health or of moral vision seems to me to be another myth which can be sustained only by looking at the past through a tinted glass, rosily.

Statistics showing violent increases in mental diseases, sexual deviations or crime need to be interpreted with great caution, as experts know. Certainly they reveal grave problems confronting modern society, but it by no means follows that these problems are rooted in peculiarly modern conditions. In many cases the figures merely reflect improved methods of diagnosis, greater public frankness and an increased interest in collecting statistics which in earlier times no one thought to be interesting. And below this salutary but rather superficial observation lies a consideration of fundamental importance, to which psychologists have begun to pay attention only relatively recently, namely, that violence, perversion and neurosis can escape attention by being built into the structure of society itself.

Instead of delinquency, which modern 'open' society worries about as a problem, the more closely integrated societies of pre-industrial civilisations took violence for granted in frequent small wars, in public executions or floggings for relatively trivial crimes, and in the savage persecution of heretics of one sort or another, all of which were considered part of the natural, ordained scheme of things by the vast majority of rulers and ruled alike. The enormities which shocked the world in Nazi Germany would have been accepted by some of the mediaeval Popes as normal business to be attended to before or after Mass. In fact the Grand Design of the traditional outlook did not prevent demagogues from wielding power, or mitigate the rat-race of ambition, or stop people from using words like 'right', 'wrong' and 'justice' to cover up their cruelty and greed: it merely provided a framework of thought in which these things could be concealed, as of course great artists showed in their works long before modern psychology was thought of. In particular, Shakespeare explored the theme again and again in his plays: although he was concerned at the dangers which would arise from the repudiation of the Grand Design, he was also at pains to make clear that this would do no more than bring out into the open evils that the Grand Design served to disguise – and bringing them out into the open would provide the first real possibility of trying to do something to cure them.

Another truth always known to artists which is now being forced into public attention by the findings of psychologists and anthropologists is that the high sexual codes of some traditional societies did not mean that sexual deviations were 'kept in control', but rather that they flourished in disguised forms behind the façades of Church, army, court and home. In this respect, too, the decline of the traditional outlook with its rooted standards of 'normal' behaviour has not led to any new outburst of hitherto controlled sexuality, so much as to the open recognition of what human feelings and needs are really like in this area of life. But perhaps the most important of all exposures now being made along these lines by psychologists and anthropologists is of the way in which whole societies can in effect be organised neuroses. It is being recognised, for example, that organised social ritual, which proponents of the traditional outlook so often fasten on as one of the great lacks of modern society, actually leaves the participants just as cut off inside themselves from real human contact with one another as the conventional neurotic of modern society is as he sits in his 'little box' performing obsessive private rituals. Equally, it is beginning to appear that people who live 'in modest harmony with nature', far from being the noble savages or peaceful peasants or contented craftsmen of popular mythology, are in fact overshadowed for most of their lives by fear of nature's uncertainties, and because of this are riddled with taboos and compulsions which are unmistakably neurotic when they are once examined objectively. For every African who suffers breakdown through being uprooted from the age-old harmonies of his tribal life under the impact of industrialisation, it is beginning to seem likely that there are at least two, and possibly a dozen, who fly to the cities not for the lure of money but in the hope of escaping from the prison of tribal existence, in comparison with which even the overcrowded slums offer the attraction of a spark of freedom.

This is in no sense to deny that the loneliness, overcrowding, noise and pace of industrial life causes mental strain and breakdown on a horrifying scale. It is simply to say that the total proportion of such suffering in society may well be no greater than it ever was, and that suffering which is recognised as such, and whose causes are known, is surely to be preferred to suffering which is disguised and which people are expected to put up with as part of some Great Plan. It is easy, for example, to see how aircraft noise or the frenzy of rush-hour commuting causes mental strain, not so easy – yet surely necessary – to reflect that these problems could never have arisen if the human organism did not have capacities which lie unused in non-industrial society, neglect of which possibly causes other kinds of frustration and strain that no one can possibly recognise until some kind of alternative to traditional patterns of living is offered. The traditional outlook discourages any expression of frustration with established ways of living, so that if these ways of living have elements in them which, on any objective view, justify the term 'neurotic' – as I believe they commonly do – then the traditional outlook ensures that the neurosis is never recognised. The modern outlook, by encouraging objective examination and experimental discovery, ensures that neurosis, whether caused by new or by age-old conditions, is recognised for what it is – sickness requiring remedy. The increase in 'mental cases' is in my view one of the most hopeful features of our society.

Moreover these psychological considerations seem to me to reveal the heart of the whole matter I have been discussing in this chapter. For if I am right in even half my contentions about the way people misunderstand the modern outlook, it is impossible to avoid the question of why misunderstanding occurs and persists on this scale. In particular, it is not necessary to be Freud in order to wonder what it is about the traditional outlook which causes so many people to want to hold on to it or reinstate it, when so many of their ostensible reasons for wanting to do so involve misunderstandings. This is a question which has to be faced honestly both by religious people and by those 'fellow-travellers' in the literary or psychological fields who have rallied to the defence of the traditional outlook, if they are to say anything really convincing one way or another about religion to children, for even if all my contentions are rejected, the mere fact that they can be raised means that many people will suspect there is some kind of neurotic defence-mechanism in the traditional outlook, leading people to find rationalisations to avoid abandoning it. The question has in any case been forced on all thinking people in the modern world by the contention of many psychoanalysts that religion is, in Freud's famous words, a kind of universal human neurosis.

As I shall try to show in the next chapter, this is a diagnosis, not of specific religious beliefs, but of the traditional outlook itself, closely related to the recognition of 'organised neuroses' in many of mankind's traditional patterns of living. It is not a philosophical judgement but a practical one, arising from actual analyses, and I shall try to show that when it is properly understood it is in no way contradicted by Jung's discoveries concerning the positive value of great religious images as expressions of major features of mankind's inner life. I believe modern depth-psychology provides overwhelming evidence, for anyone who faces its findings seriously and honestly, that the transition from the traditional to the modern outlook represents a major advance in sanity, because the traditional outlook was of its very nature a suppression or evasion of man's most distinctively human characteristic. To take full advantage of this advance in sanity, however, it is necessary, for reasons I have already touched upon in a preliminary way, to set aside not only traditional religion but also modern materialism, and I believe there is a real possibility here for a new kind of religion which is humanist while going beyond conventional atheist humanism.

6: Religion and materialism on the psychoanalyst's couch
with some autobiographical illustration

The statement that religion ought to be seen as a kind of general neurosis, which was first published by Freud in 1927, is one of the most widely misunderstood sayings of modern times. It has been misunderstood both by supporters of religion who set out to refute it and, almost equally, by people who quote it with approval; it has even sometimes been misunderstood by Freud's followers in the psychoanalytic movement. In particular, it is commonly treated, both by supporters and by opponents of religion, as if it were meant as another blow in the old 'conflict between science and religion' – akin to the claim that physics disproves the possibility of miracles or that the discovery of evolution disproves the notion of divine creation – but in fact it was something much more fundamental than that. It was an attempt to bring out and characterise the underlying psychological basis of the whole history of 'conflict between science and religion', by showing it to have been a conflict of attitudes rather than of specific beliefs, and by diagnosing the attitude normally associated with religion as one of neurotic refusal to face facts.

Most of the efforts made by supporters of religion to refute Freud's view of it have been quite beside the point: indeed they have provided unwitting evidence in its favour, since they have avoided facing the facts of what Freud actually said! For example, his well-known suggestion that belief in God the Father arises by a process of 'projecting' buried infantile images of human parents into the heavens, is frequently taken as an attempt to explain God away, and for nearly forty years religious spokesmen have devoted books, articles and sermons to demonstrating that this involves a logical fallacy. They argue that no psychological account of the internal mechanisms by which beliefs are formed in the mind can possibly disprove – or for

E

that matter prove – the truth of those beliefs: the concepts of higher mathematics are in no way discredited by the recognition that they all ultimately derive from savages counting on their toes, and if human beings are to conceive at all of being dependent on a divine creator, they must perforce use mental mechanisms formed in childhood from the experience of dependence on human parents. This argument is exactly parallel to those which were (and sometimes still are) advanced to show philosophically that neither Galileo's description of the heavens nor Darwin's description of the emergence of life on earth could in principle invalidate the idea of divine purpose behind creation, and like those older arguments is both logically correct and completely beside the point. Indeed, it is beside the point in a much more obvious and pedestrian sense than the arguments about astronomy or evolution, for the people who quoted Galileo or Darwin against religion usually *thought* they were disproving the existence of God, whereas Freud knew perfectly well he could do no such thing, and said as much. The real issue – the clash between the experimental approach to life and the whole business of believing in realities 'behind the scenes', beyond disproof, beyond experimental evaluation – remained concealed on both sides in the older arguments, whereas Freud's purpose was precisely to bring it out.

His theory about the mental genesis of the idea of a Father-God was in fact only incidental to a much more general analysis of what is actually happening in people's minds when they base their lives on belief in things that are supposed to exist even though they are beyond the reach of experimental evaluation. This analysis took its rise from the recognition that the mental processes and types of behaviour involved in such 'religious' belief are precisely the same as the mental processes and types of behaviour associated with neurotic (or psychotic) delusions in the most straightforward sense. The point may be illustrated by taking as an example that standard lunatic of music-hall and fiction, the man who believes himself to be Napoleon (although this was not an example Freud himself used, since he was writing primarily for people who would already be familiar with the phenomena of neurotic or psychotic delusion in real-life cases, which are not usually as dramatic or simple as this).

It is characteristic of a person suffering from this kind of delusion that if well-wishing friends or doctors try to cure him by producing evidence that his belief is false, or evidence of his actual identity, they are likely to find themselves countered by elaborate and often highly logical arguments to prove that the evidence can be ignored. For example, he will dismiss a history-book showing that Napoleon died a century ago as a forgery produced by the conspirators who are trying to prevent him from claiming his rightful place on the throne of France, and he will probably be able to find a good deal of internal evidence of forgery in the book. He will have similar cast-iron logical arguments to explain away any documents showing that he is in fact Joe Bloggs, born at 12, Doggetts Square, Strood, Kent, on 5th May, 1924. At the same time, he will produce clues of his own to show, with quite plausible reasoning, that he really *is* the person he claims to be, and the victim of a conspiracy: for instance, a handkerchief in his pocket bearing the initials J.B. will be advanced as a fairly obvious present from Josephine to Buonaparte, while the antipathy shown by his alleged family to his long reminiscences of the retreat from Moscow will be taken as proof that they are really actors and not his family at all. Yet he will not be at all surprised when the evidence fails to convince anyone other than himself, since he has long ago decided that all his apparent well-wishers are involved in the conspiracy. Because of this he is likely to insist on keeping up various private rituals, such as dressing up for dinner in a certain way or making regular readings from accounts of Napoleon's campaigns, in order to maintain his hold on the 'truth' in spite of the false appearances produced by the persecutors who are trying to brainwash him.

In the technical jargon of psychology this kind of behaviour is known as 'paranoid fantasy-obsession', and one of Freud's major achievements in the study of mental disease, before he turned his attention to wider human affairs such as religion, had been to show that delusions like this are more than meaningless aberrations due to mechanical brain-failure, as most medical and psychological opinion had supposed them to be before his time. He showed them to spring out of a wish to escape from the responsibilities of ordinary life, and this discovery is now generally accepted even by psychologists who are very critical of Freud's other theories, including physiologically-minded psychologists who hold on to the view that a mechanical or chemical failure is involved in bringing about the retreat from ordinary life. The Joe Bloggs who think themselves Napoleons may be suffering from a brain deficiency, or they may be simply victims of unfortunate upbringing, but the essential point is that for one reason or another they are unwilling to accept the limitations of their ordinary Joe Bloggs situation and, even more important, they are not prepared to face the responsibility of trying to improve that situation. They accordingly construct a fantasy-world which they persuade themselves exists behind the scenes of their ordinary experience, namely, the supposedly 'real' world in which they are great leaders being deprived of their rightful position by conspiracy, and this fantasy becomes the basis of their lives. Their intelligence – which can perfectly well be quite high – is used, not to improve their actual lives, but to rationalise everything that happens in terms of their supposed 'concealed truth'.

Freud's diagnosis of religion arose initially from specific cases of psychological analysis in which religious beliefs were actually found to be performing the same paranoid function for people, albeit usually in a milder form, as delusional fantasies perform in the lives of obvious lunatics. The effect of analysis in such cases was to make the whole question of the possible metaphysical 'truth' of the beliefs irrelevant, since the patients' motives for holding – and holding on to – the beliefs was revealed as having nothing to do with considerations of metaphysical truth, being entirely a matter of emotional interest in maintaining a barrier of fantasy against the practical challenges of ordinary life. This can be found to happen – and since Freud's day has been found to happen again and again in many different kinds of psychological analysis – with people who are not mentally sick in any very severe sense. Religious spokesmen often criticise Freud for generalising unjustifiably about religion from what he saw of it in minds which, being those of neurotic patients, were already sick anyhow, but this again is a criticism that misses the point of what Freud actually said. It was a central feature of his work that paranoid retreat from experience into fantasy is not a special characteristic of a peculiar class of people called madmen, but is, rather, a tendency in the minds of all of us that leads us into madness if followed. We all, in other words, have tendencies towards neurotic escape from life's challenges, and religious ideas can again and again be found to exemplify just these tendencies, as I can best illustrate from my own experience.

This particular illustration serves incidentally to rebut two other arguments that are commonly used against Freud's diagnosis, on the one hand the argument that psychoanalytic treatment is so intensive that it can brainwash people into accepting the analysts' conclusions, and on the other the argument that the diagnosis applies only to extreme forms of religious belief involving terrible notions of guilt. My own religious convictions have never been of the hell-fire guilt-obsessed kind: insofar as I had any knowledge of these ideas at all from early childhood (and it was not much) I repudiated them in favour of a vigorous H. G. Wellsian 'scientific atheism' in my very early teens. When I subsequently began to take a positive interest in religion in my university years, it was of the mildest, middle-of-the-road Anglican variety, with strong tendencies towards Modernist interpretations of theology of the kind that are often associated with the more liberal, intellectual wing of the Student Christian Movement. Its central emphasis was on divine love, and on the function of the Church as a community dedicated to expressing divine love in terms of human love, both between its own members and, even more important, in the general structure of human society. I openly despised religious people who laid heavy emphasis on guilt or personal salvation, and indeed accused them of being neurotic. I made free reference to Freud's notion of the Father-God as a neurotic projection, but argued that the true Christian idea of God was nothing like this, being a universal Ground of Being for which terms like 'Father' were merely convenient symbols in earlier ages. It was therefore a considerable shock to me to discover that my own mild, humanistic and 'healthy-minded' religious views were paranoid defence-mechanisms, but the discovery was forced on me, not by any long period of psychoanalytic brainwashing, but as a simple insight brought about largely by the circumstances of my ordinary life, mediated by very small amount of contact with an analytical psychologist of Jungian rather than strictly Freudian inclinations.

No 'mental illness' was involved: the occasion was simply the break-up of a particularly cherished personal relationship, of a kind which happens in a great many people's lives. It served, however, to make me recognise that my beliefs about Universal Divine Love were based, not on any objective philosophical considerations about the nature of the universe, but on a desire to have 'love' without the necessity of taking any real notice of other people or of their actual needs. By convincing myself that I had a revelation (from the Bible and Christian tradition) of the true, objective nature of Universal Love, I was able to convince myself that I knew what was best for everybody, irrespective of their own wishes or feelings: I also, incidentally, provided myself with an excuse to exercise a considerable natural gift for preaching, without having to give too much attention to the hard practical details of what precisely would be involved in achieving a more 'loving' society. There were no gods or demons in my theology, no Wrathful Father or Blood of the Lamb, no Everlasting Arms or hell fires, yet I was for all that living in a fantasy-world, a world where Universal Love was working away behind the scenes to bring everyone and everything to a great consummation beyond the limitations of time and space. By interpreting everything that happened in terms of its contribution to (or reaction against) this Grand Design I was able to avoid taking seriously any concrete facts I did not wish to face, from the boredom of my job to the inconvenience or pain I sometimes caused my friends. Being on the whole a naturally friendly individual, reasonably warm and kind, the discrepancy between my professions and my actions could escape notice for much of the time, and where it appeared my powers of argument (public and private) were sufficient to cover it up and deceive many other people for much of the time, as well as myself the whole time. When the moment of truth came, however, the question of the possible metaphysical 'truth' of my various arguments became completely irrelevant. I realised that the whole business of believing in metaphysical truth had been a way of avoiding the challenges and responsibilities of ordinary life.

I cannot, of course, assert dogmatically that *every* religious person would come to the same kind of discovery about his beliefs if he were really honest: what I am prepared to assert is that until the *possibility* of this kind of discovery is faced with complete honesty we can have nothing to say that will carry any real conviction to the children in this post-Freudian era – not even to children whose normal environment is totally devoid of any explicit knowledge of Freud. For the Freudian insight has begun to permeate the whole atmosphere of western civilisation, not primarily from directly personal discoveries, so much as from a dawning (if often still very obscure) awareness of the real significance of the decline of religion that has accompanied the rise of the experimental outlook over the past few centuries. This was the insight which Freud himself achieved when he went on from his purely experimental discovery of the paranoid character of religious ideas in individual psychological analyses, to a recognition of the fact that paranoid fantasy-thinking is not confined to the private lives of individuals, but can be shared by whole groups of people, even by whole societies.

This too is an insight that is now generally accepted even by psychologists, sociologists and anthropologists who are otherwise very critical of Freud's general theories. Indeed, Freud lived to see it horrifyingly demonstrated to the world in the phenomenon of Nazism, in which millions of Germans were able to escape from the humiliation of post-war depression, and from the responsibility of facing the rehabilitation of their country as an economically vital part of a politically co-operative Europe, by living in a collective fantasy of the Nordic race being kept from its glorious destiny by an evil world-conspiracy of Jews and Communists. This might be described as a large-scale social counterpart of the man who believes himself to be Napoleon, except that a better analogy would be the dangerous kind of lunatic whose paranoid fantasies can lead him into murder if he is left at large (would-be Napoleons being notoriously harmless, unlike Nazi Germany). Hitler himself was probably just such a paranoiac, with vague delusions of reincarnating the old Aryan gods, but the important point in this case is that he was able to persuade a whole society to join in his fantasy, with *collective* rituals to subdue any doubts about the fantasy that might arise. Freud first perceived the possibility of this kind of collective paranoid fantasy long before the Nazi movement had begun to establish itself, by studying the psychology of primitive religion and its relation to tribal solidarity – an insight which found dramatic fictional expression, before Freud's ideas were at all well known, in H. G. Wells' story *The Country of the Blind*. In this story a traveller stumbles upon an isolated valley inhabited wholly by a tribe of blind people, and he finds by bitter experience that the old proverb about the one-eyed man being king in such a country would hold good only if he took great care to conceal the fact of his sight while exploiting it. Wells' hero, far from being welcomed for his ability to see, is persecuted as a dangerous heretic because he challenges the blind community's religious belief in a literal heavenly dome above the world from which divine beings give orders for the organisation of life.

Wells was not of course just writing a story about primitive religion: he was concerned rather to use his fictional tribe to satirise the way Christianity, Islam and other higher religions behave, and hence to make the same point as Auguste Comte had made at the beginning of the Victorian era, that theological beliefs represent a primitive mode of thought and life. Freud too went on from his studies of primitive religion to a general diagnosis of religion as such, but his judgement was a deeper and more subtle one. Having recognised the possibility of paranoid fantasy spreading across a whole society and even forming the basis of its life, he went on to see that the paranoia was to be found, not in any specific beliefs, but in the basic act of believing in realities 'behind the scenes' of ordinary experience, of basing life on supposed metaphysical truths beyond the reach of experimental evaluation or disproof. His characterisation of religion as 'the universal obsessional neurosis of humanity' was in fact a diagnosis of the entire traditional structure of human society, the whole traditional 'way of responding to life'. Although as far as I have been able to discover Freud made no reference to Comte's earlier diagnosis, his own was similar both in recognising the radical difference of *attitude* between traditional 'religious' and modern experimental thinking, and also in bringing out the essential psychological similarity between relatively primitive or crude religious ideas and the more abstract metaphysical notions to which people of higher education commonly resort (a point which my own personal self-discovery served to bring home directly to me, inasmuch as I found that my very abstract metaphysical beliefs were serving precisely the same kind of neurotic purpose as the cruder beliefs I had so loftily condemned in more old-fashioned religious people). Where Comte had been content to describe the traditional attitude to life as primitive, however, Freud diagnosed it as psychologically diseased in the sense of being founded on flight from responsibility, with the implication that the steady decline of the traditional outlook over the past three hundred years was quite literally an advance in social sanity – not just a 'growing up' or 'coming of age' of human thought, as Comte's diagnosis implied, but a gradual escape from the bondage of an age-long state of neurotic inhibition.

Freud did not develop this implication of his diagnosis at all systematically in relation to the history of the scientific revolution, but then he lived before historians generally had begun to recognise and bring out its truly revolutionary character. His diagnosis seems to me the only way to make sense of the fact that human thought about the world's workings made such very small progress in the thousands of years prior to the seventeenth century, in spite of the existence of thinkers every bit as clever and every bit as capable as any modern scientists, and even in spite – as historians are increasingly realising – of the existence of many of the necessary mental and practical techniques. Professor Herbert Butterfield, in his book *The Origins of Modern Science*, pin-points the crucial change of the scientific revolution as 'a new feeling for matter', and when Francis Bacon first tried to express this change he did so in terms which almost anticipated Freud's diagnosis of traditional thinking as paranoid fantasy: he spoke of current religiously-approved speculations about the natural world as 'idols of the theatre', a form of mental play-acting which avoided the responsibility of practical exploration by experiment. He attributed it to a form of hypnosis exercised on scholars' minds by scholastic philosophy. Freud's insight goes deeper; it enables us to see the sense in which scholastic philosophy was psychologically of a piece with religion, and hence to see the revolution in science which Bacon pioneered as part of a wider release of human life from an age-long neurotic inhibition of human creativity in all aspects of culture and social life.

The academics of Bacon's day were not slow to try to repudiate the charge of avoiding responsibility. They pointed to the rigour of their logic and to the diligence of their labours in the study, in the field and in the alchemical laboratory. In the same way modern religious spokesmen have tried to repudiate Freud's more comprehensive version of the same charge by pointing out the positive burden of responsibility which religion imposes in moral and social life on anyone who takes it at all sincerely. This, however, is yet another argument that misses the real point of Freud's diagnosis, for the essential characteristic of neurotic illusion is that it achieves nothing real, not even the escape it seeks to achieve. Joe Bloggs still has to cope with the problems of humdrum living in spite of his fantasies of being Napoleon: the routines of workaday life could scarcely be more tedious than the rituals he imposes on himself in his obsession. The majority of Germans had to cope with even greater burdens of hardship and humiliation under

Nazism than they would have done without it. Reality is not mocked, and if real responsibility is evaded by retreat into paranoid fantasy, the fantasy exacts its price – often with interest – in terms of unnecessary burdens which bring no profit to anyone. The labours of the alchemists and scholastic natural philosophers were largely of this character, and it seems to me that the same is true of a great many of the burdens of moral and social responsibility undertaken or imposed in the name of religion.

They may indeed be as great as – sometimes even more wearying than – the responsibilities that arise out of ordinary human sensitivity or from the rational claims of social life, but they are unprofitable in the sense that moral or social action that is *not* undertaken out of ordinary human sympathy or the rational claims of social life is largely ineffective and often positively harmful. My one-time belief in the moral and social demands of Universal Divine Love was not one whit less escapist for involving me in a frenzy of benevolent and reforming activity. The burden of human relationships remained with me, but because I chose to try to escape from their real challenge into this metaphysical fantasy, my real sensitivity was far less than it would otherwise have been, and my efforts to spread 'love' often caused pain. On the wider plane of society as a whole, notions of divinely-instituted systems of social 'degree' or of 'Christian marriage' are no less escapist for being hard on large numbers of people. However different they may be from the Nazi system in detailed content, they resemble it in requiring individuals to live by a system of abstract rights and duties that are supposed to correspond to his 'station in life' in the underlying Grand Scheme, rather than by direct response to other individuals or by rational co-operation for agreed practical objectives. Under such systems the individual may well be confronted with very harsh, punishing burdens, but their effect is to meet no one's real need properly, while building up great reservoirs of repressed resentment which in one way or another finds its outlet in cruel or destructive action. Supporters of religion often argue (like Shakespeare's Ulysses whom I quoted earlier) that something more is needed, over and above ordinary human sympathy or rational acceptance of the need for co-operation and companionship, to hold marriages together or to make society work harmoniously, but the truth is that insofar as people do stay together or do their daily work for such 'supernatural' reasons they succeed only in creating inhuman situations full of repressed violence which sooner or later expresses itself, usually in disguised form.

As I indicated in the previous chapter, I believe Shakespeare was well aware of the fact that the Grand Design of traditional society which his character Ulysses described so eloquently was a sham in precisely the sense I have been describing, and in our own day the point has been made very neatly in Bertolt Brecht's play about the life of Galileo, from which I quoted in Chapter Four. In this play, the little monk who is Galileo's disciple, yet is worried about his master's new approach to astronomy even though he believes it to be correct, illustrates his worry by describing his aged parents. They have lived out their lives, he says, slaving each day in the parched vineyards from morning to night, in the belief that it has been their part in the same Grand Divine Scheme whereby the sun and the moon move unweary-ingly across the sky: if now Galileo takes away this vision, what will they have to keep them going? Galileo's reply is simply that there is no need for them to keep going: if the vineyards were irrigated instead of being tilled by the age-old ritual they could get more crops for less labour, and if they broke free from their sense of supernatural duty to their landlords they would get a fairer share of the rewards of their work. The little monk's rejoinder comes very close to Freud's diagnosis of the real emotional reason underlying the maintenance of the tradi-tional outlook and its Grand Designs: 'But they are tired, Mr Galilei.'

Freud's diagnosis would say 'scared' rather than 'tired', and the difference is important, for the little monk's plea could be regarded as having a certain amount of force, in purely human terms, in relation to people who have grown old under the traditional outlook. Indeed it is often echoed nowadays by religious spokesmen who see something of the true nature of the challenge of the modern experimental outlook, and are even prepared to grant that the traditional outlook may have involved a certain amount of delusion, but nevertheless feel that the decline of traditional beliefs is proceeding too fast for many ordinary people to bear it. Can we be so completely certain of the virtues of the modern outlook that we can allow simple people's life-plans to be shattered, they ask? Are we so absolutely sure that there is nothing in traditional beliefs at all, that we are prepared to remove their support even from those who have grown old and tired in them? In general I believe the question is unreal, because I am convinced, like Brecht's Galileo, that the traditional outlook actually makes things harder than they need be for ordinary people, but for old people I could not be so completely dogmatic, as I suspect Brecht could not either: perhaps the human organism does reach a stage when ingrained routines, however harsh, are less painful than being required to take initiative. It is a question for psychological specialists to which I would not be prepared to try to guess an answer, and for this reason I would not myself wish to upset any old person's beliefs (although my own experience suggests that old people, like children, are not nearly so much in need of protection as some of the worthy middle-aged suppose). When we are considering what to tell the children, however, the question simply does not arise, for even if we thought it desirable to protect them from the challenge of the experimental outlook, it simply cannot be done, as I have insisted from the beginning of this book (and I doubt very much if it can be done for many old people either, unless they can neither read nor watch television). The challenge of the experimental outlook *must* be faced, simply because it has become an inescapable part of our lives, and to face it satisfactorily we have to give full, serious and honest consideration to the case for believing, with Freud, that the traditional outlook now stands exposed as an age-long neurosis of the human race.

Can such an issue possibly be put before the children themselves? With older children I think there is no doubt that it can and must be, for it is an essential part of helping them to articulate the doubts and uncertainties about religious matters that they find around them in the world – the crucial task of religious education today in my view. Let me emphasise again, as I have tried to do throughout this book, that the problem here is not primarily (perhaps not even necessarily at all) a matter of talking about philosophical questions. The issue has to be posed primarily in personal, experiential terms, and I believe it is possible for the parent or teacher to declare his own personal decision on this basic question while still presenting a lively appreciation of the alternative decision and what it means. I myself, for example, have no doubt of my own decision about the nature of the traditional outlook, and have left no doubt of it in the discussion in this and the previous chapter, but I have also indicated, at the beginning of Chapter Five, that many distinguished people like T. S. Eliot and C. G. Jung have come down on the other side, and I have tried to give some glimpse both of their reasons and of how life appears to them when they have done so. In actual discussion with older children I should and do go further on this point, both developing the arguments in favour of the traditional outlook in more detail, and allowing artists like Eliot to convey the feel of that outlook with the cunning of their art, as for example in the play *The Family Reunion*, where two characters express in ritualised speech the notion that our human conflicts and guilts have their effects 'behind the scenes':

> . . . in the nether world
> Where the meshes we have woven
> Bind us to each other . . .
> . . . A curse is written
> On the underside of things,
> Behind the smiling mirror
> And behind the smiling moon.

Equally I think it is both possible and essential for a parent or teacher who, after full, serious and honest consideration of the evidence, has nevertheless found a way of rejecting Freud's diagnosis of the traditional outlook, to give a fair and lively presentation of the kind of case I have been putting in favour of it, both personal and social, in these two chapters. If he fails to do this for children who are old enough to understand at all, and who are bound to want to understand somehow when they see both attitudes to life represented in society around them, then he is failing in his duty to them.

What about younger children? I do not propose to enter here into the question of the age at which children can begin to understand issues like this explicitly, which in my view is a question for specialised psychological investigation, where at present we know remarkably little with any certainty. Instead, I want to make rather a different point. In my experience it is mainly parents and teachers anxious to put over a religious point of view who deny the possibility of presenting anything even remotely like the Freudian diagnosis to younger children, but in fact they themselves are often engaged in putting over a remarkably similar notion in the course of their own religious teaching. I am referring to the idea that mankind is 'fallen' or 'under bondage to original sin', which occurs in most of the world's religious traditions and is certainly an essential prerequisite for presenting the idea of Christian salvation. This idea – of mankind being under bondage to some kind of alienation from the beginning of history – has obvious affinities with Freud's idea of a universal neurosis, for although 'sinfulness' is defined in terms of the traditional 'theological' outlook as alienation from God, it has always been understood even within theology to carry the implication of an alienation of human beings from their own human health and potential as well. Hence if parables and stories can be used to give children some idea of the religious concept of man being 'fallen', they can equally well be used to convey the kind of thing Freud was trying to say, namely, that somewhere at the very beginning the human race seems to have turned aside from the challenge of using its power of imagination to improve life creatively, and equally from the challenge of real mutual perception of personal needs in human relationships – turned aside by using imagination to create fantasies of a hidden pattern behind the scenes into which human life should be fitted.

Indeed, the parallel between Freud's diagnosis and the religious idea of 'fallen mankind' goes even further in the case of the Jewish-Christian religion, as Freud himself, as a Jew, was well aware. If a parent or scripture-teacher is going to refer to the Bible in talking to children, then he is bound to come across the notion that at least some kinds of religious imagination – namely, the kind referred to as 'idolatrous' – are fundamentally bound up with mankind's condition of alienation or 'sinfulness'. The Bible actually says that idolatry is the essence of sin – when man turns aside from his own health and potential it is not to anything like unbelief in the sense of atheism, but rather to the worship of 'false gods', by which the Biblical writers did not mean just physical idols of wood and stone, but false *imaginations* of gods, or in other words, precisely, 'fantasies of hidden powers behind the scenes of life'. What is more, the condemnation of idolatry was not just a straight-forward demand that people should believe in one special Power Behind the Scenes (Jehovah or God) rather than a number of rival powers (Dagon, Moloch or whoever). No doubt this was all it meant on occasions, but on other occasions something more subtle must have been involved, for in the prophetic literature of the Bible we are confronted repeatedly with the notion that the Israelites (or later the Christians) were themselves indulging in 'idolatrous imagination' even though they used no physical images and professed, to themselves as well as others, to be worshipping the One True God. Unless the Jewish or Christian parent or teacher is going to omit all reference to these more difficult passages of the Bible in talking to the children, he is going to find himself having to explain that any 'brand' of belief about Divine Power governing life from behind the scenes *can* be a diseased use of the imagination, an escape from the fundamental challenge of life, however respectable its theology appears. If this is once faced, there is little difficulty in going on to explain Freud's wider application of the same principle to religion in general.

To approach the matter in this way is, however, to raise a question which Freud himself never really faced, and which never even occurs to the majority of more conventional atheists or to the majority of supporters of religion, namely of whether the prophetic writers in the Bible and in other great religious documents may possibly have meant something quite different from what we ordinarily take them to mean in their protestations about the 'true God' – something that was not really 'theological' at all in the ordinary sense, something that actually had to do with overcoming mankind's traditional outlook rather than with living in terms of it. As I have suggested earlier, something like this does seem to have been implied, however inadvertently, by Francis Bacon at the very beginning of the modern decline of the traditional outlook, when he explicitly advocated the adoption of the experimental outlook in place of the traditional *in the name of recovering a long-buried truth of Biblical religion.* I believe this question is one which must nowadays be considered very seriously in deciding what we today have to tell the children, for it is not merely of academic interest: if there is indeed something of this character in religion, it is potentially of immense importance for the future of our whole civilisation. Supporters of religion are bound to consider this possibility even if they radically disagree with my judgement that the traditional outlook was diseased, for otherwise they convict themselves of being blinkered about difficult passages in the Bible and other religious documents of the world, and hence of using them in precisely the way Freud diagnosed, to support a fantasy-system in which awkward facts (even facts about religion itself) can be ignored. More positively, no responsible supporter of religion can seriously ignore the possibility of finding something in religion that he has not hitherto suspected. But for anyone who considers, as I do, that the overcoming of the traditional outlook means a major advance in human sanity, the possibility that there is something in the world's great religious traditions that actually worked in this direction, in complete contradiction of the normal character of religion, is of even greater interest, for it may be of considerable importance in helping mankind to heal civilisation's division into 'two cultures' by bringing the revolution of the last few hundred years to fruition.

This is a point on which it seems to me that a great many atheists and humanists are quite as guilty of superficiality as religious supporters ever are of obscurantism. They tend to assume that our civilisation's problems about religion will simply disappear in due course as scientific education spreads, but in fact the overcoming of the traditional outlook is by no means proceeding as a matter of course, and, what is more important, it is not only the supporters of religion who are standing in the way of it. On the contrary, the traditional outlook exercises its most powerful sway in the modern world not in the surviving remnants of religion but in the new mental tyrannies which may conveniently be lumped together under the general name of materialism.

I am using the term here in a fairly commonsense way, to embrace all those kinds of philosophy, whether articulate or only semi-articulate, in which the theories of contemporary science are taken as descriptions of what the universe is 'really like', with the result that people come to think of themselves as mere by-products of a vast evolving system of physical forces. This notion is often used by religious propagandists as a bogey with which to frighten us into holding on to traditional ways of thinking, but the thing itself is no mere bogey. It is indeed a mental tyranny which, as the religious propagandists are wont to say, 'devalues personality', whether in the explicit political tyrannies based on Marxism, where the individual is thought of as valuable solely insofar as he contributes to the historic process of creating the perfect society of the future; or in the subtler, less articulate forms of the west, where lip-service is paid to individual value but the mechanical patterns of commercial and social practice commonly squeeze it out of existence with utilitarian bustle. Where the religious propagandists are guilty of deceiving us is in representing materialism as a product of the modern scientific outlook which can be resisted by a return to traditional values, for the truth is exactly the reverse, as I argued in the last chapter. By taking the theories of modern science as descriptions of the underlying reality of the world, and using them to create a picture of a Great System of forces in terms of which human behaviour has to be understood, materialism contradicts the basic feature of the modern outlook, the experimental principle, for which theoretical models of the world have meaning always and only in terms of human creative action, and are to be discarded at any time if experimental action finds them inadequate. Materialistic philosophies are interpretations of current scientific theories in the terms of the traditional outlook, using ideas of atoms, electrons, force-fields, evolution and the like as if they were simply alternative revelations of the underlying reality of things, in place of older revelations about angels, gods or demons – and the tyrannies of materialism are simply modern versions of the very same tyrannies which in earlier ages were imposed in the name of religion, namely, pressure of guilt and regimentation into the supposed demands of World Forces.

In fact the Freudian diagnosis of religion applies equally to materialism: materialistic schemes of thought are paranoid fantasies of invincible forces-behind-the-scenes just as surely as religious systems, and they involve exactly the same escape from the direct personal challenges of ordinary experience. This is fairly obvious in the case of Marxist materialism, and the resemblance of organised Communism to religion, with its ceremonies, its heresy hunts and its mental discipline of individuals to the cause, has often been remarked upon. The point is less obvious in the case of our western forms of materialism, but psychoanalytic insight soon reveals it, and indeed it sometimes emerges in ways almost as obvious as in the case of Marxism: for example, one of the most noted western 'scientific' materialists, Bertrand Russell, has a famous passage in one of his essays which has only to be strung out in blank-verse form to be obviously a kind of hymn rather than an assertion made in the real spirit of modern science:

> Brief and powerless is Man's life;
> On him and all his race
> The slow, sure doom falls
> Pitiless and dark.
> Blind to good and evil;

> Reckless of destruction,
> Omnipotent matter rolls on its relentless way;

Real science knows nothing of Omnipotent Matter, for it is a continual process of changing both our concepts and our experience of matter. The only constant factor in real science – the science of the experimental method – is Potent Man, man who constantly strives to use matter to express the creativity of his own inner life. Omnipotent Matter is as much a paranoid fantasy as the traditional concept of Omnipotent God, and serves the same neurotic purpose of providing grounds for not taking the inner life of human beings really seriously in its own right. Where traditional religion insists upon the subordination of man's inner life to the supposed Divine Plan behind the scenes, materialism overrides the inner life by dismissing it in the name of a 'tough-minded' assertion of man's utter insignificance in face of the inflexible laws of an indifferent universe.

If our civilisation is really to break free of the paranoid outlook – which I am convinced is the only constructive solution to its current split mind about 'the two cultures', and hence the only way of advance towards a really humane society – it must find a way to give proper articulation to the modern, experimental concept of sanity, which as I said at the very outset of this book, has as yet scarcely been done even in the scientific field where the experimental method is established procedure, and has not been done at all in other fields. We must find a way, in other words, to articulate the idea of Potent Man – and while this must by definition be a humanistic aim, it seems to me to involve considerations that very few humanists have yet begun to contemplate. For even those humanists who have recognised that materialism is an inhuman outlook when it takes forms like Marxism, still tend to have a materialistic view of nature at the back of their minds. To put the point crudely, they have mostly just removed the concept of God from the traditional kind of picture of the universe and left behind a vague concept of a Great System called 'nature', propelled by its own laws, of which man is envisaged as a part, a product of a general 'natural' process of evolution. This still has the practical effect of devaluing personal life in our minds, even though it be accompanied by ethical exhortations about 'the supreme value of personality'. Ethical exhortations count for little in determining the way people take practical decisions about the organisation of life, either at the personal or at the social level, and if our underlying picture of ourselves is of creatures who are just parts of nature's Great System, we shall inevitably tend to think always in terms of adjusting our inner lives to the 'hard facts' of external reality, rather than in terms of the real experimental spirit

which takes the initiatives of the inner life itself as its criteria of judgement of what is significant and what is not. As Auguste Comte said,
conventional atheism merely substitutes a blank for God while still
retaining the theological outlook and the habits of mind associated
with it. In technical philosophical terms, no naturalistic philosophy
can be adequate to the spirit which A. N. Whitehead expressed when
he said it was more important for a proposition to be interesting (a
challenge to action) than for it to be true (a passive acknowledgement of
supposedly unalterable fact). To be really 'humanistic', to do real justice
to the experimental outlook and its implication of Potent Man, it is
necessary, as I said in the previous chapter, to break away completely
from the whole idea of nature as a Great System, and to think of it
instead as a Great Opportunity, as raw material for human creativeness
– and this, it seems to me, means thinking of ourselves as in the most
literal sense *super*-natural beings, beings who stand *above* nature.

I have deliberately chosen this expression, which is likely to provoke
humanists by its religious overtones (rather than a less provocative
term such as 'creative beings'), because I believe there is a real challenge
here which humanists have to face if *they* are to be really honest in what
they tell the children, just as surely as religious spokesmen have to face
the challenge of the Freudian diagnosis. I am not, obviously, using the
term 'super-natural' in the traditional religious sense, implying that
man has some kind of occult entity in him called a 'soul' which has to
take its place in a supposed Great Divine Plan behind the scenes of
ordinary life. What I am doing is to raise the question of whether *some*
of the concepts and feelings associated with religion may not be
relevant to the 'positive' outlook on life – indeed, not just relevant, but
essential to its full expression – even though religion has normally been
identified with the utterly different (and in my view neurotic) traditional
outlook. This is obviously directly related to the question I posed
earlier when I was discussing the way some of the statements about
idolatry in the Bible and other great religious documents seem to
anticipate Freud's diagnosis of religion. The question I raised was
whether there could possibly have been something in some of the
world's religious traditions which was not connected with belief in a
power-behind-the-scenes at all, something that had to do with overcoming mankind's traditional paranoid outlook rather than with
persuading people to live in terms of it. I am not referring here simply
to the ethical aspects of religion, which humanists do very commonly
claim to take over (although I strongly suspect that this claim represents very superficial thinking – the kind of ethical behaviour associated
with the 'theological' outlook, whereby people behave in certain ways
because one or another divine being so commanded, seems to me

F

something humanists should be quite positively concerned to get rid of, since it involves reacting to other people in terms of an abstract scheme or myth rather than in terms of their simple human reality). I am referring rather to something at the very heart of religion, something which I can best express in humanist terms as *a certain feeling for the significance of inner, personal or 'spiritual' things as against purely external nature.* I am suggesting, in fact, that to do real justice to the experimental outlook, to be genuinely humanistic, *it may perhaps be necessary to think of ourselves and our inner lives much more in the way people in the past have thought of God than in the way most people have ever hitherto thought of 'man'* – and although this goes right against the general run of religion, with its emphasis on the virtues of humility and obedience to the Great Plan, I am suggesting that some of the great religious teachers of the world were reaching towards a really humanistic vision when they spoke of the 'true God' being 'with man in the world'.

What precisely does this involve? This is what I want to go on to explore in the next chapter, for in my view it is the most important of all questions that have to be opened up for the children if we are to do our duty by them in this vexed area. If either humanist or religious parents or teachers fail to raise this issue, I believe they will in either case find that the children recognise instinctively that what they are being told does less than real justice to the opposite point of view, and will react with confusion and distrust. Those who present traditional religious views without facing up to these questions will be recognised, even by children who have never heard of Freud, to be passing over the genuine evidence that religious culture is neurotic, the evidence that makes most atheists and humanists shy away from religious ideas in however reasonable or liberal form they are presented. On the other hand humanists who try to give children an 'objective' view of religion without raising these more difficult considerations will equally be seen, I believe, to be doing less than full justice to religion, not just historically, but even in the contemporary situation. For I strongly suspect that a great many people who today are reluctant to let religion go, and even many who jib at Freud's diagnosis, do so not wholly (and sometimes not even mainly) because they are particularly addicted to the traditional outlook, but rather because they recognise instinctively (though normally without being able to articulate their recognition) that conventional atheist humanism leaves out something of positive *human* value which religion expresses in however distorted a form. This is why they so often appeal to the hackneyed expression about 'throwing the baby out with the bathwater', and my suspicion is that if humanists were more prepared to consider this seriously, they would find at least some religious people would become less anxious to hold on to the traditional outlook, and more willing to consider the justice in Freud's diagnosis of religion.

Indeed, it seems to me that Freud's diagnosis of religion itself compels us to consider these issues, if we take it really seriously. The point was epitomised for me in a recent book of essays by leading British humanists called *The Humanist Outlook*, edited by Professor A. J. Ayer, in which Miss Brigid Brophy, the novelist, urged her fellow-atheists not to be cowed by being told that their approach to religion is purely negative: we do not, she said, blame a surgeon because his approach to a cancer is purely negative. We may admire the fighting spirit but must reject the analogy; Miss Brophy of all people should have known better, since she herself claims to accept the Freudian diagnosis of religion. For a neurosis is not a cancer, and if we are convinced that someone is suffering from neurotic delusions we should know very well that they neither should nor can be attacked in a surgical fashion. On the contrary, one of the most important features of Freud's understanding of neurosis (also now generally accepted even by psychologists who are very critical of his other theories) is that paranoid delusions have to be taken very seriously because they contain essential clues to the positive growth-processes that have to be undertaken if the neurotic is ever to achieve a responsible healthy existence. My contention is that our civilisation as a whole needs to do just this with religion – to take its leading ideas very seriously indeed as clues to the character and dimensions of healthy human existence, while recognising unequivocally that the traditional expression of those ideas was actually an evasion of healthy human existence. Unless we do this I do not believe we shall achieve real humanism, and even the theories of psychoanalysts themselves will become (as indeed they often do now) a new form of materialistic 'religion' which has the effect of belittling the very thing – man's inner life – which practical psychoanalysis is concerned to liberate.

7: Humanism and the supernatural
with an appraisal of New Theology

In the second half of the twentieth century it has become increasingly common for religious spokesmen to challenge the idea that humanism and religion must necessarily be opposed. In many cases this has not amounted to anything very profound. When Dr Ramsay, Archbishop of Canterbury, declares himself a 'Christian humanist' on the ground that the vision of love in the New Testament is relevant to the humanising of life in this world as well as to salvation in the next, he is not intending in the least to abandon the traditional notion that life in this world has its ultimate meaning in terms of other realities, hidden behind the scenes of ordinary experience. He is simply choosing to use the term 'humanism' in a vague sense which altogether fails to appreciate the real challenge of the humanist movements of the past few centuries, the challenge of a new outlook in which the world of ordinary experience is not treated as a scene at all and love has simply nothing to do with churches, sacraments or archbishops. Some other religious spokesmen, however, have really tried to meet this challenge, and one of the most notable of these also came from the Church of England – Dr John Robinson, who as Bishop of Woolwich started one of the biggest discussions of religion amongst the general public that has taken place for many decades, when he published his book *Honest to God* in 1963.

Dr Robinson himself was astonished by the popularity of his book, which he originally wrote as a tentative and rather specialised work for discussion amongst theological students. I believe the reason for its success was that it seemed to promise a way between the horns of the dilemma confronting millions of people in the modern world, the dilemma of being unable to deny the sanity of the modern experimental/ humanist outlook while feeling at the same time that conventional

74

unbelief leaves something vital out of account. In the first place, Dr Robinson put his finger very precisely on the nerve of the modern world's difficulties about religion in a single illuminating phrase – that people are becoming less and less able to attach any meaning to the idea of a God 'out there'. The significance of this expression, which communicated itself immediately to vast numbers of ordinary people, seems to have eluded most professional critics: they have treated it as a proposition about God, and have accordingly discussed Dr Robinson's work as if it were a treatise about the possibility that Christianity might dispense with the doctrine of divine transcendence in the light of modern scientific knowledge, but if *Honest to God* had been no more than that it would certainly have remained a specialised book for students. What Dr Robinson was actually concerned with was the fact that the modern outlook just does not have any 'out there' at all, quite apart from the issue of belief or non-belief in God, and his concern was to challenge the common assumption, shared by religious and humanist spokesmen alike, that Christianity can have no meaning (except perhaps in terms of its general moral ideals) unless this humanistic outlook on life is changed.

Because his book was written with a theological readership in mind, his challenge took the form of asking Christians to consider whether traditional religious attitudes and philosophies have ever really done justice to the Bible. This question has of course been asked many times before at critical points in the history of Christianity, notably at the Reformation, and some observers have suggested that *Honest to God* was just one symptom of 'a new Reformation' taking place throughout the Christian world in the mid-twentieth century – making itself felt even in the Roman Catholic church as growing numbers of Catholics argue that their church's traditional views on birth control or priestly celibacy may be distortions rather than expressions of original Christianity. Now insofar as such questioning of tradition takes its rise from experimental valuation – the experimental judgement that priestly celibacy cuts men off from valuable life-experience, or that the banning of artificial birth control imposes intolerable strain on people's sex-lives – it is bound, I believe, to lead on in due course to the more radical kind of questioning attempted by Dr Robinson. It must do so, logically, since it implies at least some acceptance of the modern outlook, in contrast to the traditional outlook from which theological judgements are normally made, wherein empirical considerations are simply made to fit the supposed requirements of the hidden Divine Plan. So far, however, most of the upsurge of new thinking in the churches – even in the Protestant churches – has stopped a long way short of challenging the traditional religious outlook as such. Indeed, not a few of those who have tried to 'bring the church up to date' in the years since the Second World War have combined their specific criticisms of ecclesiastical practice with vigorous defences of the general religious outlook, in the belief that essential human values are bound up with that outlook, as I mentioned at the beginning of Chapter Five. Perhaps most notable amongst these are the many Roman Catholics who have sought inspiration in the work of the Jesuit priest-scientist Pierre Teilhard de Chardin, with his belief that an updated version of the traditional outlook would make it possible for traditional Catholic faith and practice to be combined both with modern scientific ideas and with a general acceptance of progressive social action. Such theological 'progressives' often point to humanistic ideas in the Bible that have been neglected by their more conventional brethren in the churches: Teilhard, for example, claimed that St Paul's writings about humanity 'growing up into Christ' and bringing all nature into obedience, imply ideas of evolution and social progress in this world which conventional Catholicism has commonly ignored. But Dr Robinson went much further, and asked whether a really serious view of the Bible might not possibly imply that mankind should outgrow the traditional 'religious' outlook altogether. This, I believe, gave his book an appeal which was quite new in the new Reformation, and has led to a much more drastic kind of questioning of tradition which has come to be known as 'the New Theology' or 'radical theology'.

Dr Robinson was not, and did not claim to be, an original thinker in his own right. His questioning took its rise from a number of earlier writers in Germany, Britain and the United States, the most notable being a remarkable German pastor, Dietrich Bonhoeffer, whose affirmation of humanistic values in the name of Christianity had led him to refuse to acquiesce in the common view of the German churches under Nazism that Hitler's political actions had nothing to do with them. Arrested by the Nazis for being involved in a plot against Hitler's life, Bonhoeffer wrote a number of remarkable letters from the prison camp before he was executed, urging that 'religiousness' represented only a passing phase in mankind's development, with which Christianity had become mistakenly identified. The modern world's lack of religion, Bonhoeffer wrote, should be seen as mankind's 'coming of age', and Christianity should henceforth take a 'religionless' form. Bonhoeffer's letters were published after the end of the Second World War, but remained little known, certainly outside Germany, until Dr Robinson set out to follow up his ideas, together with certain similar lines of questioning developed by the German-American theologian Paul Tillich, and by myself in various essays and broadcasts I had produced while trying to grope my way from my early religion of Universal Divine Love to something like the diagnosis I have advanced in Chapters Five and Six of this book.

From Bonhoeffer's letters (and to some extent also from my own writings) Dr Robinson was led to ask whether the constant preoccupation of the Biblical writers with 'idolatry' and 'false religion' should not be taken to indicate that they were interested in something of quite a different order from all mankind's ordinary kinds of religious belief about powers behind the scenes of nature. From Paul Tillich's writings, Dr Robinson was led to ask whether any notion of 'God *out there*', a master mind in a world behind the scenes of ordinary experience, could possibly do justice to the constant emphasis both of the Biblical writers and of the early Christian philosophers on the fact that *they* were using the word 'God' to talk about something absolutely infinite and absolutely universal. From Bonhoeffer, Tillich, myself and a number of other post-war thinkers, Dr Robinson was driven to question whether the traditional notion of religion as something opposed to humanism could possibly be compatible with the Biblical writers' common insistence that 'true religion' (as against 'idolatrous religion') is *integrally* bound up with the achievement of better human relationships (for example, St John's assertion that anyone who claims to love God while hating his brother-man is simply a liar). Against this background, *Honest to God* set out to look afresh at the whole history of Christianity from Biblical days onwards, in the conviction that it might continue to be tenable – might indeed still come as a Gospel or 'good news' – to a civilisation which has grown out of thinking of the world in terms for which the notion of 'God *out there*' can have any meaning.

Dr Robinson's conclusion was that insofar as the Biblical writers and early Christian philosophers condemned not only the worship of physical idols of wood and stone, but even the use of mental images to represent God, they must have been trying to direct people's attention away from metaphysical belief in a separate being behind the world of ordinary life, so as to concentrate attention on the *personal attitude to life* which the metaphysical belief had served in more primitive times to induce. Seen in this light, Christianity would be firmly linked to 'humanistic' ideals, since it would imply treating personality as 'of *ultimate* significance in the constitution of the universe'. Indeed, it could be argued that without such a view of the universe, humanism makes no real sense, since the logic of a fatalistic or purely materialistic view of reality would be that people should eschew personal values – individuality, love, beauty, justice – and learn to adapt themselves to a universe which is utterly indifferent to such values. It was therefore no mere historical accident, Dr Robinson argued, that modern scientific-humanist culture, which dispenses altogether with the idea of God as a separate metaphysical being while retaining the overriding sense that personal values are significant, grew out of Christendom, with no real counterparts in other areas of the world where religious traditions were either more fatalistic or more tolerant of 'idolatry'. Christians ought to recognise that modern humanism is in a sense a logical development of their faith – but it should also be recognised that the complete rejection of faith by many modern humanists has the effect of undermining their humanism both logically and psychologically, with results that can be seen in the 'inhumanism' of much modern culture, both western and eastern. The challenge of this situation to the churches, Dr Robinson concluded, is to learn how to proclaim and defend their faith that 'personality is of *ultimate* significance in the constitution of the universe' without recourse to the idea of God as a separate Being 'out there'. They should proclaim and defend it as an experimentally-grounded conviction that the dedication of life to the service of personal values opens up depths of meaning in ordinary experience which require terms like 'divine' and 'eternal' to do justice to them – meaning which is revealed in its full, infinite depth in Jesus's total dedication of himself to unconditional love of others 'even unto death'. The churches themselves should be communities who follow Jesus's revelation by realising the divine depths of love in the relationships of individual members to one another and, perhaps even more important, by using prayer and worship as what Bonhoeffer called 'secret disciplines' to equip people to struggle for the 'humanising' of the world's whole social structure, to the greater realisation of the divine depth of meaning everywhere.

This attempt to re-state the Christian ideas of God and of the Incarnation in 'non-religious' terms seemed to many churchpeople in 1963 to amount to a complete betrayal of Christianity to modern unbelief. Looking back at it now, however, in the light of assessing its importance in relation to what we should tell the children about religion, it seems to me that the only fair criticism is the one which Dr Robinson himself anticipated: 'The one thing of which I am fairly sure is that, in retrospect, it will be seen to have erred in not being radical enough.' For although his terminology may be unfamiliar to conventionally-minded churchpeople, the ideas he expressed turn out, on close examination, to belong after all to the traditional 'religious' way of thinking rather than to the modern experimental way of thinking. Humanist critics have often remarked that from their point of view Dr Robinson's practical proposals (in *Honest to God* and subsequent writings) concerning church membership, church worship and morality, seem more like liberalising reforms of traditional religion rather than 'religionlessness', and I believe this goes back to his basic theology, which in effect reintroduces the traditional outlook in disguised form after a bold – and I believe sincere – show of trying to break away from it. This comes out most strikingly in a passage towards the end of *Honest to God* where he is deliberately setting out to show that the reformulation of Christianity in terms of 'depth' does not simply reduce it to the same thing as ordinary humanism. He points the contrast by referring to Sir Julian Huxley's scientific-humanist 'religion without revelation':

> For the humanist, to believe in a 'religion of love' is to affirm the conviction that love *ought to be* the last word about life, and to dedicate oneself to seeing that it prevails everywhere. . . . But the Christian affirmation is not simply that love *ought to be* the last word about life, but that, despite all appearances, it *is*. . . . And that takes an almost impossible amount of believing. It is frankly incredible *unless* the love revealed in Jesus is indeed the nature of ultimate reality, unless he is a window through the surface of things into *God*. Christianity stands or falls by revelation, by Christ as the disclosure of the final truth not merely about human nature (that we might accept relatively easily) but about all nature and all reality. The Christian's faith cannot rest in the capacities of man. Indeed it strikes him as astonishing that someone of Huxley's honesty and intelligence should be able to reissue his book in 1957 without a single reference to the possibility, not to say probability, that there might not, within his frame of reference, be any prospects for humanity at all. No, the Christian's faith is in Christ as the revelation, the laying bare, of the very heart and being of ultimate reality.

Now it is not only the language here which is religious in the traditional sense, but the whole attitude. Love has become a reality *out there* just as surely as the God of conventional theology ever was, and 'Jesus Christ' has become a symbolic figure, not an historical human being but a mystical vision valued for its supposed revelation of hidden reality. In terms of the experimental outlook the whole statement is simply meaningless: for example, it is certainly not 'relatively easy' to accept that Christ was the disclosure of the final truth about human nature on the basis of the actual facts either of the New Testament story or of its subsequent interpretation in Church history. In this context it does not make much difference whether we try to discern an historical human being beneath the New Testament accounts, or accept the Gospel stories whole as they stand, as composite works of art recording the total impression Jesus made on his followers. Either way, the most that can be said from the facts of the New Testament is that Jesus was a very unusual man who moved people profoundly as a prophetic teacher and healer and exercised a remarkable effect on history by being declared risen from the dead after being executed as an agitator – all of which undeniably makes him interesting, but gives no positive meaning whatever to the notion that he was a disclosure of the final truth about human nature, since human beings generally are certainly not called to be celibate teachers and we know next to nothing about the way Jesus conducted himself in most of his relationships. If on the other hand we turn to the subsequent interpretation of the New Testament by the Christian Church, the plain fact is that Christians all down the ages have simply projected their own ideals into the figure of Christ, so that there are almost as many portraits of 'perfect human nature' as there have been Christians, many of them utterly contradictory, and some of them downright unpleasant: as William Blake so neatly put it:

> The vision of Christ that thou dost see
> Is my vision's greatest enemy.
> Thine has a great hooked nose like thine,
> Mine has a snub nose like to mine.
> Thine loves the same things that mine hates,
> Thy heaven's doors are my hell gates.

In fact the statement that Jesus was a 'disclosure of the final truth' about anything presupposes the traditional outlook by treating a person as a symbol or 'window' for discerning something beyond. The experimental outlook is simply not concerned with a 'final truth' in this sense, since it is always looking towards new truth. The traditional religious outlook is also presupposed, I believe, in Dr Robinson's acceptance of the idea that Jesus's life was of special significance because of its unique display of unconditional love. From the actual facts of the New Testament portrait there is no very special evidence of loving behaviour; the portrait is of a teacher, not of a human being in depth. The idea of the Christ-life as a display of unconditional love is imported into the story from the ancient religious concept of Jesus's death as a kind of ritual sacrifice: in ordinary historical terms his death was not a laying down of life for his friends but a political execution from which his friends gained nothing.

This failure to break really free from the traditional outlook in spite of a sincere intention of doing so has, it seems to me, caused the whole movement of radical theology to fall short of fulfilling the hope it initially aroused. In general, its practitioners talk a great deal about the need to accept the fact of 'the death of God' in the modern world as a sign of 'man's coming-of-age', but fall back on thoroughly traditional 'religious' concepts in their approach to Jesus, or indeed to the Bible as a whole. Their continued identification with the traditional outlook is pinpointed by the fact that so many of them, like Dr Robinson himself in his later book *Exploration into God*, published in 1967, are prepared to link their views with those of Teilhard de Chardin, who was quite explicitly dedicated to the recovery of the traditional way of looking at the world, notwithstanding his very positive wish to embrace science and social progress. He bent his skill as a writer and his considerable knowledge of science to the task of painting a picture of evolving nature as the outward and visible expression of a vast scheme of psychic evolution underlying it, and on the practical level his objective was to persuade people to see the whole of life, including the business of science, technology and social reform, as a vast act of sacramental worship, *The Mass on the World*. True, there was one very important respect in which Teilhard did sense the modern world's real challenge to religion; he recognised that the constant factor in modern science is not the Omnipotent Matter of materialism but Potent Man, man realising himself as a being capable of standing above nature, and this made him criticise traditional Christianity, as Bacon had done long before, for playing down the idea in the Book of Genesis that man is meant to exercise dominion over nature. He had no intention of making any radical break with tradition, however, and when the Jesuit order imposed a ban on his writings he accepted it humbly as part of his vow of obedience. Since his death most Catholic authorities have come to see that such minor unorthodoxies as his acceptance of evolution and social progress were really quite secondary to the fact that he remained in general a convinced and powerful apologist for the traditional outlook, an apologist whose real affinities were not with Bacon's experimental philosophy but with the pseudo-scientific nature-mysticism of some of Bacon's strongest contemporary opponents. Significantly, Teilhard's greatest popularity outside Roman Catholic circles has always been amongst those numerous groups all over the western world who are trying to reinstate occult ideas – astrology, theosophy and the like – and are prepared to swallow his Catholicism because he seems to give the authority of 'science' to the basic occult notion of a spiritual reality underlying everything in ordinary experience.

Dr Robinson and the majority of Protestant 'radical theologians' would probably repudiate indignantly any affinities with this 'occult underground' – as indeed Teilhard himself did during his lifetime – but

81

they ally themselves willy-nilly with the occultist position whenever they quote with approval (as many of them do) such Teilhardian statements as 'Everything has an inside.' And they tend also to come out in much the same position as Teilhard in relation to practical questions of 'Christian behaviour'. For example, Dr Robinson in *Exploration into God* quotes with approval the American Robert Castle's *Litany for the Ghetto*:

> O God, who lives in tenements, who goes to segregated schools, who is beaten in precincts, who is unemployed . . .
>
> Help us to know you
>
> O God, who is cold in the slums of winter, whose playmates are rats – four-legged ones who live with you and two-legged ones who imprison you . . .
>
> Help us to touch you.

Insofar as these lines have a serious intention beyond their irony, it is of precisely the same kind as Teilhard's when he tried to persuade people that efforts towards technological and social progress should be seen as sacramental offerings, outward and visible signs of the divine Christ's self-offering to God the Father. In both cases the writers' conscious aim was to rebuke conventional Christianity for its tendency to use prayer as an escape into some remote imaginary heaven, but in actual result their references to God 'down here' in the affairs of this world are still religious in an entirely traditional sense, since they advocate living in terms of a supposed deeper truth underlying ordinary experience rather than in terms of the experience itself. To people who do not share the traditional attitude to the world, this whole way of approaching life is meaningless and, even more important, rather suspect, since there are good reasons for believing, as I argued in the previous chapter, that the effect of such an approach is actually to detract from the sense of ethical responsibility it appears to be trying to promote. If elementary human compassion does not move someone to respond to the suffering of the oppressed, he is unlikely to be made to respond by being told that God is involved in that suffering, since he can always turn to some less challenging interpretation of his religion. For anyone who does feel compassion, on the other hand, the effect of religious language like Castle's or Teilhard's could well be to divert them into a masochistic drama of 'religious concern' which avoids the responsibility of meeting people's actual needs. (This was precisely what happened with my own religion of Universal Love, and in fact many of the 'radical theologians' seem to have ended up with just such a religion.)

And in this, it seems to me, we have the clue to the way in which *Honest to God* and the other writings of the 'radical theologians' have not been radical enough – they have failed to grasp just how far away from traditional 'religiousness' it is necessary to move in order to take the modern outlook really seriously. They have treated the modern inability to make sense of 'out there' statements as if it were simply an advance in mankind's scientific knowledge, whereas in fact it is a change in our criterion of sanity, which means that if it is accepted as an advance at all, in any sense, then the traditional 'religious' attitude to life must be considered, not merely as outmoded, but as in some sense positively diseased. In this respect I believe Dietrich Bonhoeffer showed greater insight into the modern outlook and its implications than any of the later thinkers who have found inspiration in his writings, although he did not live to develop it. It is significant that many of these later admirers, including Dr Robinson, have expressed wonderment at the fact that Bonhoeffer was able to talk about mankind having 'come of age' when he himself was forced to suffer so much at the hands of modern society. This seems to me to betray a failure to grasp an essential part of Bonhoeffer's view, namely that in terms of his estimate of 'modern man', Nazism would not rate as a modern phenomenon at all, but as a profoundly reactionary movement, harking back to pre-scientific ideas of social unity that were directly bound up with the traditional 'religious' outlook from which Bonhoeffer believed mankind was emerging with its 'coming of age' – in particular, the ritual submission of individuals to a Grand Design accepted on the authority of a Leader. This was in fact Hitler's own view of the matter. His declared intention was precisely to recapture in the Third Reich a sense of national corporateness which he believed had characterised the First Reich in ancient times and the Second Reich in the Middle Ages, but had been lost by 'bourgeois-scientific' culture with its corrupt 'Jewish-atheist' belief in individualism and democracy. On the basis of this belief, the Nazis set out systematically to undermine those very features of modern European culture which led Bonhoeffer to speak of mankind having 'come of age', namely its sense of the significance and potency of human beings in their own right, which involves, on the other side of the coin, the willingness of individuals to accept responsibility for responding to every human relationship in its own right. Bonhoeffer's criticism of the contemporary German churches was that in some ways they effectively went along with Hitler, not just in the negative sense of believing that their concern with other-worldly matters absolved them from becoming involved in any active opposition, but also in the positive sense that they sought to convert unbelievers to religion by means of evangelistic techniques similar to the methods used by the Nazis – techniques based on inducing a sense of guilt to undermine people's confidence in themselves and so soften them up for submission to authority.

So when Bonhoeffer asserted that Christianity need not and should not go on being religious, he must, I believe, have envisaged a far more radical break with traditional Christian practices and ways of thinking than any subsequent 'radical theologians' have yet contemplated. This can only be a matter of speculation, of course, since he was executed just as he began to work out these ideas, but it seems to me that most of his latter-day admirers take him less than seriously when they quote his fairly traditional pre-war writings about God and Christ and Christian behaviour as if *they* provide clues to what he meant by 'religionless Christianity'. To take him seriously would mean facing the fact that the whole traditional outlook has fundamental psychological similarities to Nazism even when it is associated with radically different ethical or social views, and none of the more recent 'radical theologians' have been prepared to make as radical a break with tradition as this. Dr Robinson in particular quite explicitly turned aside from separating himself as far as this from conventional religion when he felt compelled, in *Honest to God*, to demur after quoting a passage from my own writings where I had described the traditional religious idea of God 'out there' as actively evil rather than just primitive or crude.

I had based my statement partly on Freud's diagnosis of religion, but mainly on my own experience of the fear-ridden superstition which passed for religion in the working-class district where I was born, from which I had early retreated into H. G. Wellsian atheism – the kind of superstition that made many people believe that a local bargee had been literally struck blind by God for uttering the oath 'Gor blimey'. No doubt educated religious apologists would raise their hands in horror and deny that this had anything to do with orthodox Christianity, I wrote, but this is just not good enough, for the fact is that educated apologists effectively go along with beliefs like this amongst the less educated even today in many parts of the world. They take it for granted that their duty is to oppose attacks made on religion by psychoanalytic and other humanist critics, although such attacks are mostly directed against this kind of fear-ridden belief, and anyone who seriously wanted to dissociate Christianity from such superstition would support the attacks, not oppose them. I wrote:

It is not enough to describe such beliefs as childish or primitive, for this implies that the truth is *something* like them, even though much more 'refined' or 'enlightened', whereas in reality *nothing like* the 'God' or 'Christ' I was brought up to believe in can be true. It is not merely that the Old Man in the Sky is only a mythological symbol for the Infinite Mind behind the scenes, nor yet that this Being is benevolent rather than fearful: the truth is that this whole way of thinking is wrong, and if such a Being did exist, he would be the very devil.

To this Dr Robinson replied:

That, I believe, is an exaggeration. To speak thus one is in danger, like the Psalmist, of condemning a whole generation – indeed many, many generations – of God's children. It is still the language of most of his children – and particularly his older children. There is nothing intrinsically wrong with it, any more than there was with the symbolism of a localized heaven.

At this point, it seems to me, Dr Robinson drew back from doing justice not only to Freud, not only to me, not only to Bonhoeffer, but also to the Bible itself. When the Hebrew prophets found their country-men worshipping graven images they did not merely shake their heads indulgently and put it down to childish or uneducated ways of thinking that would be grown out of in later generations. They did not say 'there is nothing intrinsically wrong with it': they condemned it as part of the world's disease. This was what led Freud to say that he felt considerable kinship with the prophets of his race, to the point of sometimes almost wishing he could make use of their language to denounce modern thinkers, like his renegade disciple Jung, who urged the recovery of mankind's traditional 'religious' outlook. And it is precisely this element in the Bible that gives ground for believing that a new Reformation might, if pursued radically enough, succeed in meeting the challenge of the modern experimental/humanist outlook. Bonhoeffer seems to me to have been trying, just before his death, to take this aspect of the Bible really seriously even to the point of considering that it might mean repudiating many of his own earlier convictions and aligning himself with modern critics of religion against many things that are commonly thought of as fundamental to Chris-tianity (although as far as I have been able to discover from his writings he had no acquaintance with Freud's ideas). Because subsequent 'radical theologians' have not been prepared for this, the new Reforma-tion that has actually occurred in the churches since the Second World War has not really met the modern world's challenge at all, in spite of the hopes which Dr Robinson's initial diagnosis of that challenge aroused.

To be specific, the challenge of the modern outlook cannot be met by any merely philosophical reformulation or 'demythologisation' of traditional Christian beliefs, not even by the kind of reformulation that implies a more positive attitude to humanistic social action than Christians have generally taken in the past. The only kind of Reformation that could really meet the challenge would be one which discovered traditional Christianity to be a paranoid distortion of a movement that was originally concerned with something utterly different from belief in realities behind the scenes of the world of ordinary experience, even though its pioneers used terms that are ordinarily assumed to imply such belief, like 'God', 'heaven', 'sin' and 'salvation'. The possibility of such a discovery is hinted at not only by the vehemence of the Hebrew prophets' denunciation of any kind of belief that could permit of 'images' (even mental images) of God, but equally by the famous statement of Jesus (which had long before been anticipated by other Hebrew teachers) that 'the Sabbath was made for man, not man for the Sabbath' – a statement which, if taken seriously, surely implies treating religious observance as an experimental business to be judged by its results in human life, not as a ritual process whereby people adapt themselves to some Great Divine Plan. The question that has to be asked is whether the 'supernatural' language which Jesus and other great religious pioneers used could possibly have any meaning in terms that are genuinely experimental, in the sense of being concerned with suggestions for action *in* the world of ordinary experience rather than with statements about supposed realities behind it.

It seems to me that Dr Robinson came very close not only to formulating this question, when he spoke of breaking away from the idea of 'God *out there*', but also to indicating the lines along which an answer might be found. If supernatural terms are to be anything other than statements about occult realities, it can only be by virtue of their asserting *something very special* about the world of ordinary experience and its potentialities for creative action – something moreover with a direct bearing on people's willingness to pursue such values as love, beauty and justice. Dr Robinson went back on his own formulation of the problem, however, by assuming that to say something special in this context must mean saying something about hidden personal character in the universe at large, which as I have shown is just as much an appeal to supposed occult reality as the more traditional kind of theological statement, even though its form is vaguer. But there is no necessity for this. As I said in the last chapter, it is possible to talk about life being super-natural in an entirely experimental sense, simply by virtue of the fact that when people take up the experimental attitude they actually do stand 'above nature' to change or control nature. I want now to propose that religious statements about the supernatural could have truly experimental meaning *by being suggestions about the scope and character of creative action, about the relationship between personality and the universe which is involved when creative action is undertaken, and about the rules that govern creative life both in individuals and in their relations with each other.*

For example, the idea of God as personal supernatural power over against man could have experimental meaning as a suggestion that human life, like the rest of nature, can be seen as subject to control and change by the power of personal creative action, a power which goes beyond our past or present conceptions to an unknown degree, perhaps having no necessary bounds at all. This may not sound, at first hearing, like anything that we normally think of as 'religious', and indeed it is certainly not a 'theological' idea in the traditional sense, for it has nothing to do with any notion of a power behind the scenes of life. It is a profoundly humanistic idea, both in the positive sense of implying an overriding obligation to respond to personal creativity wherever we encounter it, in ourselves and others, and hence to treat people as ends rather than as means, and also in the negative sense of denying that there is any Grand Design beyond personal creativity to which human life has to be adapted. Yet on the other hand it *is* a religious idea, inasmuch as it is concerned with transcendence, with the possibility of worlds unrealised, with the possibility of new dimensions of experience, and with the awesome drama of alienation and reconciliation arising from the fact that we are free, by virtue of personal creativity, to deny or evade personal creativity. It would be well-nigh impossible to express this kind of suggestion about life in non-religious language like that of conventional naturalistic humanism, which inevitably conveys the assumption that personal creativity is a function of various natural processes such as the electrochemistry of the brain or the evolution of society. The whole purpose of the idea of God, on this reckoning, would be to urge people to take precisely the opposite point of view – to take personal creativity sufficiently seriously that electrochemistry, evolution, social forces and so on are thought of simply as intellectual tools for realising personal objectives: more generally, to see the whole natural universe as a Great Opportunity rather than any kind of Great System, and so to refuse to accept any natural limitation on personal creativity as final, however unyielding it may seem at a particular time.

Now of course it would be totally misleading to use the word 'God' in this way if it had no relation at all to the way in which it is or was used in at least one of the world's major religious traditions, but I believe careful study of the records reveals evidence of just some such usage at the heart of several traditions, including Judaism and Christianity. For example, when the Hebrew Rabbis of classical times condemned idolatry even to the point of forbidding mental images of God, yet at the same time used verbal images in profusion – the Ancient of Days, the High and Holy One, the column of smoke going before the people through the desert, the Consuming Fire and so on – it can only have been, it seems to me, because they meant those images to be understood as inspirations to be pursued rather than symbolic statements of truth. Centuries of traditional theological interpretation have made us read the Hebrew scriptures (which Christians call the Old Testament) as accounts of belief in a Great Power behind the scenes who was supposed to watch over the Jewish people, guiding their fortunes in war and laying down rules for their behaviour, but it seems to me that this was precisely the kind of belief the prophets were concerned to condemn as idolatrous. Their complaints against idolatry were very commonly linked with condemnations of self-righteous nationalism and mechanical observance of rules. Their exhortations to 'true religion' imply a belief of exactly the opposite kind, namely, an essentially practical conviction that the inner creative power which impelled the Jewish people to try, fitfully, to build a community-life based on 'righteousness' (the mutual respect of individuals for each other as centres of creative life), can actually be the strongest power in the universe, before which all things must finally be as clay to a potter. Thus the prophet Isaiah was able to sum up true religion in a tremendous vision of a future 'Kingdom of God' wherein personal creativity would have such dominion over nature that the wolf could be tamed to lie down with the lamb. For the nearer future, he and other prophets urged that the Jewish people should not allow the apparently greater power of 'unrighteousness' to deter them, since all communities founded on the exploitation of man by man must inevitably fail through the inner contradiction of allowing personal creativity to turn against itself, while those who pursue 'righteousness' even in the face of adversity have the reward of living at the highest intensity, perhaps even in some way being raised above fear of death.

The same kind of conviction seems to me to have been at the root of the great religions of India, inasmuch as their major teachers commonly insisted that beliefs about gods, heaven, hell, reincarnation and so on should never be taken as final truths, but must always be capable of being discarded if they interfere with the practical pursuit of wisdom and compassion. These religions are normally interpreted as embodiments *par excellence* of the traditional outlook, inasmuch as they rest on the assertion that the world of physical nature is a complete illusion, but modern scholars have cast doubt on this view. They have come to the conclusion that the Sanskrit word *maya*, which is normally translated 'illusion' in western versions of Hindu scriptures, is actually from the same Indo-European root as the word 'matter', the fundamental connotation of which is not 'hallucination' or 'mirage' but rather '*stuff with no identity in its own right*', or, in other words, 'material' for creative use. Hence I believe the Indian religions' affirmation of the essential identity of the human soul with God, the supreme reality of Universal Consciousness beyond the illusion of the physical world, was not originally a doctrine about a supposed reality behind the scenes of nature at all: it was an experimental proposal that the inner life of man be treated as the most significant thing in the universe, inasmuch as physical nature is opportunity, not substance. When the great Indian sages went on teaching elaborate reincarnational cosmologies while insisting that they must finally be regarded as 'optional', it could only have been because they were not meant as revelations of truth for people to obey but as experimental hypotheses about the aspirations and dynamics of the inner world. For instance, the doctrine that consciousness 'falls' into the world of illusion was in my view not originally a metaphysical assertion but an attempt to describe how creativity continually gets bogged down in believing that the world of nature is a Great System with laws of its own before which man must submit. The doctrine of reincarnation itself was basically a pre-scientific speculation about how creativity gets bogged down in different people to such different degrees, but its original religious use was probably as a stimulus to the imagination to envisage creative 'changes of identity'. On this view the use of the doctrine in popular Hinduism to justify acceptance of one's lot in the caste system was a total distortion of the idea into its own opposite.

The attitude of the great Indian sages to their cosmologies seems in fact to have been precisely the same as the attitude which Jesus took, standing in the general tradition of the Hebrew prophets, to the elaborate moral/ceremonial system of the Jewish law. Here too we find the insistence that the law should be taught as important, yet must finally be regarded as optional ('the Sabbath was made for man . . .'). The conventional modern Christian interpretation of the Hebrew prophets is that they were struggling to lead the Jewish people from a relatively primitive to a nobler view of the Master Mind behind the scenes and his wishes, but if this had been so they would surely have tried at each stage to modify the law in which the will of God was supposed to be expressed, perhaps abolishing the ceremonial laws altogether as primitive superstitions. In fact they did nothing of the kind. What they did was continually to attack the people's compulsive, ritualistic, self-righteous *attitude* to the law, and in the light of modern psychology I believe this kind of attitude is an inevitable concomitant of any kind of belief in a Master Mind behind the scenes, inasmuch as it is a characteristic of the paranoid approach to life. Hence Jesus and the prophets must have been trying to recapture an original view of the law *as a whole* which had nothing to do with any such 'theological' belief, and the principle 'the Sabbath was made for man, not man for the Sabbath' seems to me to point unmistakably to an experimental attitude whereby ceremonies were meant to be used as psychological disciplines for helping people come to terms with the super-natural fact of creativity, both in personal and in social life.

The Hebrew scriptures were actually put together as collections of stories and poems to be read on ceremonial occasions, both private and public, and I suspect the various Hindu scriptures were drawn up for the same kind of purpose, though perhaps with more emphasis on private meditation. The object in both cases, I believe, was originally to help people gain insight into the scope and dynamics of creativity. Historical stories like the Biblical Books of Kings or legends like the Book of Job or the Bhagavad-Gita would aim to show how communities that deny creativity are doomed by their internal contradictions, and also how creative initiative might overcome the limitations of circumstance, possibly to degrees undreamt of in the world's everyday philosophies. For example, a common theme of both Hindu and Hebrew scriptures is that creativity might, in the right conditions, be able to exercise psychosomatic control over bodily functioning for the healing of disease. Side by side with these historical or quasi-historical stories were set meditative poems like the Psalms or cosmological epics like some of the Vedas or the opening chapters of the Book of Genesis, whose purpose I believe was to express, usually in symbolic form, the inner dramas of challenge and response, alienation and reconciliation that make up people's experience of creativity. For instance, the story of Adam and Eve, as I shall try to show later, is a remarkably insightful parable of how human beings can use creativity to evade the challenge of creativity, and one of the interesting things about it is that if it is approached psychologically, rather than as a statement of historical or moral truth, it seems actually to portray conventional religion as an aspect of man's alienation. It starts, that is to say, by portraying 'God' as an inner power urging human beings to exercise dominion over nature, but as soon as Adam and Eve evade this inner voice they start thinking of 'God' as a Great Power behind the scenes demanding subservience to nature.

In this fashion I personally believe that at least some of the world's religious traditions embody ways of thinking about life which are not only compatible with the modern experimental outlook, but actually essential to it if it is to do itself full justice rather than have its humanist ideals overwhelmed by the narrow prejudices of materialism and naturalism, as I described in the previous chapter. Inasmuch as the experimental outlook does mean taking creativity seriously, I believe Bacon was quite correct in thinking that his proposed revolution could be a fulfilment rather than a denial of religion's original purpose; and insofar as modern civilisation embodies that outlook and its humanist ideals I think it is closer to the intentions of some of the great religious teachers and prophets than were the so-called 'Ages of Faith', when religion's original purpose was almost wholly overshadowed by the 'idolatry' of the traditional outlook. Insofar, on the other hand, as our civilisation rejects religion as such in the course of reacting against the traditional outlook, I believe it really does, as many people fear, run the risk of throwing out the baby with the bathwater. To stop short of Bacon's vision of fulfilling religion's original purpose is to risk losing what we have gained, as Comte saw when he urged that to do justice to the positive outlook mankind cannot rest with atheism but must achieve a 'religion of humanity', giving experimental expression to insights which the older religions had distorted into 'theology'. Comte's own attempt to create such a religion failed, I believe, simply because he himself did not take his own idea fully seriously, and stopped short at the notion of using prayer and ritual to help the individual integrate himself with society, which is one of the least human functions of traditional religion. The experimental vision that is actually to be found underlying the 'theological' distortions of traditional religion is in my belief something at once grander for humanity as a whole than Comte imagined, yet focused on individual inwardness rather than on social collectivity – namely, the super-natural vision of personal creative power.

This is what I believe our 'new Reformation' would have discovered if it had been radical enough, and it may yet go on to do so. I was interested to see that one American writer on the 'new theology', William Miller, traced the spiritual ancestry of the movement back, not to John Robinson or Paul Tillich or even Dietrich Bonhoeffer, but to that extraordinary prophet-like figure William Blake, who erupted on to the English scene at the end of the eighteenth century proclaiming that the churches were distorting the basic truth of religion and so allowing the world to succumb to inhuman materialism. Blake, I would say, was a genuine modern prophet, seeking to recall people to religion's original purpose as the prophets of old did, with no mincing of words about the distorted character of conventional religion; and he also seems to me to have shown remarkable insight into the real danger of materialism, which few writers have done since.

He attacked materialism for reducing human experience to an abstract mechanical pattern and thereby denying man's most distinctively human capacity: creative imagination. This, he contended, led naturally and inevitably to the practical inhumanities of industrialism – the 'dark Satanic mills' – yet it actually had no warrant whatever in real scientific discovery:

> As to that false appearance which appears to the reasoner
> As of a Globe rolling thro' Voidness, it is a delusion . . .
> The Microscope knows not of this nor the Telescope: they alter
> The ratio of the Spectator's Organs, but leave Objects untouch'd.

Blake mistakenly attributed the materialistic outlook to Bacon: in fact he was inclined, like many people today, to be so concerned about the danger of materialism that he attacked the scientific outlook as such on many occasions. More careful study of it would have told him that the spirit of new outlook, Bacon's experimental principle, is precisely the means whereby the abstract patterns of the scientific mind are put in their proper place as temporary hypotheses, intellectual tools for achieving limited practical ends in the interests of the imagination. But Blake was at no point a defender of the traditional outlook, as most critics of science are; on the contrary, he denounced conventional religion as vehemently as materialism, and indeed anticipated Freud's analysis in denouncing them both as examples of *the same* universal human sickness whereby the challenge of creative imagination is evaded or denied in being forced to adapt itself to some supposed revelation of a hidden pattern behind the scenes. In one well-known poem he even anticipated Freud's diagnosis of religion in detail, when he referred to the God of the churches as 'Old Nobodaddy' – the unreal father-image who is supposed to be allowed to rule our lives even though he is totally concealed behind the scenes and beyond the reach of empirical valuation:

> Why art thou silent and invisible,
>   Father of Jealousy?
> Why dost thou hide thyself in clouds
>   From every searching eye?
> Why darkness and obscurity
>   In all thy words and laws, –
> That none dare eat the fruit but from
>   The wily serpent's jaws?

Or is it because secrecy
Gains feminine applause?

Where Freud admitted only a kinship of feeling with the Hebrew prophets, however, Blake set out to proclaim what he believed to be their original message, that Nobodaddy-worship is a neurotic distortion of 'true religion' – and he defined 'true religion' as recognition of 'the divine body, Human Imagination', without which he believed society would degenerate into tyranny and self-destruction. He devoted his whole life to the creation of elaborate symbolic paintings and poems in which the ideas of the Bible, of Greek mystical mythology, of Norse religion and of Hindu mysticism were all interpreted as insights concerning man's alienation from 'divine imagination' and its consequences for mental health, politics and morality. In fact I believe that Blake, without really understanding the new scientific movement, embarked a generation before Comte on the task of hammering out the pattern of that very 'religion of humanity' which Comte diagnosed as necessary to the new outlook yet had insufficient imagination to work out in practice. So if our contemporary New Reformation really harks back to Blake, it may yet break free from its present limitations and go on to lead or push the churches towards the experimental vision of the super-natural which our civilisation needs, not to counteract its humanism but to fulfil it.

However, this is not in my view an issue that can simply be left to the 'experts' – the professional philosophers, theologians and clergy. It is an issue which I believe must be put fairly and squarely before the children by anyone who sets out to tell them about religion, so that they themselves can embark, if they choose to do so, on their own personal quest for some such way as this between the horns of the modern dilemma about religion. The 'experts' may well prove to be too wedded to traditional ways of thinking to be capable of this degree of radicalism, and the New Reformation as a movement within the formal structure of the Christian churches may peter out in minor liberalisations of traditional religion, but I do not believe this should or will stop young people from being driven by their own insights to try to press on to something else. Even quite young children could, I believe, embark on this kind of inner quest with the help of a teacher or parent who is prepared to face the quest himself, and there are signs at the present time that older children will drive their would-be mentors to explore new approaches even if the parents or teachers themselves feel inclined to settle either for some conventional religion based on the traditional outlook or for conventional atheist humanism based on the rejection of the traditional outlook.

As I said at the end of the last chapter, modern children – even the less academic ones – are liable to ask awkward questions about religion that can embarrass both the conventional believer and the conventional humanist. Amongst older children particularly, the spread of esoteric religious ideas in the world of pop music during the last few years has given an impetus for asking such awkward questions which only a few highly educated people would have had in previous generations. On the one hand, conventional believers are liable to find themselves faced with questions about the contrast between the basic ethical teachings of great religious leaders like Isaiah or Jesus, or of the great eastern scriptures, and the unholy practical behaviour of organised religions throughout history with their wars, persecutions or caste systems. Does this not indicate that somewhere along the line, traditional Judaism and Christianity and Islam and Hinduism have distorted the intentions of the great teachers in some absolutely radical way? On the other hand, conventional unbelievers are equally likely to be challenged with questions about whether it is really very sensible to reject out of hand claims of some religious people all down the ages to have had experiences in which they seemed able to reach beyond the ordinary limits of space, time and matter. Are not such claims worthy of serious consideration by all of us, considering that the very best we can hope to do with present techniques in technology, art and social reform is bound to leave the majority of individuals subject to a great deal of pain, fear and frustration, notably the pain of loss and the fear and frustration of death? To take such questions as these seriously is to be plunged, I believe, into an exploration of the experimental roots of religion in which the traditions of the past – not just of Christianity, but of other religions too – are taken as guidelines, but no more than guidelines, for the discoveries of the future.

For parents or teachers who approach the problem of religious education with strong views about the authority of Christianity or some other religious tradition, this whole idea may seem like opening the doors to chaos in the children's minds, but the truth is that the chaos will come anyhow in our contemporary situation. If the parent or teacher shies away from the task of helping the children in their explorations, he will simply leave them to speculate far more wildly in private, with none of the help that an adult can provide in terms of greater knowledge of life, of history, of scientific and psychological facts and of the religious traditions themselves. If the task of exploration is undertaken consciously, on the other hand, the parent or teacher will have the opportunity to try to justify his own belief in authority in terms which make sense to the children. He may not succeed in convincing them as he argues out his case, but he has no hope whatever of convincing them in any other way. On the same principle, a staunch atheist has the chance of convincing young people that their inclinations to religious speculation are all nonsense if, and only if, he allows those speculations free play and joins in the exploration himself as honestly as he can.

The exploration I am suggesting here is not primarily an historical exercise in trying to discover what particular doctrines, traditions or passages of scripture may originally have meant. This *would* be a task for experts, and moreover could never hope to be conclusive. What I am suggesting is something much more comprehensive and flexible. I am suggesting that Freud's diagnosis of the neurotic character of conventional religion should be properly understood and squarely faced, including the corollary which I mentioned at the end of the previous chapter, that in Freud's view of neurosis, paranoid fantasies are not just meaningless mental vapour, but reflections of those very aspects of experience that have to be given more conscious attention if neurosis is to give place to health. On this basis, I suggest, it becomes sensible – indeed important – to examine *any* religious notion that comes down to us in traditional form, to see if it could be a distorted statement of an important experimental insight in relation to that aspect of life from which religion as collective neurosis seeks escape, the exercise of real responsibility for creativity. It is sensible and important to do this *even if it is impossible to establish that the notion in question was ever actually understood in an experimental fashion at any time in past history*. On the same basis, it is equally sensible to re-examine the ideas of modern thinkers who have tried to reinstate the traditional outlook in original ways, such as Jung and Teilhard de Chardin, to see if they too are pointing to experimental insights about personal creativity and the inner life which could be expressed in other terms. In the next chapter I propose to illustrate how such an examination might actually work out in practice, not in order to propagate my own particular interpretation of some of the great doctrines of religion, but to exemplify in the only way that I can – by personal example – a process which I believe is likely to become increasingly common in the future, and upon which the future health of our whole society may in fact depend.

8: Exploration and encounter
An outline course of religious discussion

The task of trying to explore what religious traditions can mean to people demands intellectual and emotional honesty, imagination, and openness to the possibility of meanings quite different from those we ourselves have hitherto taken for granted in either accepting or rejecting any particular tradition. During the decade of the 1960s there began to develop in the United States a movement for introducing these qualities into the whole process of education, although the primary emphasis was not on the academic education of children so much as the emotional education of adults. It has come to be known as the 'human potential movement', and in the late 1960s it began to spread to many other countries. It might best be described as an attempt to take some of the leading insights of psychotherapy – particularly group psychotherapy – out of the hospital and consulting-room into ordinary life. One of its main manifestations has been the creation of 'encounter groups' in which ordinary people with no special psychological problems try to help each other achieve emotional growth by getting rid of artificial defences, abandoning habits of rationalisation and self-justification and openly acknowledging feelings of need, dependence, fear, resentment and so on. I believe some of the techniques developed by these groups can be of great help in any process of teaching or discussion about religion, for if such discussion or teaching is to be at all meaningful it must, in my view, be a real encounter between the people involved.

In particular, I believe teaching or discussion about religion would be enormously helped by the basic encounter-group rule that anyone who takes up any kind of dogmatic or ideological stance should be challenged to say openly what that stance is 'doing for him' personally. In most ordinary encounter groups the stances in question are not usually religious at all, of course, but they are often ethical. For example, in one which I attended I expostulated, 'I believe people ought to control their anger; it's only this that distinguishes us from savages.' I was then pressed into admitting that I had all my life held back my own anger because I feared outbursts of anger from others. partly because they reminded me of the rows between my parents, which I dreaded as a child, and partly because my mother had brought me up with a quite inordinate fear of even the tiniest physical hurt, which made me anxious to transfer all conflicts to the verbal level where I could beat almost anyone. This revelation has totally transformed my subsequent discussions of the question of violence, quite apart from its practical value in making me realise that in many cases people treat me with more rather than less respect if I allow feelings of anger to show. In another group, a young physicist asserted, 'Science is the only reliable guide,' and when challenged was forced to admit that he had from his university years taken refuge behind the label 'scientist' as a way of gaining an authority which he felt he otherwise lacked because he came from a very poor home, had a working-class accent and believed he looked unattractive. The other group members then went on to make him recognise that his defence-mechanism was largely unnecessary and in any case totally ineffective: he would be treated with respect precisely insofar as he carried some personal authority of his own, which to some extent he had already achieved in spite of the limitations of his background and superficial appearance, whereas the stance of 'scientist' in itself gained him nothing worth having. This led him both to take more trouble about his appearance and personal attitude to others and, incidentally, to be far less rigidly dogmatic about scientific materialism.

Our normal tradition of academic teaching and discussion tries to separate questions of truth and falsehood from 'personal considerations' like these, but during the present century it has come to be recognised not only by psychologists but also by philosophers and logicians that an absolute exclusion of personal considerations merely renders discussion useless. For example, logical analysis shows that general philosophical propositions like 'Mind is merely a by-product of the brain' can be neither true nor false in themselves, since it is necessary to know the full context of a statement before its truth or falsity can be determined. In this particular case, a brain physiologist engaged on examining the mental effects of stimulating the brain with electrodes would be perfectly justified in treating mental phenomena as by-products of physical events in the brain while he was actually doing his work; whereas poets talking about 'the marriage of true minds' would find it quite irrelevant to do so, a spiritualist would be out of business if he did so, and a Jungian psychologist believes his patients get better if they think of 'mind' as something that pervades all nature. Hence the proposition 'Mind is merely a by-product of the brain' boils down in practice to something like the assertion 'We can trust what brain physiologists tell us about human behaviour but many of the things poets, spiritualists and Jungian psychologists tell us are quite untrustworthy' – and it is on this kind of level that evidence for or against the philosophical proposition about mind and brain should be considered if. the discussion is to get anywhere. To apply this principle fully, especially to propositions like those of religion or politics whose emotional overtones can often be very strong, I believe it is necessary to go beyond the kind of general considerations of 'practical meaning' that the logical philosophers deal with in their textbooks, and to carry the question 'What exactly is this belief doing for you?' through into the everyday lives of all of us.

The tradition of trying to separate teaching and discussion from 'personal considerations' was mainly concerned with avoiding 'argument from authority' on the one hand ('This is true because our forefathers believed it and who do you think you are to contradict them?') and the dismissive *argumentum ad hominem* on the other ('You only believe in hereditary intelligence because you are a filthy snob'). The encounter-group movement is equally anxious to get away from these kinds of argument, but it does so, not by trying to 'raise discussion above the level of mere personalities', but rather by insisting that every individual must be responsible for his own statements and has no right to thrust them on anyone else. Thus if any member of an encounter group makes a statement about another, like 'Now you are being hostile', he is made to 'take full responsibility for it' by changing it to 'I *feel* you are being hostile.' The same applies if he makes a general appeal to authority, like 'But nobody believes in astrology nowadays' or 'Everybody knows that Jung's psychology has superseded Freud's', He is made to change the statements to 'I *feel* anyone who believes in astrology – and specifically you over there who have just used an astrological term – is silly,' or 'I feel Freud's psychology is too restricted, or too messy, to apply to me.' If anyone in the group uses an *argumentum ad hominem*, like 'You're only criticising me because I remind you of your father,' or even 'You remind me of my father,' he is challenged to recognise that he is actually 'putting the other person down', by saying in effect 'I'm not taking you seriously at all.' Psychoanalytic interpretations are discouraged for the same reason: the group challenged me to ask *myself* what my pacifist views were doing for me, but if any other member had tried to *interpret* my pacifism as a defence-mechanism he would have been asked why he was trying to put me down by explaining my statements away instead of listening to them. Had someone felt strongly that he wanted to press the point, he would have been told to take responsibility for his statement by saying 'I *feel* you are using pacifism as a defence against fear of violence,' and I would have been free to reply 'That's your privilege.' It is by using safeguards like these, I believe, that a discussion about emotive subjects like religion can be meaningfully personal without degenerating into slanging-matches or blind assertions of authority.

Being open and honest is not easy, and even those who are sincerely trying to do so can often fail to express themselves because they lack the right words. For this reason, encounter groups have developed a number of simple devices to assist the processes of self-disclosure and self-discovery. For example, members are told not only to listen to words but also to be sensitive to tones of voice, posture and bodily gesture: hence if someone is arguing violently (as I did) about the evils of violence, someone else in the group can say to him, 'What I actually *hear* you saying is . . .,' putting forward what he has received as the underlying message. The speaker is then free to accept or reject the attribution. If an argument develops, members of the group sometimes try to bring out what they believe to be the unexpressed or badly expressed feelings of the person with whom they sympathise by getting behind his chair and speaking as an *'alter ego'*. Here again, the person is then free to accept or reject the ideas or feelings attributed to him by his would-be allies. Most important of all, there is a continuous counterbalancing of words with physical action or with silence. If tensions are running high, then instead of everyone struggling like mad to control them and maintain 'civilised argument', the whole group may stop talking and have a few minutes' exercise in which people who have been getting across each other stand face to face, jump up and down and scream at each other as hard as they can, perhaps making grimaces while doing so. At other times, or perhaps immediately after such a session of physical tension-breaking, the group has a short period of silence in which people close their eyes, go inside themselves and try to experience 'where they're at'. If some issue has arisen that most members of the group seem to find particularly emotive, there may be a different kind of silent period in which everyone explores that issue for himself in fantasy with his eyes closed. This last technique I believe could be particularly valuable for preventing discussions about religion from running away into abstract intellectualism, with the participants either getting bored or getting worked up about points of apparently abstruse argument without quite understanding why.

I am not trying to suggest that every religious education class or school assembly should be turned into a full-blown encounter group, still less every discussion about religion in the family. I am simply suggesting that the basic principles of encounter are essential if religious teaching or discussion is to be made really meaningful, and that some of the specific techniques I have described are likely to prove useful from time to time. It is against this background that I propose now to try to show how the general approach of this book might be worked out in a practical scheme for exploring what religion can mean to people. It is a scheme that could, I believe, be adapted by skilled teachers for children in almost any age-group over about twelve years, but its most immediate use is probably for senior children, for teachers in training or for other adults who want to work out where they stand in trying to present these matters to the young.

I propose to develop the scheme as a series of discussions round the leading questions that in my experience normally present themselves once the subject of religion has been raised. In these discussions I shall continue to follow the principle of making my own view clear while doing my best to set it in the context of the most important alternatives. In fact I shall be presenting something of the story of my own personal attempts to explore the meaning of religion, but I shall try to do it in such a way that it will be useful, as an illustration, even to those who have no wish to follow some or any of my conclusions.

The basic question: why religion at all
The traditional and the experimental approaches

I believe the best starting-point is to set the whole question of religion in historical perspective by bringing out the fact that until a few centuries ago the question 'Why religion at all?' could scarcely have arisen, since religion of one form or another was practically universal and was moreover taken for granted as the central focus of all life, both individual and social. The basic facts of the rise of 'doubt' over the past few centuries should also be cited, including the fact that open admission of irreligion remained a subject for public scandal in many parts of the world until relatively recent times, so that professing atheists were forbidden to hold public office (and even now find themselves at a disadvantage in obtaining some posts such as head teachers). Some statistics about the extent of irreligion today as reflected in opinion polls and other surveys should be given.

With older children, or adults from any but the most sheltered religious backgrounds, it is almost certain that someone will raise the hoary old myth of the 'great conspiracy', whereby religion is supposed to have been invented by wicked rulers as a means of keeping the common people in subjection through superstitious fear. It must be made clear that this is no longer believed by any serious scholars even amongst Marxists who regard religion as the opiate of the people. The furthest they would go is to hold that *in relatively recent times* there have been members of the ruling classes who were sceptical themselves but encouraged public observance of religion for the 'moral guidance' of the less educated masses – in much the same way as many parents even today believe that religion is good for the moral training of children even though they believe little in it themselves. In earlier ages, it is now generally accepted, priests and kings were ultimately as much caught up in the religious systems that gave them their power and privilege as were the common people under them. If they had any greater freedom at all, it was only to the extent of knowing more about the technicalities of the religious system and being able in consequence to find their way round some of the prohibitions which to less educated people seemed inflexible. Moreover, the other side of the coin was that priests and rulers were often in danger of far greater penalties, if they were ever caught out in violation of the system, than the common people over whom they ruled. Insofar as religion *has* served as the opiate of the people – and this will nowadays surely be conceded to some extent even by the most devout, for they can see it to be true of religions other than their own even if they refuse to allow it in their own tradition – then it must be seen as functioning for the most part like a neurosis which bound rulers and ruled alike into their roles, rather than as a 'great conspiracy' by the rulers to keep their subjects in order.

In establishing this point, it is important that anyone who has raised the 'great conspiracy' theory should not feel that he has been merely 'put down'.* On the contrary, it is probable that anyone who takes the trouble to put the idea forward, feels strongly about it because he has, somewhere in his background, felt personally oppressed by religion, and this is something that should if possible be brought out into the open and discussed, since it can lead on to some very fruitful exchanges of experiences. It is my guess that a great many people who are anti-religious are reacting against the kind of life-denying, fear-dominated experience I had in my own childhood as mentioned in Chapter Seven (p. 84), even though they may have experienced it only at second hand in family reminiscences or in observing the lives of peasants in less

* In fact I think it would be a salutary experience for anyone learning about or discussing religion to see the 'great conspiracy' theory given a real run for its money in Nigel Dennis's irreverent comedy *The Making of Moo*, in which a religion is actually synthesised for reasons of political expediency.

developed countries. If this kind of reaction against religion is once brought out, it provides an ideal starting-point for raising the question of why all reasonably enlightened people do *not* feel repelled by religion on these grounds. In fact I would urge that in the modern world this is really the only sensible starting-point for any positive discussion of religion, so much so that if by any chance a group of pupils is so docile that none of them spontaneously raises the Marxist attack on religion or some more personal variant of it, then it is the teacher's duty to raise it himself, even if he is a believer.

In other words, the only sensible basis for discussing religion today is to begin by asking how religious people justify their position in view of the undeniable fact that for a great part of mankind all down the ages, beliefs about higher spiritual interests have been responsible for oppressive, life-denying social systems here on earth – systems all of a piece with, even if not always involving, such ultimate inhumanities as the Inquisition, the caste system, blood sacrifices and holy wars. This approach to the subject serves to bring out right at the start that two quite distinct kinds of religious position are possible, which get hopelessly confused with one another in most ordinary discussions of religion, although in reality the difference between them is as important as the difference between religion and unbelief.

On the one hand, anyone who remains attached to any of the organised religious traditions must, if he is honest and logical, believe that it does have insight into higher spiritual interests which can demand discipline and sacrifice from people, even though he may consider some religious authorities gravely mistaken in some of the sacrifices they asked people to make and in some of the methods they used to enforce discipline. This kind of religion is opposed to humanism in principle, inasmuch as it claims insights (about the will of God, about the true purpose of sex, about the nature of the soul's spiritual evolution after death, or whatever) which are beyond ordinary human criticism since they cannot be evaluated by experimental results in common human experience. On the other hand there are some religious people, especially today, with the new wave of interest in mystical religion amongst a younger generation that has had little or no organised religious background, who would consider that the historical record of the organised religions proves them devoid of any spiritual insight worthy of the name. People in this position may use the same words and phrases as the organised religions (about God, the spiritual evolution of the soul after death, prayer and so on) and they may even go to formal worship from time to time, but their claim is to have penetrated to a kind of religion totally different from that which has served to organise people into oppressive social systems, a mystical or esoteric or original kind of religion of which the organised religious traditions represent radical distortions. They may not ordinarily think very much about their disagreements with organised religion, and they are likely to consider themselves to be in a different camp from humanism, yet when pressed about their attitude to the life-denying role which religion has so often played in society, their criterion of judgement will turn out, I believe, to be a fundamentally humanist criterion – and not a whit the less humanist for being the criterion enunciated by Jesus when he said that men do not gather figs of thistles.

I believe that if these two approaches to religion are thought through properly, they will prove to be not merely different but totally incompatible, notwithstanding the fact that the majority of religious people never fully appreciate the distinction and veer uncertainly from one approach to the other without realising what is happening, while most critics of religion never grasp that the distinction exists at all. In essence it is the divergence of outlook on life which I have been explaining in the earlier chapters of this book. It is probably most succinctly described as the difference between a conformist attitude to reality, which sees man's ultimate good in terms of some kind of obedience, and an experimental outlook which takes for granted as its fundamental starting-point something that seems like dangerous pride to the other – namely the right of the human spirit to explore, to create and to challenge any aspect of reality that seems less than its own highest vision. Terms like 'spiritual', 'supernatural', 'God', 'soul' and 'life-after-death' have utterly different meanings for people who take these different attitudes to life, although the ordinary kind of religious discussion probably never brings the difference out. The result is that arguments about whether God exists, or whether there is life after death, or which religion gives the best insight into the supernatural, are often completely at cross purposes. Encounter-style discussion, on the other hand, throws up the basic difference of outlook very rapidly, and makes clear how many differences of theological or philosophical belief are really determined by differences of feeling and attitude, rather than vice versa as is commonly supposed. I can best illustrate this by a concrete example from one of my own 'encounters' with a group of 16–18-year-olds.

I had been talking to the group about my own early adolescent experience, just prior to the Second World War, of coming upon the fiercely atheistic works of H. G. Wells in the school library and feeling immense relief, as I followed his demolition of religion, at the thought that there was not after all a God watching my every action with a stern eye, as my whole background had hitherto predisposed me to fear. A girl in the group who came from a theosophical home could not

H

understand this at all: when she had begun to doubt *her* parents' religion, she said, it had been a matter of immense sadness to her, to think that human life might have no meaning beyond the all-too-limited span of our earthly existence. She had recently begun to recover belief in mystical religion through the new culture of the pop world, inspired largely by people's experiences of altered states of consciousness induced by pot-smoking, L.S.D. and meditation, and she felt great happiness at getting back something of her earlier convictions. At first sight, this looked like a simple matter of different religious backgrounds with different ideas of the character of God or supernatural reality, and a boy in the group who described himself as an evangelical Christian proceeded to try to explain to me that my parents' idea of a wrathful, punishing God was mere superstition which proper knowledge of the Christian revelation would have replaced by a joyful faith. 'I know that I can hold my head high and approach God in confidence,' he said, 'because Christ died for me and revealed God's love towards me.' At this the girl, far from accepting him as any sort of ally, rounded on him with a passion that was of precisely the same emotional character as my adolescent rejection of God in the name of H. G. Wells. 'To hell with that,' she exclaimed. 'I'd approach God in confidence anyhow. Any God I couldn't approach in confidence wouldn't be worth calling God.'

She became positively vituperative when the boy tried to argue that God's infinite goodness made it necessary to approach him first and foremost in fear and trembling. 'How can you possibly believe in a God like that?' she asked, whereupon I had to remind her that for most of the human race throughout history it had seemed self-evident that God should be approached in fear and trembling: why did she think she could be out of step? We here had to get a version of the 'great conspiracy' red herring out of the way, with some of the group arguing that people in earlier ages had modelled their ideas of God on the tyrannical rulers of earth. After a certain amount of discussion and consultation of references in history, anthropology and psychology, we agreed that the order of psychological priority was the other way about – absolute rulers on earth had been able to hold their power only because people believed it to derive from supernatural authority. When we returned to my question about what made the girl so certain that all these people had been wrong in their view of the supernatural, her reply was that people in earlier ages had gone in fear and trembling because of the threat of hell, which no intelligent modern person could share because our greater scientific knowledge showed it to be absurd. She was quite astonished when the evangelical boy, supported by a couple of Roman Catholics in the group, argued – with a logic she could not fault – that no scientific discoveries could ever disprove, or even cast doubt on, the possibility of hell in some quite different dimension of existence after death. Only revelation, they asserted, could give assurance that God was merciful, and they told her, to her considerable indignation, that she was cashing in on the inherited capital of the Christian revelation without realising it.

Most of the group were taken by surprise at this turn in the argument, since we had not previously discussed the 'science and religion' issue in any detail. After going into it a little, we were brought up against the common *impasse* which I described in Chapter Three, whereby a large number of people in the group found themselves unable to dispel the *feeling* that science had rendered a lot of traditional religious ideas obsolete, yet were forced to admit that in terms of strict logic, the religious apologists were correct in saying that science cannot in the nature of the case prove or disprove anything important about the supernatural. I then suggested that the most constructive course would be for the religious apologists to stop trying to put this common feeling about science down by logical argument, and try instead to understand it, at the same time coming more out into the open about the feelings underlying their own position. As a start, I proposed the experiment of a fantasy. I asked the theosophical girl and one or two of those who called themselves agnostics or atheists to imagine what they would do if they died and discovered that the universe really was managed by the kind of God my parents had felt to be watching over us all. How would they react, I asked, when hauled up before the judgement seat and condemned for disbelief or for some sexual misdemeanour which they had hitherto considered relatively harmless? Their replies were very similar, in spite of the fact that she considered herself religious and they did not – and I was again reminded of my own feelings in the days when I first came across H. G. Wells. The girl said she would spit in God's face, and one of the boys said he would haul Him down off His throne and take over. When I asked how they could possibly contemplate this when God was omnipotent, they all agreed that a being who could send people to hell for heresy or disbelief must be less than man and so could not possibly be really omnipotent, however powerful He might appear. 'I'm sure we could organise a revolution against Him even from hell,' said the girl, 'but if we couldn't – if He really could see everything we were thinking and had just been playing cat-and-mouse with us during our lives on earth – then I'd rather go out cursing Him than knuckling under.'

This brought out very nicely the true logic of the modern world's refusal to be browbeaten or overborne by fear of hell or any other nasty supernatural fate. Although the modern feeling normally finds rational expression as a conviction that the whole idea of hell is absurd, its real root is a sense of man's right, ability and indeed responsibility to challenge any prospect he finds inhuman, no matter how weighty the arguments may be to show that the challenge seems like folly. It was this rebellious, 'non-conformist' spirit, not scientific knowledge, which inspired the great atheist humanists of the eighteenth and nineteenth centuries – and many humanistically-minded reformers within the ranks of religion as well – to denounce the doctrine of hell as an infamous invention of perverted human imagination. Of course, once the challenge is thrown down, the first thing that becomes obvious is that there is absolutely no positive evidence for believing in hell in the first place, and at *this* point scientific advance comes in to reinforce the conclusion, not so much by casting doubt on the idea of a localised hell below the surface of the earth, or anything of that sort (for serious theologians would never have been restricted by this kind of literalism anyhow), but rather by showing that human beings can get away with challenging all kinds of *earthly* fates which had hitherto been regarded as divinely ordained, like poverty or disease, without bringing down immediate wrath from on high. To those who do not have the spirit of challenge, however, lack of positive evidence for hell or for divine retribution is no reason at all for daring to doubt what great religious authorities of the past have taught about these things. For what I have called the 'conformist' outlook, the threat of awful supernatural consequences remains always a haunting possibility in principle, even for those who, like the Christians in my group, believe that *as a matter of fact* God is loving rather than wrathful. To the 'humanist' or 'experimental' outlook, on the other hand, it seems self-evident that a universe which could condemn people to hell or to an inflexible *karma* would not be super-natural but sub-human, so that it is not to be taken seriously without very strong positive evidence indeed, and if by any horrible chance it were to turn out to be the case, it would be a matter for defiance or attempts at alteration, not humble acceptance.

In putting the matter in these terms I am obviously betraying my own definite prejudice in favour of the modern outlook, and I am glad to say that some of the Christian members of my group were quick to tell me so. With the evangelical boy as their spokesman, they said I was now putting *their* position down, not so much by my argument as by using the term 'conformist' with its modern overtones of cowardice. The Christian martyrs under the Caesars or the Nazis undoubtedly believed themselves to be conforming to the will of God against pagan tyrants, but they were the very opposite of what most people nowadays mean by conformists. I accepted the criticism, and asked the members of the group who felt themselves on the side of the traditional religious view to try to find a more positive way of expressing their position.

They began by talking theology, but the rest of the group said this made no sense to them, so I suggested they might try to define their position, at least as a start, by saying what they thought about my fantasy-exercise. After some discussion this produced an answer which proved very illuminating to everyone. They said the fantasy totally ignored the fact that if God were really the creator of the universe, He must by definition be wiser than us and know better than we do what is good for us, however arbitrary His actions might seem to our pitifully limited minds. It would be sheer arrogance, they argued, for human beings to rebel against the conditions God has laid down for our lives just because they seem unpleasant or unfair to us. It would be like petulant schoolchildren deciding that the headmaster's threats of chastisement for smoking were due to sadism when in fact they are signs of his wisdom about the ultimate consequences of smoking to health in the grown-up world beyond the school, which the children have to take on trust because their limited minds cannot begin to conceive it.

Some of the humanist members of the group naturally came back at this, asking what reason there is for believing that the universe *is* under the control of such a supernatural wisdom, considering the immense amount of pain and waste in the world. One of the Roman Catholics, a girl, replied that this was exactly the kind of arrogant attitude that had caused scientific man to make such a mess of the world over the past few centuries. Nature may have many features beyond our understanding, she said, but overall the universe manifests a design of such awe-inspiring proportions that it behoves us to be humble about the things whose meaning we cannot grasp, especially as the Christian revelation warns us that our minds are not only very limited but blinded by sinful pride into the bargain. The evangelical boy added that the humanist trust in man is in any case futile because there is really no such creature as man: there are only lots of individual men and women, whose notions of what is good for them are both muddled and mutually contradictory because their dominant motive is selfishness, so that every attempt by mankind to determine its own fate is foredoomed to chaos.

Here we had a very clear confrontation of the two attitudes to life I had been trying to define, in terms which enabled everyone present to see their implications and decide where they themselves stood. At bottom it is a dichotomy between two radically opposed estimates of man – or, more precisely, two radically opposed feelings about the nature of human creativity, the distinctive characteristic of our species, rooted in imagination, which confronts us with the need to make choices and also enables us to be dissatisfied, as other species are not, with the way things happen to us in the ordinary course of nature.

On the one hand is the feeling that the main feature of this creativity or freedom in man is that it opens up the possibility of chaos unless people learn to discipline themselves to some kind of overriding pattern which will relate them to each other and to the rest of the universe. In terms of this outlook, which has dominated the human race for most of its history, religion has its traditional dictionary-definition meanings of 'submission to higher powers' and 'binding together'. Religion in this sense is essentially a social phenomenon, but as far as cosmology is concerned it is perfectly possible in principle to have an entirely naturalistic religion, in that a society can decide to base its life on adjusting its members to the ordinary patterns of biological existence, with no hope of any life beyond except the general organic life of nature and the race. It is in this sense that Marxism, Nazi racialism and certain other forms of modern dogmatic materialism can be called religions of a kind, and my reading suggests to me that certain kinds of atheist Buddhism and Stoicism also come in this category, although I am not an expert on these religions and may have misunderstood them. For most human societies, however, it has seemed self-evident that other parts of nature must have the same kind of conscious 'inside' as human beings have: hence as a general rule religion assumes some kind of spiritual order underlying the material universe, but when the subject is approached in this conformist frame of mind, the *a priori* assumption is that the unknown of the spiritual order is likely to be as fearful for human beings as the unknown in the natural order. On this subject, as on the subject of the purpose of drama (see Chapter Two), Shakespeare puts a classic statement of the traditional outlook into the mouth of Hamlet:

For in that sleep of death what dreams may come
When we have shuffled off this mortal coil,
Must give us pause . . .
For who would bear the whips and scorns of time,
The oppressor's wrong, the proud man's contumely,
The pangs of dispriz'd love, the law's delay,
The insolence of office, that patient merit of the unworthy takes,
When he himself might his quietus make
With a bare bodkin? who would fardels bear
To grunt and sweat under a weary life,

But that the dread of something after death,
The undiscover'd country from whose bourne
No traveller returns, puzzles the will,
And makes us rather bear those ills we have
Than fly to others that we know not of?

The hope that the supernatural world might offer boons rather than (or even as well as) terrors can be given, on this view, only by some kind of revelation, and any such revelation will come to human beings as a 'gospel', 'good news'. Such good news will inevitably go hand in hand with demands for repentance and discipline, however, since if death *is* the gateway to spiritual bliss then our sense of death as loss is yet another indication of something radically wrong with our minds.

For the outlook I have called humanist, on the other hand, the whole matter looks entirely different, because human creativity is itself taken as the standard by which order is valued, whether in society or in the universe at large. (This was shown up very clearly in the confrontation in my group, by the way those who shared this outlook took for granted, in my fantasy-exercise, that a universe which fell below human standards by condemning people to hell after death must by definition be something less than supernatural.) The only ethical criterion of human interrelationship that can be admitted as ultimate on the humanist view is that of mutual respect between persons for each other's creative initiative: more general rules for social harmony are seen, not as ends in themselves, but as means. The end which such rules must serve is the essentially practical one of giving individuals a stable base from which to explore new creative possibilities in physical life, in mental life and in ways of relating to each other; and this means that the rules themselves must always be open to revision. Harmony with the universe at large is seen in the same way, as a means to creative exploration rather than as a valuable end in itself. Practical common sense dictates caution about flying in the face of what seem like laws of nature or forces of superhuman dimensions, whether in the ordinary physical realm or in any other realms that may exist beyond it, but it is a basic assumption of the humanist outlook that no one will ever know how far human beings can go in pursuit of their aspirations for more abundant life unless there is continual experiment. It was the rise of this outlook over the past few centuries which brought about both the experimental revolution in science and the social revolution of declining 'bondage' to religious authority – but this did not by any means always mean a lessening of interest in the human aspirations which are commonly associated with religion, such as the hope of life beyond the confines of ordinary physical existence. For a not inconsiderable number of people, both within the ranks of organised religion and in a host of new mystical groups, it meant a new kind of approach to these age-old aspirations, and this was in no sense a mere compromise with the old outlook. There is nothing inconsistent with the humanistic outlook in entertaining such aspirations, or in considering prospects of their fulfilment. On the contrary, the kind of dogmatic naturalism or materialism which denies any such possibility is as much a denial of the basic principle of humanism – the experimental principle of acknowledging no *a priori* limits to human creativity – as is the kind of dogmatic religion which claims a definitive revelation of the supernatural world, as I argued in detail in Chapters Five and Six.

This last point is in my judgement probably the most important thing that needs to be brought out in all teaching or discussion about religion today. For I suspect that what the great majority of people are looking for is a way of pursuing religious aspirations without succumbing to what I have called religious bondage. Not all, of course. There are still many religious people, like the little band of defenders of orthodoxy in my group, who fully accept the traditional outlook. For them, the answer to the question, 'Why religion?' is basically 'Because when we weigh the matter up, we believe the traditional outlook represents sanity and the humanist outlook a kind of madness.' After that, their specific religious allegiance – evangelical Christian, Roman Catholic, classical Hindu, orthodox Jewish, Mohammedan, occultist or whatever – will be determined by which revelation of the nature of things they find convincing. This is also in effect the position of some adherents of dogmatic ideologies which do not ordinarily call themselves religions, as is evidenced by the way some Marxists treat Marxist/Leninist orthodoxy or Chairman Mao's little red book. For many other people, however – especially, as I have said, many young people today who are taking an interest in mysticism even though they have no background of parental religious tradition – the answer to the question 'Why religion?' is quite different.

For some, though probably only a tiny minority, it is simply, 'Because I have had religious experience which makes me certain of a transcendent reality.' For others – and this is nowadays, I believe, a growing proportion of the population both inside and outside the ranks of organised religion – the answer is rather vaguer, but goes something like this:

> Because I have a strong feeling, like Walt Whitman, that I am not contained between my hat and my boots. Because I cannot believe our sense of purpose is just the cruel joke it so often seems to be

when lives or relationships are cut short by death long before we have had time to learn much about living. Because something in me resonates to some of the great poetry of religion in words or paint or music or stone, and to some of the things people have said about religious experience. Because I think it would be foolish to ignore anyone who claims to have real insight about these things when the best our science and technology and social reform can ever do in the foreseeable future will still leave most people dying unsatisfied.

Because such concerns as these have in the past been almost wholly identified with the traditional religious outlook, people who feel like this, and even sometimes people who have had actual religious experiences, are prone to think they *ought* to put themselves under bondage to some religious tradition if they are not to betray their deepest feelings. And, of course, the traditionalists urge them (quite properly, from their own point of view) to do just that. Religious yearnings, they say, are the pangs in man's soul that show his hunger for the True Faith, and mystical experiences are messages from heaven calling people to embrace the Master's yoke. For some they may be right, in that what these people really *are* wanting is the obedience of some traditional kind of religion, but for a great many others, as for me, I am sure this is not the case.

People like this commonly find themselves confused, often even torn in two by the feeling that they have to choose between betraying their integrity by accepting a bondage they find impossible, or betraying it just as much by trying to forget their religious concerns. To anyone in this situation, the insight that transcendental concerns are in no way incompatible with a humanist outlook, and can be pursued by taking a purely experimental attitude to the received ideas and practices of traditional religion, will come as real 'good news'. I believe, as I argued in Chapter Seven, that any normal group of young people setting out to discuss religion freely today will find itself, as did the group I have been describing, pushing towards this conclusion almost irrespective of its leadership, although it may not follow anything like the line I have taken.

This insight – that transcendental concerns are in no way incompatible with a humanist outlook – is equally important, I believe, for those who consider themselves atheists or agnostics, for I suspect a great many such people have rejected such concerns not for any really logical reason, but simply because they cannot accept the traditional outlook with which such concerns seem to be identified. Indeed, I believe it is a matter of considerable importance for our whole culture, quite apart from religious education, that there should be a much wider appreciation than there is of the fact that the experimental/ humanist outlook which gave birth to the modern movement in science is essentially creative, open-ended and person-oriented – not dogmatic, mechanistic or materialistic. Dogmatic materialism, whether in Communist governments, in capitalist economic planning or in psychology departments where 'soul' is a dirty word and 'dreaming' a period of rapid eye movements, needs to be exposed for what it is: a bastard form of authoritarian religion with no claim whatever to the title 'scientific'. If a class or discussion-group on religion succeeds in clarifying this issue alone, it will have done a valuable service for the whole educational curriculum. Greater clarity on this issue would make many young people think again before adopting a totally anti-religious stance in the name of science, and, on the other side of the coin, it might do something to stem the now rising tide of young people who believe it is necessary to repudiate the whole scientific approach to life and get back to some traditional religious obedience if our world is not to become a mechanised hell where everyone is sacrificed to the Moloch of materialistic progress.

Of course, the choice between the traditional and the humanist attitudes must always remain an open one, in the sense that it can never be settled by any kind of knock-down philosophical argument. The important thing for anyone conducting any sort of religious discussion is to ensure – irrespective of his own decision in the matter – that the whole subject is thoroughly explored with all its implications, and that the group is fully aware of the real issues on both sides. In particular it is up to him to see that people are not being misled either by straight errors of logic (like the belief that science has somehow disproved the traditional religious position or, on the other side, that humanism means materialism) or by simple errors of fact (like the idea that religion is merely a great conspiracy or, on the other side, that pre-scientific societies were paradises of creative individuality). I have presented the essential philosophical and practical arguments, as I see them, in Chapter Five. If the subject is to be considered properly and not just superficially, however, the most important considerations are probably the psychological ones outlined in Chapter Six, where I have tried to show how the traditional outlook (as distinct from any specific religious concern) *can* be a kind of personal or collective neurosis based on avoidance of the responsibility which is implied once human creativity is taken seriously. In discussing *this* subject in a group, it is important that no one should be allowed to use this argument to 'put down' anyone else's beliefs. The important thing is for those who espouse the traditional outlook, and those who wonder if they should espouse it, to consider honestly what in practice it 'does for them', facing up to the kind of possibility I outlined from my own experience in Chapter Six, where religion was definitely shown to be providing *me* with a neurotic escape from human responsibility.

These issues should, I am sure, be opened up and explored pretty fully fairly near the outset of any instruction or discussion about religion, since otherwise the discussion of more specific issues will almost certainly be at cross purposes. On the other hand I think it is likely that many people will be unable to decide properly where they stand until they have looked at what is implied by the two contrasting attitudes, in relation to such issues as belief in God, life after death and morality. I therefore propose now to examine some of these, still in terms of leading questions as they are likely to arise in an 'encounter' context.

Why God? *And what prospects of eternity?*

Most discussions about God are bedevilled by the fact that people do not start by clarifying what they mean by the term, and to do this properly it is necessary to go beyond dictionary-style definitions and establish just what the idea of God is doing for people in practice when they either accept or reject it.

My own experience, from working with groups of many different kinds, is that the great majority of people in modern society take it for granted that the word must mean something like 'the creator and sustainer of the whole universe' or, possibly, 'the infinite ground of all being'. They are normally prepared to argue about whether Dr John Robinson was justified in using the term 'God' to mean 'ground of being' rather than an individualised Master Mind, but it is much rarer, in my experience, to find people bringing forward the possibility of a divine reality quite independent of the natural universe. Even those people who take a very personal approach and speak of a 'God within' will still usually be found assuming, as soon as they come to spell out a little of what they mean by this, that the divine reality they believe to be within them is a manifestation of a universal reality behind all things. It comes as quite a surprise to most groups, in my experience, to be reminded that Tennyson could ask the question, 'Are God and nature then at strife?', and that the early centuries of Christianity were occupied with debates against a whole body of Greek 'gnostic' religious traditions which maintained as a matter of basic principle that the physical world, including the human body, is an evil creation with which their God had nothing to do.

I think it is important to get this point on the table right at the outset of any discussion about God, because the conventional Christian approach to the subject of religion, which begins by arguing that the universe must have a creator and then tries to show how the Bible depicts a progressive revelation of the character of the creator, is quite alien from any real living religious concern in most people, including most Christians. Even those traditionalist Christians for whom religion *does* mean belief in a divine plan underlying all things to which human beings should adjust, did not, in practice, actually *arrive* at their belief in this way, at least not in the vast majority of cases. It is much more likely that they started out with some kind of sense of divine presence, or some feeling of divine authority, in their own personal lives, in most cases derived from their home background, and only later came to explain it in terms of Christian theology. This means that arguments about whether the universe does or does not show evidence of an underlying design or plan probably never touch the personal core of anyone's religion, not even that of the most traditional kind of theist. Such arguments have one and only one value, as I see it, and that is to spell out why unbelievers do not accept the universal authority which traditionalist Christianity claims to embody.

I find most conventional Christians who have not read much philosophy are very surprised, sometimes almost shocked, at the fact that unbelievers are so totally unimpressed by arguments about the universe needing an explanation in terms of some kind of creator or designer or ground of being. I think a key feature of any serious process of religious education or discussion must be an understanding of the fact that unless someone starts out with the presumption of the traditional outlook – that is to say, the presumption of wanting to find an underlying plan in things which will show people how to relate to each other and to the rest of nature – no argument from the actual evidence of experience can ever give grounds for *believing* in a universal creative mind or divine ground of being behind everything. The very most such arguments could ever do in principle would be to suggest the idea as a hypothesis, but hypotheses are not for believing in, they are for trying out in action, and that is scarcely possible in any serious sense with the idea of a universal creator or divine ground of being. Some Christians try to claim that they are being experimental, living by what they believe to be God's will and finding out whether or not they do subsequently enjoy harmony with other people and the universe at large; but in my experience close examination always shows that they are really *making* the experiment come out right by approaching it with the prior conviction that whatever happens to them *will* be right, even though on the surface it seems anything but harmonious. Failures of harmony with other people are put down to failure really to live up to the revealed standard, while frustrations or tragedies in material life are explained as 'events sent to try us' or signs that God is choosing for our own good to move in a mysterious way. This, as I said in Chapter Four, is reasoning of exactly the same class as that of the astrologer who claims every success as evidence for astrology but maintains that predictions which appear to fail are really true at some deeper level – or the Azande chiefs whose oracle was infallible because its apparent failures could always be accounted for by saying that something had not been done properly.

In other words, any really serious belief in a creator and sustainer of the universe or a universal divine ground of being implies the traditional approach to life, for which evidence is ultimately irrelevant, since its beliefs are taken as authoritative revelations with which all evidence whatsoever must somehow be 'squared'. It goes without saying that such a belief gives a sense of meaning and purpose in life to anyone who can accept it, and the same is true of any other belief of the same logical type, whether it be primitive magical theories of the world as a continuum of occult forces, astrological belief in underlying cosmic rhythms, or Teilhard de Chardin's notion (reminiscent of some eastern cosmologies) of the universe as a great system of psychic evolution towards a final divine consummation, the Omega-point. The questions that are worth discussing about any belief of this type seem to me to be three:

1. How do believers face up to the problem that puzzles unbelievers, that there are so many different belief-systems in the world, each capable of backing up its claims with arguments which, to the outsider, are just as good as each other?
2. How firm in practice do believers feel their assurance of meaning and purpose to be, in the face of evidence that appears to the outsider to contradict the belief, especially, of course, personal tragedies which on the face of it seem to indicate that the believer is anything but in harmony with the ultimate purpose of things?
3. On the obverse side of this, how far is assurance of meaning and purpose purchased at the price of having to believe, and ask others to believe, that everything that happens in the course of nature or traditional custom necessarily has divine sanction, as contrasted with anything which involves new human initiative? For example, how far does the belief that nature is rooted in the will of God or the divine ground of being lead the believer to accept for himself, and try to impose on others, rules forbidding birth control, abortion, relief of pain, bottle-feeding of children,

artificial fertilizers or other supposedly 'unnatural' attempts to improve life? How far does belief in divinely-instituted rules of social life lead to taboos on strikes, divorce, mixed marriages, protests and similar attempts to change society?

I do not think believers can possibly lose anything by free and honest discussion of these issues, or by exposing to unbelievers just what it is in practice that their beliefs 'do for them' in life. After all, their position is, of its nature, unassailable if they choose to make it so, and they only give themselves unnecessary problems if they try to maintain their beliefs without facing up to the difficulties other people find in them. In particular, they get themselves into unnecessary difficulties if they try to put over any beliefs they may have about divinely-sanctioned limits on behaviour, on the presumption that certain kinds of behaviour are self-evidently 'natural' or 'unnatural'. This is a straight fallacy and should be exposed as such. Mankind has never, from the beginning of its history, lived in accordance with 'nature' except in the trivial sense that everything is in accordance with nature, including such products of human artifice as birth-control and technology. Man has always, even from the most primitive times, used his intelligence to impose new order on the patterns of sub-human nature – to cultivate his garden, to put it at its lowest. If religion claims – as almost all traditional styles of religion do – to set limits to this creative cultivation of nature, it can do so only on the basis of some supposed authoritative revelation that some kinds of cultivation are legitimate and others are not. The only other basis for suggesting limits to human action is the humanistic one of appealing to experimental evidence, and this can be done only (*a*) when there really is acceptable evidence available (which there certainly is not in the case of religious rules about sex, birth-control, abortion etc.); and (*b*) on the recognition that anyone who chooses to dispute the interpretation of the evidence is entitled to do so, since an experimental rule has no authority beyond the evidence on which it is founded. The common religious idea of 'natural law' as a norm for human behaviour is completely phoney.

In practice, I find that the effect of looking frankly at the difficulties associated with belief in God as 'creator and sustainer of the universe' or 'universal ground of being', is to make many people realise that such belief is not really the essence of their religious concern at all, though they have hitherto thought it was and have expended considerable mental energy on trying to convince themselves that the belief was reasonable. When Tennyson asked 'Are God and nature then at strife?' he was using the term 'God' to express his conviction that human history showed evidence of a supra-human spirit continually influencing the race in the direction of certain values such as justice and love, which at first sight at least seems totally opposed to the general pattern of sub-human nature 'red in tooth and claw'. I find that something of the same general kind (though without Tennyson's moralistic Victorian overtones) is the real basis of what many people today are getting at when they use the word 'God', including many who consider themselves fairly conventional believers. They have a sense, or feeling, or hunch, that something in human experience – love, beauty, justice, creative aspiration, mystical ecstasy or perhaps just a kind of stillness at the centre of the human mind – is so significant, so supremely valuable, and in some strange way so 'numinous' that it must be a glimpse of a power or presence which is somehow superior to man as we ordinarily know him. They may go on to speculate and hope, just as Tennyson did, that this power or presence may in the end turn out to be of universal significance, proving that our lives are not merely meaningless eddies in the bloodstained flux of nature, but their religion does not *start* from belief in a universal creator or ground of being, either logically or psychologically. And if their speculation or hope becomes an article of authoritative belief, they have left their original experience behind in favour of something quite different, probably without ever quite realising what has happened.

Some people may really want to do this, as I have already said in discussing the basic question 'Why religion?', and convinced proponents of the traditional outlook will of course urge that this is the right and proper course, but there is absolutely no logical necessity for it. Even when the original experience itself carries a sense of communion with something in nature, like Wordsworth's 'sense sublime of something far more deeply interfused, whose dwelling is the light of setting suns, and the living air, and the mind of man', there is still no logical compulsion to translate this into any kind of traditional religious belief in a revealed creator and sustainer of the whole universe, or a universal ground of being. On the contrary, such a transition is logically quite unjustified, as is any move from the particular to the general. When the term 'God' originates from an attempt to do justice to some experience, then it is perfectly possible to use it as the basis for a truly experimental 'faith', by seeing how far the original experience can be followed up, both with further experiences of the same kind and by illuminating and enriching other aspects of life with the inner quality of the experience. This would be every bit as legitimate a use of the term 'God' as the traditional one, but it would be a move in totally the opposite direction, namely towards the humanist outlook. It is not, to use the language of my earlier chapters, belief in a power or meaning hidden behind the scenes, to whose supposedly revealed will or character human life has to be adjusted: it is a decision to try to expand experience, and to explore the world in search of new experiences here and now. This is the kind of thing that religion means to quite a number of young people today, as I have said, and in my opinion, based on many years of discussion, a great many people who consider themselves conventionally religious would be interested in it too if they had not been brought up to identify religion with the traditional outlook. The same applies, moreover, even to some people who at present consider themselves unbelievers.

However, in many of the groups of young people with whom I have discussed this, the objection is raised at this point – usually by a self-styled unbeliever who is sympathetic to the line of argument I have just presented because he is interested in unusual human experiences, like those obtained under certain drugs – that it would be better to avoid using the word 'God' in this kind of 'religious' quest, because it is so very loaded with traditionalist overtones. I have a great deal of sympathy with this point of view, and am indeed not sure that this is not the way things will go in the next two or three decades – the word 'God' being left to the (I suspect ever-dwindling number of) traditionalists, while humanistic 'religious' concerns are pursued in other terms. The objection to this course of action is that it ignores what many of us feel to be a real possibility, even probability, namely that some or all of the world's religious traditions, even the most apparently rigid and authoritarian, originally derived from the kind of experiential interest I have been describing and consequently enshrine doctrines and practices which can be of real value in a humanistic pursuit of those experiential interests today. (I think, incidentally, that many traditionalist theologians would agree that their traditions originated in 'religious experience' of some kind or other, but they of course hold that the tradition represents a legitimate development of the 'revelation' which was given in the original experience; whereas a humanistic approach would see the idea of an authoritative revelation as a total departure from the original experience and a perversion of an original experiential concern.) Even the most authoritarian-sounding of doctrines, like the doctrine of hell, could embody an important practical insight if it is taken to refer to an experienceable state of extreme deprivation or alienation from the goodness of life. I believe this possibility – of finding experiential meaning in the doctrines and practices of some of the world's religious traditions – is the most important topic for discussion in the whole business of religious education, once the general background I have been outlining has been established.

Such discussion must combine a certain necessary minimum of

historical and theological scholarship about the world's religious traditions, with an imaginative exercise of cross-checking with people's own personal experience of 'religious' or 'numinous' or 'transcendental' concerns – or even in some cases ordinary moral or aesthetic concerns – which doctrines or practices enshrined in the traditions might help to develop. In this, the personal experience of those who call themselves unbelievers is as important as that of those who actually call themselves religious. It is not insignificant, in this context, that one of the most important British books on mystical experience in recent years was written by a self-styled atheist – Marghanita Laski's *Ecstasy*. I would myself hold, as I said at the end of Chapter Seven, that in this enterprise, experience must have priority over historical and theological scholarship, precisely because the object of the exercise is to expand experience rather than to find authority (in addition to which there is the practical consideration that historical and theological scholarship is always a terribly uncertain business, with constant shifts of opinion and disagreements between experts). If someone finds that a religious doctrine or practice 'resonates' with his personal experience in such a way as to prove useful as a practical guide to some kind of experiment in achieving more abundant life for himself, then I believe he should be allowed to have discovered a legitimate meaning of that doctrine or practice, *even if there is no evidence whatever that it was intended to be understood in that way by the religious authorities who originated it*. There is an instructive parallel here from the realm of science, where great advances have sometimes come from someone taking an old theory and using it in a new way. I see no reason why the same creative possibility should not be kept open in religion also, if we are approaching it in an experimental/humanist rather than a traditionalist/authoritarian spirit.

All the world's major religions have, of course, well-developed mystical traditions within their own orthodox structures, in which doctrines and scriptural texts were taken as formulae for helping the human soul on an inward voyage of spiritual illumination. But these will be of no more use in the quests I am describing than orthodox theology unless they resonate directly with people's real experience and give concrete practical help in the development of that experience. Some of the great mystical writings of east and west should certainly be looked at in the course of any serious programme of teaching or discussion about religion, and so also should one or two of the unorthodox mystical traditions which have developed during the last century or so, drawing electically on doctrines and scriptures from several religious traditions, such as theosophy and Vedanta. It must be clearly recognised, however, that mystical interpretations are merely another form of traditional authority if they are taken – as they very commonly are – as descriptions of spiritual realities 'out there' towards which people are expected to direct their minds in order to adjust themselves to what has been revealed. The great mystical masters themselves were frequently concerned to warn would-be followers of the tendency to believe you were undertaking a mystical adventure and moving from stage to stage along some path described in the literature, when what you were really doing was simply to think about doing so. (The frequent occurrence of this warning in the great mystical literature of the past is one of the things that convinces me of the existence of an 'experimentalist' strain underlying even the most traditional ortho-doxies. It stands in marked contrast to the traditionalist view – which other mystical writings embody all too often – that if prayer or medita-tion produces some kind of results, whether material or spiritual, this is a sign of God's generosity, but if no results are forthcoming it merely proves that God knows it is good for us to go on in blind faith unrewarded.) A truly experiential approach to religion means some-thing much more palpable, much more concretely life-enhancing, than most of what usually passes for mysticism in the mystical sects or groups I have come across; and this means that doctrines – including mystical doctrines – will be of value only if they gear in with concrete personal experience at the most down-to-earth level, susceptible of real experi-mental testing.

The modern writer who has probably done more than any other to give concrete meaning to the mystical side of the world's great religious traditions is the Swiss psychologist C. G. Jung, to whom I have referred several times in the earlier chapters. His leading ideas are well within the grasp of older children, and some reference to them should certainly be made. In particular, I find most people experience con-siderable resonance to his suggestion that the idea of God arises from an inner urge towards growth in the human psyche which makes us very uncomfortable in various ways if we try to settle down in a state of compulsive dependence on family or friends or institutions or ideologies, or if we develop one aspect of life, such as intellect, say, or masculinity, at the expense of others. This gives an immediate practical meaning to the Christian mystical doctrine that we all experience God as wrath unless we follow the will of God for us, which inevitably involves a path of sacrifice because it is necessary to give up compulsive attachments and one-sided ways of living in order to move on to a more mature, authentic 'individuated' existence. Traditional religious practices such as prayer, meditation or mystical worship in the Catholic Mass may have a real part to play in this psychological development, Jung holds, but the development itself has to be worked out in absolutely concrete terms by achieving new levels of relationship with specific people and bringing into action long-neglected parts of ourselves which we fear because their neglect has kept them in an infantile condition. The man who has always been terribly kind to everyone, for example, will have to learn to use his aggressive instincts constructively, instead of repressing them – for repression merely ensures that when they do burst out, as they always do from time to time, they are frighteningly nasty and ruthless – and on the other side of the coin, a very driving person has to develop his tender feelings which at present he fears because, precisely so long as they are repressed, they are frighteningly sloppy and sentimental. Jung suggests that this need to bring out repressed functions is what all the great religions refer to when they say that the way to the God-life lies through the dark land where evil spirits have to be wrestled with, not in order to be put down, but in order to be redeemed. The almost ubiquitous mystical symbol of the goal of the religious quest as a diagram with a cross or a square inside a circle – the *mandala* as it is called in India, and the 'four-square city' as it appears in the more social imagery of the Book of Revelation in the Bible – Jung interprets as an inbuilt psychological awareness that a fully balanced human life, both for the individual and for society as a whole, is one in which there is complete equilibrium between the four basic functions of thinking, feeling, sensation and intuition.

The above is merely a lightning thumbnail sketch of Jung's ideas, and I hope no one will attempt to judge their value on the basis of this totally inadequate highly personal summary. In my own discussions of religion with young people I always try to go into them fairly thoroughly, mostly on the basis of Jung's book *Psychology and Religion: East and West*. I find they arouse considerable interest, but sooner or later I almost always get the same critical comment, usually from one of the more orthodox Christians present: 'That's all very well, and probably very valuable, but are you saying that religion all boils down to a process of psychological development?' And at this point my own personal feeling resonates to some extent with orthodoxy, even though I am prepared to defend Jung by saying that he never pretended to be providing a full account of religious truth, but was concentrating on one aspect particularly relevant to his own work as a psychotherapist, with the added faith that if people got as far as following out this practical side of religion, all kinds of other things might turn out to be added unto them, such as, for example, an entirely new relationship to the forces of nature, or to time and space. This added faith comes over from Jung, not so much in his professional writings, as in his auto-biographical meditation *Memories, Dreams, Reflections*, which is in my view a modern mystical text of some stature. However, for me the problem of man's relationship to the physical world is as central as the problem of his inner growth. That is to say, such issues as bodily health, sex, work, play, politics, pleasure, pain and death are central, and in no sense merely secondary, in what I feel to be my own religious concerns; and I also find them taking a central rather than a merely peripheral place in the doctrines of the religion I know best, namely Christianity. So while I am personally quite out of sympathy with the traditionalist position from which orthodox Christians usually speak when they find Jung wanting, I believe they are pointing to a real one-sidedness in his approach to religion – a one-sidedness which in my view he shares with all purely inward-looking psychological or mystical interpretations of religious doctrines and practices.

I can express this in another way by saying that for me the experience which seems to demand the use of the word 'God' to do it justice is not any special experience like mystical ecstasy, love, beauty etc., but the basic experience of human creativity itself, the experience of having imagination which sets us all these problems of choice and discontent that other species do not have. Occasionally I have experienced creativity as something directly numinous in my own personal life, so that I know what Wordsworth meant by 'that awful power' which 'rose from the mind's abyss' – a power which is not confined to genius, but is known to every human being that has ever made a real breakthrough in doing his own creative thing, whether it be writing a poem, inventing something, developing even a small new theory in mathematics or philosophy or science, working out a new social organisation or a new pattern of family life, overcoming a neurosis, achieving a new psychological balance *à la* Jung or even just devising a book on religious education. Over and above this direct personal experience, however, I have a much more general sense of awe when I stand back from human life and stop taking the astonishing fact of creative imagination for granted, which we have mostly been brainwashed into doing by deterministic philosophies that really have no logical claim to validity at all. (To refute the deterministic claim that creativity is merely a natural function of the human brain, it is only necessary to consider the fact that we have reached the point today, in an age of organ transplants, where it is possible to *imagine* that if anyone wanted to, he could use his inventive skills to devise ways of extending his brain – which is simply a crude practical example of what philosophers mean by 'transcendence'.) I find a sense of awe both from immediate contemplation of the elementary fact of creativity in myself and the others I see around me, but even more from an objective contemplation of the way the human species as a whole has never ceased to struggle for new levels of health, knowledge, aesthetic beauty and civilisation, in spite of the immense conservative forces of fear, prejudice, stupidity, meanness, selfishness and hypocrisy. In fact I get a sense or a hunch of 'a power or presence which is somehow superior to man as we ordinarily know him', not so much from particular humanistic concerns like beauty or ecstasy or love or stillness, as from the very basis of all humanistic concern, the power of imagination, the creativity of the human spirit itself. And I have already tried to indicate, in Chapter Seven, how I find evidence of just such a concern at the back of several of the world's great religions, including some of the supposedly mystical eastern ones, but most particularly in the Judaic tradition of the Bible, which is founded on a definition of God as creative power breathing into man to inspire him to have dominion over nature – an expression which as I see it means not just agriculture or weather control, but *dominance over circumstances*.

In historical Judaism, Christianity and Islam this definition has been translated into a traditional-style belief in a great creator 'out there' who provides an authoritative plan for every human life, but I believe there is evidence, behind all three traditions, of a practical humanistic-style faith. This might best be summed up as the faith that the creative power that seems to breathe into man is actually infinite, so that the whole universe before it becomes potentially plastic, a Great Opportunity rather than any kind of Great System. This would be an experimental hypothesis that insofar as human beings do not alienate themselves or each other from their creativity by trying to avoid the responsibility that goes with it, then it will always eventually triumph over all obstacles, whether in the vagaries of human nature or in the inertias of biological nature – although since this *is* an experimental hypothesis, it cannot by definition predict in advance precisely how the triumph is to be achieved in any particular case. On the other side of this coin is the correlative social hypothesis that the only true basis for human interrelationship is the mutual response of creativity to creativity, which implies that any social organisation whose structure frustrates creativity in any of its members must sooner or later break down. The only hope for social stability, on this hypothesis, is for the whole social structure to be based at every level on 'justice' in this fundamental humanistic sense.

What can this idea of God do for people in practice? I can only give a personal answer. I find it sufficiently vindicated in my reading of experience, both in individual lives and on the plane of history generally, that it gives me a sense of meaning and purpose, as well as practical inspiration, at both levels – as a person in working out my life in intimate relationships, and as a member of the larger human community. In individual life, I find it vindicated in my experience that living by the humanistic ethic really does give 'life more abundant' in the sense of greater vitality, both mental and physical. I shall be going into more detail about what this means in terms of some concrete moral issues later. The basic point I want to make here is that I observe, both in my own life and in society generally, that greater life comes from finding out with intelligent psychological insight what your own creative thing is and then doing it, subject simply to the constraint of not frustrating other people from doing theirs. (The kind of psychological process Jung describes is in my view an essential part of learning to do your own authentic creative thing, and in this I myself accept his ideas as a valid and important interpretation of *one aspect* of the doctrines and practices of the great religions.) By contrast, I find that depleted energy, neurosis and sickness comes from playing psychological games of pretence, of seeking status in terms of some supposedly accepted plan of social life, of avoiding responsibility, of masochistic denial of your own needs or self-righteous attempts to deny the needs of others. This experience is sufficient vindication of my faith that creativity is 'a power or presence somehow stronger than man', 'significant and supremely valuable', that I am prepared to go on to believe, as a continuing experimental hypothesis, that this God in each of us can eventually triumph over all the frustrating circumstances that restrict our lives, even to the point of finding some way in which the creative consciousness in each of us can overcome the apparently insuperable biological necessity of death.

Because my faith is a humanistic one it cannot, as I have said, in the nature of the case predict in advance how frustrations will be overcome, especially not this final frustration which St Paul called 'the last enemy'. Certainly it is relevant that mystics of all religions all down the ages have reported experiences which seemed to them to give unshakeably convincing evidence of the possibility of a change of consciousness to a state in which time and space have no longer the same kind of limiting power as they have in ordinary biological existence. On the other hand I do not know how people who have not experienced this kind of consciousness – or for that matter even those who have – may be expected to enter it at the dissolution of their bodies. My own personal hunch is to think that the individual's hope of triumph over the frustrations of the physical world is in some way bound up with the meaning and purpose I find in life on the wider social-historical plane. Here I find my faith in the infinite power of human creativity vindicated first and foremost in the immense material progress that has been made over the past few centuries since the human race really began to take the humanistic outlook seriously.

I want to make the point here that even the technological developments which have come to be matters of fear or dubiety or downright horror for us, because of our lack of social and psychological progress, are no less vindications of my faith at this level than the more obviously beneficent developments. Looked at in a detached way, it is a matter for astonishment that human beings could ever release the fundamental energies of the material world, and not at all surprising that the age-old military hierarchies promptly took up this new power for weapons. It is quite amazing that man has found out how to transform the basic materials of the world to make new ones with strange properties, and not at all unnatural that the first ones to be mass produced were hard and ugly. It is quite illogical to allow the triviality of most of what is communicated by radio and television (which is no more trivial than most human communication has ever been) to detract from the wonder of our ability to see at a distance, as once it was believed only angels could do. Considering what has been achieved in such an incredibly short time, historically speaking, in the way of ascendancy even for ordinary people over man's age-old natural limitations of disease, time, distance, mechanical weakness and intellectual inertia, it is unreasonable to assume that there need be any limits to what human creativity can do.

In this context it is important also to remember that by the standards even of today's scientific potential, most of what we ordinarily think of as technological 'wonders' are desperately crude and mechanistic: already it is possible to see that the technology of tomorrow can be something infinitely subtler and organic, leading to undreamt of extensions of the range both of our bodies and of our minds. One of the most flourishing new areas of psychological research is known as 'A.S.C.' – the systematic study of 'altered states of consciousness' in dreaming, meditation and drug experiences, and alongside this it must also be recognised that there have in our own time grown out of the scientific movement the first schools the human race has ever known of non-dogmatic, humanistic disciplines for helping people to achieve psychological health and growth – a development which is also only in its infancy as yet with psychoanalysis, group therapy, encounter groups, etc. So I do not think it absurd to believe that creativity in the life of the human race could perfectly well be moving towards a consummation in the not-too-ridiculously-remote future for which the Biblical imagery would not be inappropriate – a raising of the whole earth to a new level of life which is no longer under bondage to death (or for that matter to the limitations of time, space and charity which at present make the prolongation of human life a problem rather than a hope). And I am accordingly inclined to consider that the Bible's imagery may also be the most appropriate for speculating about the way in which individuals may be able to overcome death – namely, by some kind of mutation of consciousness which enables them to transcend the barriers of space and time to participate in the consummation of the race as a whole.

This is of course the vision which has given the works of Teilhard de Chardin such an appeal in our time. What is less well-known, though certainly worth noting, is that a crude science-fiction-style version of the same vision was popular amongst speculative Marxists in pre-Revolutionary Russia: they considered that the establishment of a truly classless society would so liberate man's creative energies that the scientific achievement of eternal youth would soon be forthcoming, and after that the resurrection of the dead (by providing glorious bodies for the thought patterns which could be reconstructed backwards generation by generation from their resonances in the brains of the living). I see no reason why our amusement at the naïvety of their social optimism and the slapstick character of their imagined technology should cause us to deny the value of their vision as a crude poetic expression of a vital humanistic hope. At the same time, it is instructive to note that in their vision there was no mention of the word 'God', although the character of the vision was undoubtedly derived from the apocalyptic Biblical imagery deeply entrenched in the minds of all educated Russians at that period. This serves as a reminder of the point I made earlier, that it is perfectly reasonable for humanists to decide that the term 'God' is so indelibly associated with traditionalist authoritarianism that it is better to find other terms in which to express any far-out, transcendental human concerns – for example, by asserting the transcendental or 'super-natural' character of the *human* spirit itself. I personally find it more meaningful to use the term 'God' for two reasons.

In the first place, my own personal experience of creative imagination, especially that which takes place in altered states of consciousness, which I have known to a small degree, leads me to want to emphasise that there may well be possibilities open to human beings which are even more way out than the resurrection of the dead. In this area too I have a certain resonance with some traditionalists in spite of being opposed to their outlook. Their emphasis on the idea that the supernatural is 'wholly other' than man's ordinary life, and their willingness to envisage many different orders of spiritual reality in worlds behind the scenes – angels, demons and the like – seem to me to be valid reminders of aspects of human imagination which even the most broad-minded humanist has a strong tendency to discount, although to do so is really to be false to the basic principle of humanism, of taking the creativity of the human spirit seriously. So when I say that my own experience of creative imagination combines with my vision of creativity in human history to make me feel inclined to use the term 'God', rather than simply to say 'man is a transcendental animal', I have no wish to impart overtones of traditional religious authority, but I *do* want to bring in some of the overtones of otherness, holy awe, ecstasy, magic, even of terror and ghostliness, which are commonly associated with the supernatural. I believe it is an essential part of a really full humanism to keep in mind that the creative power in man is likely to have mysteries in store for us quite beyond anything that we ordinarily conceive of when we talk about the enhancement of life. What I want to insist is that such mysteries are from a humanist point of view no more 'realities behind the scenes' than little green men on Mars would be, or a cure for cancer that is still awaiting discovery. If they are possible, they will be realities of *this* world, even if not yet dreamed of in the philosophies of most scientists.

And then, on the obverse side of this, I believe that the word 'God' does justice, as terms like 'transcendent man' do not, to the fact that creativity in man never seems to flow uninhibitedly, but has all through history been blocked and thwarted by alienation. This is of course a central theme of all the world's major religions, and I believe they have valuable insights to give us about the causes, the consequences and the cure of alienation. In the Biblical tradition the technical term for man's alienation from God is 'sin', and it is associated with the idea that humanity as a whole has in some way undergone a 'Fall'. The eastern religions also have the idea of the Fall, but do not always have equivalents to the Biblical idea of sin. I now propose to turn to this aspect of religion, which is likely to come up in most discussions once the idea of God has been explored to a reasonable degree.

Naked ape or fallen angel? *Is the sense of sin neurotic?*

The ideas of sin and the Fall are probably the most unpopular of all religious concepts with unbelievers, and even with some religious people. Any champion of orthodoxy who finds this unpopularity puzzling should be referred to Professor E. B. Castle's book *Moral Education in Christian Times* and Gordon Rattray Taylor's *The Angel-Makers*, which give massive documentation of the way in which the concept of sin has been used as an excuse for the most dreadful sadism in punitive systems, especially in the upbringing of children.

This is one of the grim features in the history of organised religion which in my view the champions of orthodoxy should not be allowed merely to brush aside as primitive perversion, as they are normally inclined to do. It is an important part of true education in this matter for everyone to recognise how easy it is for this kind of thing to happen in the context of the traditional outlook, which almost by definition is concerned to discipline individuals to a pattern of life that is believed to be divinely sanctioned, and can therefore easily be held to justify strong measures against those who prove recalcitrant. It is also an undeniable fact that champions of the traditional outlook tend even today to be much more inclined than others to believe in the virtues of punishment in general, even though it has been demonstrated beyond question by psychologists that punishment (even at the non-sadistic level) is actually counter-productive as an educational process. A direct, immediate slap on a child's wrist as it reaches for a precious vase may be valuable in teaching it not to touch, just as a mother bird cuffs its young in teaching them to fly, but such immediate 'negative reinforcement', as the psychologists call it, is not punishment in the normal planned, premeditated sense. Even negative reinforcement only works if it is an occasional event in a much wider context of 'positive reinforcement', or encouragement. If used as the sole method of education it rapidly begins, even in animals, to produce perverse behaviour, and there is overwhelming evidence in human psychology that planned, premeditated punishment *always* produces a perverse response, whether it be applied in the home, in school or in prison. The fact that so many champions of the traditional outlook continue to ignore this evidence is one of the things that serves to convince me personally of the soundness of Freud's diagnosis of this outlook as a mechanism of escape from reality, and in any serious religious discussion this point of view should be fully faced – not, let me repeat, with the objective of putting down the traditionalists if they really want to stick to their guns, but simply to bring out fully, for them and for others, just how they themselves deal with objections of this type.

One point that should certainly be brought out, in all fairness, is that there is no reason in principle why the ideas of sin and the Fall *in particular* need give a punitive character to the disciplinarian aspect of the traditional outlook, even though there is no doubt that it was these ideas which, historically, provided the justification for the punitive sadism described by Professor Castle. On the contrary, some Christian writers – notably, in recent times, the English playwright and literary critic Charles Williams – have actually maintained that the idea of sin was originally meant to mitigate the (supposedly 'natural') human tendency to cruelty in punishment, by warning the would-be punisher that he too is a fallen, sinful creature, who should suspect his righteous indignation of being sinful pride and his disciplinarian zeal of being an excuse to gratify sadistic lusts. This seems to me a useful point for getting a discussion about sin and the Fall started on a practical basis, since it raises at once the question of what exactly these ideas do for people today. Do they still give some people the feeling, as they undoubtedly did in Victorian times, that there is a basic viciousness in human nature which has to be beaten out or sweated out, or do they, *per contra*, make people feel sensibly suspicious of their own self-righteousness, as Charles Williams maintained? Do they make people feel more oppressed by guilt than they otherwise would, or do they simply gear in with a sense of guilt that is already there for other reasons, neurotic or otherwise? Do they even perhaps sometimes help to make people reproach themselves less for peccadilloes, by enabling them to think of themselves as part of a general fallen world rather than individually responsible for every hurt done to others? Until questions like these have been looked at, theological or metaphysical discussion is likely to be at cross purposes.

On the other hand, it is desirable at a fairly early stage to do some clarification of the use of terms, and I think it best to start with the term Fall, because it is common to almost all religious traditions, whereas the term sin, with its overtones of guilt, is not so common (except in the trivial sense of just another word for 'doing wrong'). The basic essence of the idea of the Fall is simply the notion that mankind as a whole, throughout history, has in some way or other always lived at a lower level than human beings are considered capable of by the religious tradition in question. This does not necessarily imply that human beings were once perfect, some time at the beginning of history, and then committed some error which plunged the race into subsequent default. This is the conventional Christian notion, but even within Christendom the idea of an historic fall on the part of some perfect ancestors of the human race has never been universally held. In almost every period of Christian history, long before anyone considered questioning the conventional doctrine on historical grounds, there have been theologians who insisted that if the idea of an historic Fall were taken literally it would imply a very poor view of God, as a creator prepared to allow a whole species to be disadvantaged by some mistake or misdemeanor of their ancestors. Such theologians interpreted the conventional doctrine, and the Adam and Eve story on which it was based, as a parable (perhaps a living parable once acted out by real-life ancestors, but nevertheless a parable) indicating that *in every human being* the essential principle of humanity has somehow taken a wrong turning. One common speculation, all down the Christian ages, was that this might possibly mean that human beings have existed in some spiritual form on some heavenly plane, from which they fell into their present alienated state at the moment of birth. This is very close to the notion found in many eastern religions, and also amongst the mystical religious sects known as Gnostics in ancient Greece, that there is a divine spark in every soul which is literally a fragment of an eternal divine being, who has fallen from a higher heavenly realm into the world of space-time and become imprisoned there in a divided, scattered form.

I think a great deal of fruitless argument will be saved by recognising from the start that all the apparently widely different Fall-ideas, with apparently totally different cosmologies, come back to the same basic psychological root, namely, a sense that there is, and has always been, a potentiality in human beings for something very much more than the ordinary levels of life which mankind has managed to achieve in any society in history. There is even an underlying agreement, cutting right across the many theological, philosophical and ethical differences, about the character of this unexpressed or suppressed potentiality: it is felt to involve much less frustration of spirit by the limitations of matter, and some kind of transcendence of the barriers that separate individuals in life as we ordinarily know it. It is a secondary issue, it seems to me, whether this sense of dissatisfaction is expressed as the yearning of separated parts of a god for reunification to a heavenly life, or as the yearning of human souls for a unity of love in a Garden of Eden or a Mount Zion, where there is no ageing or death because man has dominion over nature. The basic sense of dissatisfaction is the same in all cases, and it comes very close to being the psychological root of religion itself, as I spelt out when discussing the question 'Why religion?' In fact the idea of the Fall in this sense is actually a more fundamental religious concept than the idea of God, as witness the fact that at least one major religion, Buddhism, has no idea of God in any ordinary sense, but is certainly based on a Fall-concept (specifically, on the notion that man is subject to perpetual frustration because his mind falls into the illusion of believing itself an individual entity, distinct from the rest of reality or nature, and thereby develops individual desires which can never be satisfied).

The modern school of philosophy and psychology known as Existentialism maintains that this basic sense of dissatisfaction is a necessary concomitant of human consciousness, an inevitable result of the disparity between the infinite desires of the imagination and the limitations of all earthly existence, of which disparity death is the paradigm. People who claim never to have suffered this sense of 'existential alienation' are on this view simply suppressing it, either by burying themselves in the *minutiae* of physical life at some near-animal level, or else by adopting the 'manic defence' of some ideology which gives them the illusion of meaning and purpose when they lose themselves in it. I think this point will have to be talked out at some stage in any discussion of religion, and my experience is that most groups of people are divided about it. Most atheist humanists claim that the existentialists are merely generalising from their own position – 'putting their own trip on the rest of us', as encounter-jargon calls it. Of course pain and death are awful, they say, but not infinitely awful for the vast majority of people, and can therefore be accepted without undue fuss while every possible practical effort is made to improve life. These are the people whom Colin Wilson, in that great modern study of existential alienation, *The Outsider*, called 'once-born', borrowing a term coined by William James in his classical study of *The Varieties of Religious Experience*. Such people are often inclined to accuse those who are in any way preoccupied with the problem of existential alienation, of being neurotic, turning ordinary unhappiness into infinite dissatisfaction because something went wrong in early childhood, when all desires are felt to be infinite. Growing up, on this view, is essentially a matter of learning that there is no *need* for imagination to make desires infinite, and a really mature person will be no more upset by unhappiness than animals are – he will simply use his higher mental powers to improve his lot where he can. On this matter I think it must be insisted that although the 'once-born' have every right to their own view, they have no right whatever to put down the feelings of the others, the 'twice-born', as merely neurotic. To do so is simply playing tit-for-tat with the 'twice-born's' charge that anyone who does not feel existential alienation is burying it. It is for each person to try to be really honest about *himself*. In the effort to do this, the 'once-born' needs to be on his guard against the possibility of mediocre complacency, of letting the good be the enemy of the best, while the 'twice-born' needs similar vigilance against escaping responsibility by indulging infinite feelings, letting the possibility of a best be the enemy of the good.

It is important to note in this context that Wilson and James apply the term 'once-born' not only to atheist humanists who think the limitations of natural life can and should be accepted without fuss except when something immediate and practical can be done about them, but also to the majority of religious people who feel the same way in practice because they have faith that man's infinite desires will be coped with after death. On the existentialist view such faith is just as much a mechanism for escaping from the sense of existential alienation as political ideologies are. Both alike enable enthusiasts to lose themselves in prosyletising or organisation, and their mass of followers to bury themselves in 'the daily round, the common task', however it may be conceived, in the conviction that it all has meaning – but the hollowness of the whole operation is betrayed, so the existentialists hold, by the fierceness with which believers react to any outsider who in any way threatens to disturb the certainty of their faith. Here it seems to me that the existentialists have an unanswerable case in general, although I think they overstep the mark when they extend it to apply in a blanket fashion to absolutely everyone who is not consciously plagued by the sense of existential alienation. Such blanket generalisation seems to me to come close to turning existentialism itself into an ideology, which is a betrayal of its basic value, the value of individual authenticity. On the other hand, the extent to which heretics, questioners and nonconformists have been persecuted all down the ages, right up to the absurd persecution inflicted on hippies and drugtakers in most western societies in our own day, is surely massive indication of the fact that *for a very substantial proportion of the population* religion and ideology fulfils precisely the function the existentialists say it fulfils, of covering up a deep, basic dissatisfaction with the ordinary conditions of human life. And this incidentally proves that such dissatisfaction is not *just* a neurotic aberration of the 'twice-borns' themselves, or a piece of self-indulgence on the part of the existentialists.

Although most modern existentialists identify religion completely with ideological escape, many of them still feel impelled by the logic of their position to elaborate something like a Fall-doctrine – a Fall-doctrine which, in the absence of any notion of the supernatural, must necessarily be of the Buddhist type, a doctrine of the fall of human consciousness into alienation from the uninterrupted simplicity of nature's lack of consciousness of itself. This, as I understand it, is for example what the best-known existentialist philosopher of them all, Jean-Paul Sartre, is doing in his elaborate description of the 'split in reality' that occurs when nature, which exists solely in itself (*en soi*), produces in the course of evolution a creature who is capable of looking at things in a detached way and making them objects of his own individual desires (the *pour-soi*). Some such view of man is implied, it seems to me, by any 'twice-born' standpoint, even if it is not actually articulated as a religious Fall-doctrine. The 'twice-borns' of earlier ages were mostly prophetic or heretical figures *inside* the religious traditions, but they frequently criticised conventional religion as escapist in very similar terms to those used by the existentialists, and very often got themselves stoned, which to anyone with any insight merely served to prove that their criticisms had gone home. These religious 'twice-borns' often used the Fall-doctrine of their religious traditions quite explicitly as one of the chief ways of articulating their criticisms of conventional religion, for nearly all the great myths and stories that have been used to express the Fall-idea in various parts of the world include as a key element the notion that fallen man can use a kind of religion – usually described as idolatrous religion or superstition – as a way of trying to cover up his sense of being fallen. This is stated explicitly in most of the great eastern Fall-myths, where the various gods of popular religion are dismissed as no more than parts of the general illusion (*maya*) of the ordinary world, nothing to do with the original divine being who has fallen into this world. The same theme occurs, in a rather different form, in some of the Nordic myths. It is not explicitly stated in the story we in the west know best, that of Adam and Eve (although I believe the idea is implicit in a most interesting way, as I have already hinted in Chapter Seven; I shall return to this point shortly), but the Rabbinic tradition surrounding the story always insisted that idolatrous religion was a key feature, possibly the key feature, of the life of fallen man. The Hebrew prophets frequently got themselves into trouble by saying that their country-men's own religion had become nothing but a form of idolatry. And the features of Hebrew life they picked on as evidence for this were precisely those which the existentialists single out as evidence of people's wishing to escape their sense of alienation, namely, preoccupa-tion with the *minutiae* of sensual life, ideological passion against other tribes, and a tendency to stone prophets.

At the opposite end of the scale from the 'twice-born' view of man as *in some sense* a fallen creature, stands the 'once-born' secular view which has been described as the concept of man as 'a great ape trying to make good'. (The atheist existentialist may think of man as a jumped-up ape rather than any sort of fallen angel, but not as an ape who has it in him to make good in any real way – rather, a cruel sport of nature, fallen in the sense of being a mistake in the evolutionary process.) Sometimes this evolutionary-progressive view of man acquires a kind of religious flavour by being tagged on to some sort of mystical view of the forces of nature: this kind of thing was very common in the late nineteenth century and lay at the back of such apparently opposite movements as the racialist philosophy of Ernst Haeckel, with its doctrine of the master-race which inspired Hitler, and various kinds of socialistic belief in progress through education for all. Insofar as such philosophies can be described as, after a fashion, religions for those who follow them, then they are the only kinds of religion that have no Fall-idea. What they have instead is a notion of *natural imperfection* which is used to explain why some people are less advanced in the 'making good' process than others. In some schools of thought the differences are all attributed to genetic defects, and the result is necessarily some kind of racialism, which in its most general terms simply means a belief in a determinate, identifiable kind of hereditary aristocracy. Alternatively, all differences are attributed to lack of will or lack of opportunity: on the positive side this leads to belief in the virtues of education and environmental planning, but on the negative side can easily pass over into a tendency to write off large numbers of people as lazy or neurotic – all 'twice-borns' being, of course, included in the last category, since they remain stubbornly dissatisfied with the best that education and environmental planning can offer.

However, it is essential to remember that these are only *possible*, not *necessary* consequences of the 'great ape trying to make good' view of man. Apologists for traditional religion frequently try to advance their case by claiming that faith offers the only way between the Scylla of existentialist despair and the Charybdis of secular progressivism in which lurk the seeds of totalitarianism, but this is sheer sophistry, and should be exposed as such in any honest course of teaching or discussion about religion. One very popular version of this argument (which I first came across in the knockabout Christian apologetic writings of C. S. Lewis just after the Second World War, but has since been used in the works of serious moral philosophers) tries to turn the tables on the critics who remind the Church of its sordid record in the matter of punishment. This argument asserts that the modern secular view of man is far more dangerous than the old-fashioned religious ones, because the secularists believe their job is to improve people who fail to come up to standard, and to this end are free to resort to any measures whatsoever – if necessary brainwashing, compulsory sterilisation or castration, compulsory leucotomy, or mass extermination of the unfit – whereas the old-fashioned religious idea of punishment, however harsh it may sometimes have been, was always limited in principle by the consideration that it was retribution for some specific wrong, to be meted out only according to what the culprit had deserved. A glance at history, however, will show that this principle never in fact deterred many people in the great ages of faith, least of all the religious leaders, from indulging in torture and mass extermination of a ferocity which has rarely been equalled, let alone surpassed, by the worst tyrants of the secular twentieth century. The truth is, I believe, that if people indulge in this kind of thing at all, it is hardly likely to be for theoretical reasons alone: their main motives are emotional, and if ordinary humane feelings do not restrain them from going to excess, no doctrine of any kind is likely to do much about it. But if any doctrine were going to do so, then modern secularism is if anything likely to be less prone to excesses than traditional religion, precisely because its horizons are more limited. If you are merely trying to build a slightly tidier society on earth, you have less reason and less excuse for putting people to extremes of torture than if you believe there are infinite issues at stake.

A more sophisticated version of the C. S. Lewis argument, which tends to be popular amongst conservative politicians (of all parties), is that faith is the only ultimate safeguard against totalitarianism because it makes us realise that the really worthwhile human good lies beyond anything that can be achieved by society. People who take this line sometimes add that the doctrine of the Fall and Original Sin is socially useful, quite apart from its theological value, for reminding would-be reformers and progressives that people are prone to turn any social advantages they are given into perverse directions. Now I personally believe there is a grain of truth in these arguments, which serves to make them sound plausible, although they are actually quite specious as arguments in defence of any orthodox faith. I myself would hold that the tendency of human beings all down the ages to perverse behaviour is indeed an indication of something in man which cannot be satisfied in ordinary 'earthly' terms: the tendency to fanaticism and the persecution of doubters is just one example of this. On the other hand there is no evidence whatsoever from history that faith in general, or belief in Original Sin in particular, provides any safeguard against human perversity, nor, specifically, against totalitarianism. On the contrary, the totalitarian power of Hitler and Stalin was merely based on natural fear, whereas the Tsars and the Popes had the added power of super-natural fear, which does not seem to have been mitigated in the slightest degree by any self-doubts arising from their subscription to the Christian doctrine of the Fall and Original Sin. The only valid con-clusion to be drawn from the fact of human perversity, it seems to me, is that human beings – perhaps not all, but certainly many – have a sense of existential alienation *which will lead them into totalitarian ideologies when they try to escape from it*, and it is palpably obvious, from history, that religious faith has actually provided this kind of totalitarian ideology just as effectively as, and rather more often than, secular 'faiths'. If there is anything to choose between the two at all, then I would say that theological ideas of human nature are somewhat more likely to lead to totalitarian regimentation of people than naturalistic ones, because their proponents are more likely to be led into assuming that they know in advance, by revelation, how people ought to live on earth. If perverse behaviour is ascribed to Original Sin, history suggests that the powers that be are prone to conclude that it deserves punish-ment, whereas those who regard man as simply a great ape trying to make good are on the whole more likely to decide that social conditions and education are not yet adapted to the great ape's needs in his next stage of progress.

In general, I would say that the 'great ape' view of man is if anything less prone to lead to totalitarian regimentation of people than theo-logical concepts of human nature, because it derives from the world of science and so stands further away from the traditional outlook – for in my view it is the traditional outlook which inevitably tends towards wanting to discipline people into a preconceived pattern, as I said at the beginning of this section. The evolutionary-progressive view of man can be and has been the basis of totalitarian philosophies, but only insofar as it has been taken out of the context of the experimental-humanist outlook from which, as a scientific concept, it originated, and transferred to the traditional outlook in the form of a naturalistic or materialistic faith about Nature or History having certain goals for mankind. And on the other side of the coin, if there is any truth at all in the claim that the idea of man as in some sense a fallen creature serves to hold totalitarianism in check, it is in my view not because the concept has any inherent philosophical or ethical superiority over the 'great ape' view, *but simply because, or rather, insofar as, it is directly rooted in experience rather than in any general theological scheme of belief.* The 'twice born' for whom the idea of man as a fallen creature expresses a direct personal experience of existential alienation, does not need a doctrine to remind him of the vanity of worldly power – he himself finds it unsatisfying. He can never believe that he or anyone else has a universal or blanket solution which entitles them to push others around, and so he is an experimentalist even though he has never had anything to do with science. If he forsakes this principle then he must have forsaken his experience of existential alienation in favour of some faith, which as I have said, makes him as much a 'once-born' as any political leader or self-satisfied bourgeois. Colin Wilson gives several examples of powerful 'outsiders' copping out in this way, notably George Fox, the founder of the Society of Friends.

It is against this general background that all specific Fall-doctrines have to be considered. Like doctrines about God, I believe – and I think most traditionalist theologians would nowadays not disagree – that all Fall-doctrines originated in the first instance in experience, either the direct personal experience of existential alienation or, at very least, a consideration of general human experience as reflected in history. Where the traditionalists would think it perfectly proper, however, that religious traditions should have moved from the original 'revelation' in experience to doctrines which were part of traditional-style systems of belief, I consider, looking at the matter from the standpoint of the humanist outlook, that this transition represents an avoidance of the challenge of the original experience. From the humanist point of view the Fall-idea, like the God-idea, can and should remain an experimental hypothesis, and I believe all the specific Fall-doctrines of the world's religious traditions can in fact be treated in this way, as experimental diagnoses of the nature of man's existential alienation, to be evaluated in practical experience, as I shall try to show in the next sections. I do not dispute that the transition to traditional-style belief is 'right' for some people, in the sense that for them, the experience of existential alienation is just one factor amongst many that go to convince them that the only way to sanity lies in adopting the traditional outlook and seeking the authority of a belief-system, of which a Fall-doctrine will simply be one element. There is no logical necessity for insights about existential alienation to lead people this way, however, and my personal conviction, from a great many discussions with people of all ages, is that a lot of them – including many who think of themselves as fairly conventionally religious – are very interested in the alternative approach of taking Fall-ideas as experimental hypotheses, once they realise it is possible to do so.

In fact, as I see it, the existentialist movement arose in Europe from precisely this interest, for its acknowledged originator was not an atheist at all, but a prophetic 'twice-born' Christian with an almost obsessive concern with the idea of man as a fallen creature – the nineteenth-century Danish writer Sören Kierkegaard. It also derives much from Nietsche, another 'twice-born' of the same period who invented his own Fall-idea, cast in theological language, to challenge the smugness both of the contemporary churches and of the intellectually fashionable scientific progressives. These two men's passionate assertions of existential alienation caught the mood of many people in Europe after the Second World War and created the whole climate of opinion that came to be known as existentialist, and although most of the best-known figures in the movement, like Sartre, rejected religion totally as ideological escape, explaining Kierkegaard away as merely a compromise with his time, there were some who remained convinced that a religious answer to existential alienation could be found which was *not* ideological escape. This was in fact Colin Wilson's purpose when he wrote about 'the outsider', not only in the book with that title but in the whole series of books which followed it; but long before that it had also been the aim of many restless 'twice-borns' in or on the fringes of the churches, who called themselves 'Christian existentialists', of whom the best known were Gabriel Marcel, Pierre Emmanuel and Paul Tillich. Parallel with this, existentialist ideas began to penetrate the world of psychoanalysis, and here produced a whole spate of new thought in which the idea of the Fall provided the starting-point for a number of 'twice-born' psychologists who wanted to insist that purely materialistic theories about feeding difficulties and the like in childhood were not enough to explain human neurosis, since they left a whole dimension of depth out of account.

However, in my experience the possibility of finding experimental insights about human problems in the world's various Fall-doctrines or Fall-myths appeals to a far wider circle of people than would call themselves existentialists – in fact to many people who, from a purely temperamental point of view, would hesitate to call themselves 'twice-borns', although they are not content with ordinary commonplace life by itself and are left feeling vaguely dissatisfied with conventional religions and ideologies. In fact I suppose I myself would come into this category. I am not greatly plagued with a personal sense of existential alienation: for me, interest in religion springs first and foremost from an imaginative conviction that man has infinite poten-tialities, and this conviction could I suppose in principle be compatible with a view of man as a great ape being inspired to transcend himself by infinite creativity. Nevertheless I find the idea of the Fall interesting both at the psychological and at the social/historical level, because I cannot escape the conviction that creativity gets continually thwarted to a far greater degree than need be the case even allowing for all possible inertia on the great ape's part. I find both heights and depths in human life, both in personal experience and on the plane of history, to which a purely naturalistic model does not seem to do justice, and as I am driven on the one hand to think of something like a divine power of creativity inspiring man, so on the other I am driven to the notion of man continually falling – not just falling short of what he might be, but falling far below the worst he need be on a naturalistic model, as if there were an infinite creative energy in him being some-how turned back on itself to suppress itself. So in spite of my temperament I am forced to think of man as more like a fallen angel (or more accurately a falling angel) than a struggling ape, but I see no reason in this to want to embrace the traditional outlook, and so I turn to the world's Fall-stories and Fall-doctrines in a humanist spirit to see what diagnoses of the nature of the human condition they might have to offer on an experimental basis.

It is at this stage that the idea of Original Sin may come in, inasmuch as many of the Fall-stories around which religious traditions have grown up depict some Primal Fault from which man's fallen condition arises. Before discussing this, however, it is essential to clarify some of the difficulties of terminology which surround the word 'sin' itself.

Fatal flesh or sinful spirit? *The quest for enlightenment*

Insofar as the term 'sin' is used as anything more than a straight synonym for 'wrongdoing', it is essentially a religious term directly connected with the Fall-idea, for it implies some kind of offence against man's higher potentialities, whether or not these are defined in terms of the notion of God. One of the most fundamental reasons for man thinking of himself as in some sense a fallen creature is precisely that he feels somehow morally wrong when he commits certain actions, like killing others of his own species, which in animals could be considered perfectly natural, and the fact that most human beings are continually prone to commit actions which they feel to be wrong in this way is the origin of the notion of sinfulness. In this sense the idea of man as a great ape trying to make good abolishes the concept of sin, since it recognises only *failures* to live up to generally accepted values. Even when human beings are destructive or cruel to an extent unknown in the animal world, which is one of the phenomena which most often leads people to a Fall-idea and a 'sense of sin', the purely naturalistic view of man ascribes it to some defect in genetics or upbringing or environment, the origin of which is ultimately purely accidental. The one thing on which all religions, and even atheist existentialists, are agreed is that this view fails to do justice to the facts of human life.

Beyond this basic point, however, the diversity of usage of the word 'sin' is enormous. The biggest divergence is between those who hold that man's sinfulness, or tendency to sin, is simply a symptom of his alienated state, and those who see the alienated state as itself in some way the result of sin. The atheist existentialists come in the first group (although they may prefer to use some other word than 'sin' for the same essential concept) and so do all those religions which ascribe man's fallen condition to simple error. In many of the eastern religious traditions, for example, the primary Fall is often described as not truly a Fall at all, so much as a descent. The divine being is said to become immersed in the physical world either for fun or even, some traditions hold, in order to accomplish some new kind of creation, and then the dispersed sparks of the divine life, which have become human souls, forget their true nature and become immersed in life at the animal or even sub-animal level, with only an occasional sense of sin to remind them that they are really meant for something altogether higher. Other versions of the same basic idea speak of the divine being descending, not into any real physical world, but into a kind of sleep, in which separated parts of the divine consciousness fall into the error of mistaking the figments of the dream-world, including their own individual separateness, for reality. It was this kind of cosmology that originally lay behind Buddhism, but the Buddha seems to have introduced a more severely practical note of discouraging cosmological speculation on the ground that there is little point in a deceived mind trying to work out what things are really like – the important thing is to get on with the job of breaking out of the deceived state, after which efforts to convey the true nature of reality to those who are still deceived will be like trying to tell a man blind from birth what it is like to see. As a result of this severely practical orientation, Buddhism seems (as far as I can tell) to have come in practice often to have only the same very basic kind of Fall-doctrine as the atheist existentialists – the notion that man's imaginal consciousness introduces a split into the stream of nature's unselfconscious spontaneity which allows him to fall into the error of thinking that his separate individuality has significance in its own right, thereby condemning himself to the perpetual tragic frustration of trying to find infinite satisfaction in a finite context. All sin, on this view, is simply man's futile attempt to treat the world as if it existed for him, with growing frenzy as satisfaction eludes him.

The practical implication of all these versions of the Fall-idea is that man will overcome his alienation and begin to do justice to his higher potentialities *by achieving enlightenment through detachment from his worldly preoccupation.* This holds good even of the atheist existentialist, who has little hope that man's fate will ever be anything other than tragic, yet nevertheless seeks a kind of dignified acceptance of that fate in an authentic existence, without illusion, pretence or self-deception, in which human beings pursue their highest human goals and values without becoming identified with the prospect of worldly success either for themselves or for their work. This seems to me to come very close in immediate practical terms to certain kinds of Buddhist teaching which have become popular in the west in recent decades in the writings of men like Alan Watts and D. T. Suzuki, according to which enlightenment is sought not only through the traditional eastern method of meditation but also through various kinds of shock-tactic like answering a beginner's deep philosophical question by a rude gesture, or asking questions like 'What is the sound of one hand clapping?', designed to jerk the mind out of its habitual preoccupations and assumptions. These writers often express the practical objective of enlightenment as the restoration to man of the joyful, calm spontaneity characteristic of the rest of nature (known in eastern thought as *Tao*), by which the broken arm knows how to mend itself without taking furious thought, and everything lives its own life without assuming that it has a privileged position in the universe from which it can expect other things to exist for its satisfaction. But these writers emphasise, just as strongly as the existentialists, that the solution to man's alienation does *not* come from trying to lose his individual distinctively human consciousness by plunging into merely biological existence, either in a life of total sensuality or in total dedication to some supposedly larger life of tribe or nation or race. The 'split in nature' which characterises man's imaginal consciousness is not in itself the Fall, these writers insist, for it has itself been produced by nature's own *Tao*, and there is no salvation for man in trying to go back on it either by living like a pig at the trough or an ant in an anthill. Man must pursue his human goals and human values if he is to be true to himself: the illusion he has to overcome is that of thinking that he is a privileged entity who can achieve satisfaction for his own separated selfhood. So an enlightened man, on this view, will pursue his human goals and values – art, politics, science, teaching, friendship, gardening or whatever – but will see them simply as his way of doing his own authentic human thing, of no more and no less significance than the lion's roar, the heart's beat, the sun's shining or the bird's song, through all of which the joyful life of reality flows.

This is an altogether more optimistic picture of life's possibilities than that of most existentialists, and moreover tends as I see it to take for granted, what other eastern traditions like Hinduism affirm explicitly, that the divine life in nature with which man gets in touch through enlightenment has dimensions and proportions far beyond anything we can imagine in our unenlightened state. Hence on a practical level, Buddhism and other eastern religious traditions tend to assume things that most modern existentialists would probably suspect of being wishful thinking, such as that acceptance of the frustrations of material existence may sometimes mean not only that the pain of the frustrations is lessened or removed, but that the frustrations themselves grow physically less. I personally think this bolder view of man's potentialities is perfectly justifiable. It seems to me that many existentialists have allowed their view of nature to be overborne by the coldness of modern materialism, in spite of the fact that the existentialist viewpoint recognises in principle the fallacy of turning modern scientific theories into statements about what the cosmos is really like underneath. As I see it there is actually ample evidence from medical science itself to support the eastern religious notion – a westernised version of which is found in the modern religion called Christian Science – that if a person can cease to be frantically self-concerned about a disease, the disease itself often recedes or even disappears (though I should be totally opposed to turning this idea into a dogma about how all diseases should be treated). I would even be prepared, as I made clear in writing about God, to go along with the thought that more authentic existence can sometimes open up levels of spiritual power which modern western thought tends to discount completely, such as telepathy or the control of mind over matter outside the human body (although here too I would resist any attempt to turn this idea into a *belief*). Above all, I see no reason for dismissing the view, which the Buddhists seem to me to take for granted and other eastern religious traditions actually assert, that insofar as people become enlightened death can lose its sting for them, not merely in the sense of becoming capable of dignified acceptance, as most existentialists hold, but in the much more positive sense of being swallowed up in a wider consciousness that knows it is not limited by ordinary space-time conditions. Nevertheless, at the fundamental level it seems to me that the existentialists and the religions I have been describing have the same essential prescription for the practical treatment of the human condition, based on their common basic diagnosis of the Fall as a kind of mistake, and this carries with it for all of them the same essential view of sin, namely that enlightenment will lead towards the abolition of sin by detaching people from the frantic desires and ambitions which seek gratification at the expense of others.

A darker tone seems to me to enter the picture in those religious traditions which suggest that some actively evil agency, and not just accident, is responsible for bringing about man's fallen condition. There is a hint of this in the Biblical story, with the serpent tempting human beings to commit an 'original sin' which brings about their loss of Eden. This has very commonly been interpreted by Hebrew, Christian and Mohammedan teachers alike as a reference to a powerful evil spirit which continues to exercise a sinister influence over human life. Nevertheless the main focus of the Biblical story is on what the human beings themselves do: Satan remains a relatively minor character throughout the Old Testament, and if he is sometimes represented as having achieved some measure of control over the world, it is usually assumed to be through his influence on human beings. In the later Jewish writings of the Apocrypha and the New Testament, however, an altogether more sombre note is sounded, similar to that sounded by other religious traditions of the near east, notably that of ancient Babylon and the Zoroastrianism of more modern Persia, a note which also had its influence on many of the Gnostic sects in ancient Greece. This is the idea that nature itself is evil in some way, possibly actively evil in the sense of being controlled, perhaps even created, by some evil power with the express purpose of harming the divine being from which man's higher potentialities derive. The New Testament speaks of Satan as 'the Prince of this world', and although theologians have argued that in Greek the term really means 'Prince of the present age of human history', there is no denying that many passages of the New Testament, like the 'apocryphal books' written between the Old and New Testament periods, have an obsessive sense of nature being haunted through and through with evil forces. In the religion of ancient Babylon there was the legend that the world had originally been created from the body of an odious female dragon, something of whose character remained in all physical nature. In the Zoroastrian tradition the world was held to be the scene of a vast cosmic battle between light and dark deities, who also fought for the possession of each human soul. In certain Greek Gnostic sects, as also in certain Hindu and other traditions of the far east, the physical world was held to be the creation of an evil minor deity or demiurge ('my mad mother Kali', as a Hindu hymn puts it), from whose captivity the human soul had to escape in order to regain its true home in the supreme godhead.

From the practical point of view, the message of all these Fall-ideas is the same, namely, that man's alienation from his higher potentialities can be overcome only by putting down all love of physical nature and all those parts of the human personality that are believed to be connected with physical nature – the physical body, the sense of physical pleasure, the aesthetic sense and even, in the extreme case, all ordinary feelings of love, tenderness or compassion for other people. I find something of the flavour of this harsh dualism in the more pessimistic of modern existentialists, with their insistence on the total meaninglessness of the whole natural universe and their consequent conclusion that the only truly authentic attitude to all physical reality is one of disgust. The most vivid modern description of this view of life I have come across, however, is in a strange, little-known novel of the 1930s which purports to be an interpretation, not of eastern or Greek religion, but of the Nordic tradition found in some of the Eddas and Sagas – *A Voyage to Arcturus* by David Lindsey. It is cast in the general form of science fiction, as the title indicates, but after the first couple of chapters it gives up all pretence of offering even vaguely scientific explanations of the strange adventures that happen to the anti-hero, Maskull and his mysterious companions Nightspore and Krag on a planet of the star Arcturus. The style is entirely mythological: although the three leading characters are introduced in the context of a séance-party in Hampstead, for example, none of them have any first names, although the other characters at the party do (who are dismissed after the first chapter).

Maskull wakes up from the sleep of their journey to Arcturus to find his companions gone and himself in a kind of Garden of Eden, where a delightful couple live in complete harmony, enjoying not only all the pleasures of innocent physical life as we know it but also the added delight of special organs of sympathy which enable them to commune with others in a state of blissful love. They tell him the world is ruled by a divine being called Surtur (the saviour-hero-god of Nordic mythology) and Maskull has a vision of a glorious many-coloured being named Crystalman who claims to be Surtur. Then, suddenly, Krag erupts into the scene and strangles the idyllic couple, and as they die a horrible sickly grin comes over their faces. Krag departs without explanation, and Maskull wanders off to a series of further encounters with other couples, each slightly nastier than the last. In the course of his trip most of these other characters come to sticky ends, usually violently and sometimes at Maskull's own hand, and always as they die their faces assume the horrible grin. Meanwhile Maskull has various further visions, including one of a glorious sea of white fire, and another of sparks of fire trapped inside balls of quivering dark matter. Then at last Krag reappears to a now tortured Maskull and explains. The white fire, called Muspel-fire (again a direct reference to the fires of Muspelheim which the saviour-hero Surtur brings to burn up the world in Nordic mythology), is the divine life, but Crystalman lied in claiming to be Surtur: actually he is the devil, who has created the whole world in order to trap some sparks of Muspel-fire in the heart of human bodies. The essence of the trap is pleasure, which tries continually to seduce the sparks into remaining separate. The ghastly grin which appears on the face of a dead body is simply a revelation of the true character of all physical existence, 'a ghastly mess of slobbering pleasure'. (Although the author does not say so, Crystalman's name is presumably a reference to the way white light gets broken up by prisms, and so evokes Shelley's 'Life, like a dome of many-coloured glass,/Stains the white radiance of eternity,/Till death tramples it to fragments'.) So, Krag explains, man's only hope of salvation lies in escaping from all attachment to physical life, and the happier people are in this evil world, the more deluded they are: the wicked are in that sense actually one stage nearer enlightenment than the innocent. Krag therefore strangles Maskull, who as he dies promptly becomes Nightspore (the name being presumably a reference to the secret personality, spore of the night, which each man has buried in him). As the two of them float in a boat across the sea of white fire, Nightspore recognises Krag as the true Surtur (or saviour), and asks his real name, whereupon Krag replies 'Pain'.

The message seems a savage one, worlds away from what Alan Watts calls 'The Joyous Cosmology' of Buddhism, yet on closer analysis the line between the two may not always be at all easy to draw in practice. After all, it was the discovery of the sordid horror of poor people's lives that first shocked Gautama, the gentle, cultured prince, into a realisation of the need for enlightenment through detachment from the desires of this world, and it did so because his imagination was able to extrapolate from what he saw to the recognition that even if, by what would then have had to be a miracle, poor people could be suddenly raised to his own princely level of physical comfort, the relief of their suffering would be only temporary, since old age and death would still come to expose their happiness as a hollow sham. Since then Buddhist teachers have not hesitated, as other eastern religious teachers before and since have not hesitated, to rub their disciples' noses in the facts of ugliness, pain and death in order to urge the need for detachment: they have insisted on meditation in graveyards, they have called for contemplation of the fact that the body's greatest pleasure, sex, is closely muddled up with urine and faeces, and have even inflicted severe punishments on backsliding disciples to drive the message home. In other words, the proponents of the joyous cosmology are prepared – on occasions at any rate – to see pain as a saviour, in the sense that it serves to remind human beings of their higher potentialities which (on the Buddhist and kindred views) can be achieved only by detachment from ordinary worldly cares, whereas pleasure and comfort can have the opposite effect of making people forget about this.

Moreover it is necessary to emphasise, in this context, that the word 'remind' is the operative one here. David Lindsey's apparently savage view of the human situation is actually saying no more than is implied in *any* view of man as in some sense a fallen creature, namely that for human beings, simple innocent enjoyment of ordinary life is (usually) a sham. Liberal-minded humanists, rightly disgusted with some of the outrages committed by organised Christianity, have sometimes painted a picture of religion sadistically thrusting the claims of a so-called higher life on people who would be far better off left in simple pagan innocence: Somerset Maugham's play *Rain* is an example, evoking a sense of anger in the audience with its hypocritical missionary forcing the natives to feel guilty about their innocent sex-lives in order that he can offer them God's forgiveness through Christianity. I have considerable sympathy with this criticism of organised religion, as I shall make clear later (as I said in Chapter Seven, Dietrich Bonhoeffer was so incensed by the way the German churches indulged in this tactic that he classed them with the Nazis), but I do not think we should allow justifiable anger on this point to make us idealise the noble savage, whether we see him in primitive society or in the so-called simple souls of our own world. The evidence of both psychology and anthropology seems to me to support the 'twice-born' view that simple souls usually are burying a large part of their nature, and because of this will often show an altogether nastier aspect at the first hint of anything that seems to threaten their way of life – witness the fact that primitive people have often attacked missionaries, and at the other end of the scale, the simple American middle-class citizen wanting nothing but the right to his own innocent pursuit of happiness becomes a savage killer at the distant rumble of Communism or the first sight of a long-haired hippie. Lindsey's novel could be read as an allegory of this process, the apparently simple innocence of the first couple being shattered by pain not as the sadistic act of some punitive deity but just as a fact of life, and the subsequent couples, each nastier than the last, depicting the gradual degradation of human relationships in a world where people continue to try to live their lives at the ordinary level of getting and spending, retreating with ever-growing frenzy from the sense of existential alienation. In this sense the idea of nature as somehow inherently evil is simply the reverse side of the coin of the joyous cosmology. For once the basic idea is accepted that unenlightened human beings misperceive the world by seeing everything from the point of view of their own individual satisfaction (*pour soi*), it is perfectly possible to hold that ultimate reality, including the ultimate reality of nature and the human body, is good and joyous in itself, while also recognising that the world *as we perceive it* needs to be treated (at any rate at times) *as if* it were the creation of an evil being, since the world as we perceive it is an illusion (*maya*) constantly liable to seduce us from enlightenment.

I emphasise this because in my experience a great deal of time is wasted in religious discussions in argy-bargy about some religious traditions being 'life-affirming' because they hold that the physical world is inherently good, and others being 'life-denying' because they think of the world as inherently evil. The futility of this kind of discussion is proved by the fact that precisely the same arguments can be used by Christians against the eastern religions as are used the other way round. I have heard a great many young people in recent years maintaining, as Alan Watts does, that the eastern traditions have a relaxed, joyful attitude to nature in general and sex in particular, in contrast to the sin-obsessed gloom of Christianity: they sometimes throw in the added comment that the eastern religions do justice to femininity because they go along with nature, whereas Judaism, Christianity and Islam, with their severely masculine God, have been responsible for promoting the warlike and manipulative male virtues out of all proportion. On the other hand, it is still a common argument in Christian circles that the eastern religions must be world-denying because they hold that the physical world is *maya*, whereas the Biblical tradition maintains that God created the world and thought it very good: such Christian apologists frequently add that the western religions give both femininity and sexuality a dignity which they lack in eastern cultures, by holding that God recognises no distinction of male and female, and that the human body is the temple of the holy spirit. Both sides in this kind of argument point to the fact that the other side has a tradition of asceticism which begins with celibacy but can often be pushed to the point of graveyard meditations, disgust at the body's natural functions and self-inflicted pain.

The truth is that people's attitudes to nature, bodily life, sex and the so-called male and female virtues are not mainly determined by metaphysical or even by ethical philosophies, and a wide range of attitudes can coexist within any one tradition. The main determinants of these attitudes are practical and emotional considerations, and probably the most important distinction of all in this area, as everywhere else, is the distinction between the traditional and the experimental attitudes to life as a whole, which cuts right across almost all differences of metaphysical or even ethical doctrine. Thus the traditional outlook assumes from the start that people's primary need is for some general discipline within which both the inner imaginative and intellectual life and outer physical activities can be controlled, so as to enable man to fulfil his proper destiny (whatever this is held to be) in the total plan of the universe as a whole and to find his proper relationship to his fellow-creatures. Since one of the major problems of human life is the frustration we feel, because of our imaginative consciousness, at the experience of pain and death, the traditional outlook will always involve some kind of discipline for lessening the impact of pain and death, usually by giving the same kind of positive meaning within a larger framework. In these terms, the question of whether man's ultimate goal is seen as enlightened re-integration with the inner life of nature, or as total transcendence of nature in some spiritual heaven, is from the practical point of view merely a difference of emphasis. The darker metaphysical philosophies will in general tend to lead to harsher ideas of what life's practical disciplines should be like, but the spectrum of differences between one religious philosophy and another in this matter is probably no wider than that to be found within any one religious tradition at different times and in different places. Thus it was the Hindu tradition, with its doctrine of man's ultimate spiritual goal of evolving through incarnation after incarnation towards the final re-unification of joyous Godhead, which in practice imposed the severities of the caste system and many horrible customs like the burning of wives on their husbands' funeral pyres, all for the soul's ultimate good in its future evolution. On the other hand the puritan Christian tradition, which in theory held that this world was a vale of tears designed for the purification of souls, did more than almost any religious or ethical tradition before it to raise the life of the common people above the squalor of subsistence living, and the sin-obsessed Bach wrote music of enormous sensual beauty, including the rhythm of the dance. Overall, the general life of the average citizen, peasant or aristocrat in Buddhist and Hindu countries differs far less from that of their counterparts in Christian, Jewish or

Muslim communities than their widely different beliefs-systems would suggest. All traditions alike encourage domestic peace through obedience to the powers that be in society, bless ideological strife, discourage theft and regulate sex mainly by the demands of reproduction. All alike recognise that alongside ordinary social life, the Great System asks some people to undertake special lives of religious devotion, usually involving celibacy, asceticism, prayer, meditation and ritual, in the last of which the community as a whole is expected to participate from time to time.

In saying this I am of course speaking from my own point of view, which is one of opposition to the traditional outlook, but even so I am not wishing to put down anyone's specific beliefs by saying they do not matter. From my particular experimental point of view it may seem that wide differences of belief count for little in practice, but from the point of view of the traditional outlook such differences will be all-important because they will be matters of truth or falsehood. All I am urging is that people should recognise the facts and not try to score debating points on illegitimate grounds. Perhaps this point could be put more positively by saying that I think in the modern world, where religious toleration is a practical necessity, traditionalists of different faiths might well find that there is real ground for such toleration even within the most conservative interpretations of their traditions, if only they will analyse their doctrines carefully enough and not be misled by superficial differences of terminology.

If on the other hand religion is approached in an experimental spirit, as I believe some people have approached it in all traditions all down the ages, and as growing numbers are now seeking to do all over the world, then doctrinal differences in general, and differences about the good or evil character of physical nature in particular, are essentially practical matters, to be evaluated strictly according to what works in achieving some real experience of fulfilment of higher human potentialities. At this level I believe a maximum degree of openness of mind is essential, in view of the wide range of differences between people. For example, I am personally suspicious, both from temperament and from psychological considerations, of attempts to achieve enlightenment through asceticism or the infliction of pain, but there is no doubt at all that for some people a real experiential breakthrough can come in this fashion. The best way to illustrate this is by quoting from a recent book by a young American, John E. Coleman, who after a long quest in many countries finally achieved his enlightenment under instruction from a Buddhist Master in Rangoon: he calls his book *The Quiet Mind* but the crucial passage starts off with anything but calm:

At this point the teacher made me take a vow to remain perfectly still for one hour periods without moving. I was to make no movement of any kind, not even flick an eyebrow. Knowing this would be an extreme test of will I agreed. The heat and pain became intense. The suffering was more than unbearable, it was searing and terrible, but persistence and perseverance had been demanded and I had agreed to it.

Buddha's teachings on the nature of suffering became clearly experienced through my entire being. It was like fire, burning and scorching. And naturally the desire to be free from the agony was intense also. The slightest movement of the body would bring instant relief, but only for a moment, after which the agony would return when I sat still again.

As the days passed the pain persisted, and as the pain persisted so did my desire to be free from it. But there was to be no relief – perhaps a gradual simmering down, but no relief so long as I desired relief. My mind reflected on *anicca* again and it occurred to me that if everything was subject to change so was *dukkha* or suffering. As long as the mind was functioning in its usual egocentric fashion suffering was bound to continue.

There was an intense desire to be free from suffering and this very desire was perpetuating the suffering. This must have been the turning point, my moment of truth. Suddenly, at a point of supreme frustration, my mind stopped functioning for it realised it could not bring about a cessation of *dukkha*. The desire to be free from suffering ceased as the realisation occurred that it could not be sought after and brought about. There was an infinitesimal attachment to the self and suddenly, like a bolt of lightning, something snapped and when the search stopped there was relief. It was an extraordinary and, for me, totally unprecedented experience.

'There was an indescribable calm. There was cool equanimity that seemed to fill and encompass entirety. There was everything and nothing, a peace which passes all understanding. The mind and body were transcended. The mind was quiet. It was not pleasure as we understand the word; joy comes nearer to expressing the experience. There are no longer any words to carry on with.' These were the sentences I wrote down later in a quite inadequate attempt to record the superb moment of my enlightenment.

I cannot, and never will, lose the memory of that moment. It will always remain absolutely unforgettable and ineradicable in my mind. It was the culmination, rich beyond all my expectations, of the search. It was the fulfilment and justification of all my hopes.

Coleman makes it clear that this breakthrough did not, and was not meant to, lead to a life of withdrawn contemplation. He has returned with his wife to very active life in America, and his Master in Rangoon is an active civil servant as well as a contemplative, who loves good food and beautiful flowers. What the Master passed on to Coleman through this experience was an inner detachment which makes pleasure a matter of the eternal moment, not part of an organised way of life, in the spirit of Blake's famous verse:

> He who bends to himself a Joy
> Doth the winged life destroy;
> But he who kisses the Joy as it flies
> Lives in Eternity's sunrise.

This detachment was achieved for Coleman through pain, because he used pain as the means of learning to renounce his 'bending to himself' attitude to life. On the other hand neither he nor his Master would, I am sure, try to say that this is the way for everyone, and it is in these practical terms – of trying to discover what other ways there might be for people to pursue their higher potentialities, and of evaluating which ways are most likely to succeed – that I believe we should consider the question of whether, or how far, the kind of Fall-doctrine presented in extreme terms by David Lindsey represents a valid diagnosis of the human condition. To the traditionally-minded of course it will seem strange, even absurd, to speak of evaluating a whole cosmology in terms of practical psychological considerations; the traditional outlook sees a cosmology as an attempt to state the Truth of the Universe in terms of which man must try to live. From the experimental/humanist point of view, on the other hand, Truth lies in experience and action, not in theories of any sort, and the only point of a cosmology is to provide us with an experimental hypothesis about the way we may seek to live in the world in order to have life more abundant.

The essential point that has to be considered is whether, in the light of the fact that experiences like John Coleman's undoubtedly occur (and in fact for some mystics seem to have come only after even more severe deprivation lasting over many years), it is sensible to say that the natural universe *as we ordinarily perceive it*, and in particular the human body with its pleasure-pain orientation towards the rest of nature, should be *treated as* inherently evil, in the sense of being something which continually distracts us from our higher potentialities by causing us to seek restlessly after pleasure and run away from pain. This is another key issue which I believe needs to be talked through thoroughly in personal terms in any teaching or discussion about religion, and I cannot do better, by way of illustration, than quote from a letter I had from a Buddhist friend with whom I had been discussing these matters, *apropos* the way in which the modern encounter movement tends to take precisely the opposite attitude to nature and the human body from the one I have been describing. I had been telling her of the work of the Esalen Institute in California, one of the pioneer centres of the encounter movement, where the prevailing philosophy is that our main problem in the modern world is the maltreatment of the body, and of physical nature generally, by the mechanical routines of technological society. She wrote in reply:

> I am against the Esalen venture . . . I think, from a Theravada Buddhist background, that one should let the body go hang: if it is maladjusted, probably so much the better. Probably you will call me anti-life but I'm not really. It's just that I think matter is transformed if one starts from the other end. (I don't like using that hackle-raising word spirit: but there is *some* other end, whatever one may call it). But you may prove me quite wrong . . .

This, it seems to me, is what David Lindsey's view of the Fall really means, and what all the great 'dualistic' cosmologies mean which put down physical nature as the enemy of the spirit. I do not think they necessarily imply that man's spiritual potentialities can never be achieved this side of death, nor even that heavenly life is devoid of relationships, aesthetic values or some kind of 'embodiment'. What they *do* imply is that all our ordinary *concentration* on the comfort, health and pleasure of the physical body, or on the enjoyment of beauty and relationships, is a denial of the spirit: our aim should be to let all that go hang, to accept maladjustments as signs from heaven, to detach ourselves completely from life as we ordinarily live it and leave all questions of health and happiness to start 'from the other end'. My friend's letter is evidence, incidentally, that this view does indeed occur within at least one branch of Buddhism's joyous cosmology, as well as in the overtly dualistic religions. Is it possible that it might be proved wrong? I believe it can.

In the first place, I think there is ample evidence from experiments like that of Esalen, which are now spreading all over the world in what is significantly known as 'human potential' movement, that people can be freed from the '*pour soi*' attitude (of seeking to bend joys to themselves) as much by 'going through' real bodily pleasure as by 'going through' pain after the fashion of John Coleman. It should be noted that Esalen itself was founded by a young American psychologist, Michael Murphy, after he had experienced the joyous cosmology of Buddhism on a pilgrimage to the east, but his development of the insight he gained there went in precisely the opposite direction from that taken by my Buddhist friend. Under the influence of renegade psychoanalysts like Frederick Perls, William Schutz and Alexander Lowen, Esalen has discovered that when people begin to open themselves to the immediate here-and-now joy of such physical activities as dancing, bathing, massage, hugging someone, wrestling or even just looking at something, there can be a breakthrough into a less ego-oriented attitude to life. The experience on such occasions seems to me, from all accounts I have heard and from what I have myself encountered, to provide a direct refutation of the Lindsey view, in that *the body itself seems to know that it does not want sensual indulgence.* It takes only a small amount of real sensory awareness to awaken the body to the fact that it is being biologically maltreated by the way the mind organises life, and this maltreatment happens as much when the individual wallows in self-indulgent sensuality as it does when he strives neurotically for wealth and power, regiments himself to mechanical work-routines or suffers extreme poverty. When the body breaks out from such artificially-imposed regimes of living the result is anything but a ghastly grinning mass of quivering flesh: it is much more like John Coleman's experience of transcendent joy, or in Lindsey-terms, like Nightspore's self-abandonment to the white fire of Muspel – an experience in which the higher human potentialities seem to come nearer, not to retreat.

A very good account of the Esalen experiment, and of several kindred experiments in America (including some more orthodox offshoots of Buddhism), is given by a woman journalist called Rasa Gustaitis in her book *Turning On.* In this she quotes Michael Murphy as saying that for many people in the past decade, the possibility of breaking through into a realisation of man's mystical potentialities has been first of all opened up by drugs like L.S.D., which shatter the stereotyped mental attitudes that normally bog us down into routines of getting and spending, pursuing power or burying ourselves in sensual indulgence. All the evidence goes to show that the L.S.D. experience is normally, under the right conditions, an enormous explosion of sensuous awareness, often including a pulsation of energy through the whole body which is at one and the same time the summation of everything that is ordinarily thought of as erotic pleasure, and also a mystical awareness of something holy, marvellous and awe-inspiring. I have myself experienced something of this in the course of taking part in a research programme on mescalin, the drug described by Aldous Huxley in *The Doors of Perception.* Huxley's experience seems itself to have been, as far as it went, a direct contradiction of the Lindsey-diagnosis of the human situation, in that, like the experiences at Esalen, it was both an intensification of visual, tactile and auditory awareness of mundane objects in the room yet also, at the same time, a mystical sense of contact with transcendent reality. For Huxley, however, the mescalin vision lacked the erotic overtones often described in L.S.D. experiences, but my own had them in full measure, and provided me with a total experiential contradiction of Lindsey *in his own terms*.

My whole body was filled with intense erotic pleasure, but it was in no sense reduced to a quivering jelly of animal lust. It went out to the whole world in a kind of spiritual ecstasy a hundred miles removed from promiscuous sexual indulgence, and incidentally brought a realisation of the truth of the claim made by psychologists like William Schutz and Alexander Lowen, that sex in ordinary life is actually a very pale thing (particularly for those who indulge in sexual athletics) compared with what it can be if the mind is freed from its ordinary worldly routines. But the most striking thing of all about the experience was that when I closed my eyes the spiritual-erotic energy that seemed to be pulsing through me seemed like a sea of white fire: in fact it was this experience which reminded me of reading Lindsey's book many years before, though I had totally forgotten it at the time. I saw crystals, too – in fact the whole world seemed to be a vast crystalline structure of which human bodies were the coloured nodes of inter-section – but for me the white fire was in no sense trapped in the crystals and trying to get out. Rather it was pulsing through the whole structure giving every point its own particular incandescent colour, yet in itself the white fire remained whole and undivided, totally giving itself yet totally contained within its own numinous integrity. I have since heard several people say that they have had remarkably similar experiences as a result of meditation, and most of them confirm the erotic character of the experience, so foreign to what most people in our world would associate with the idea of transcendent holiness. This leads me to wonder whether the highly erotic language often employed by mystics did not have a more direct emotional connotation for them than is commonly supposed by ordinary religious readers who treat it as mere analogy.

These experiences seem to me to gear in with the growing recognition by depth-psychologists of most schools that all positive psychic energy in man seems to have an erotic character, and this is a further consideration which seems to me to prove the dualistic diagnosis of the human condition is wrong. For under analysis it turns out that there is a complete continuity in man's inner life, so that our highest spiritual intuitions – including the sense of existential alienation and the desire for enlightenment – are shot through and through with body-awareness, and vice versa. Indeed it is this very fact that gives rise to the problem of existential alienation which (as far as we can tell) is foreign to other species: if our instinctual life were not shot through and through with 'spirit' (or in more prosaic language, the imaginative capacity) we should not find ourselves apparently cursed with infinite desires (including the desire for personal meaning and immortality) which can find no satisfaction in ordinary worldly existence. And on the other side of the coin, every image or word we use to express our sense of potentialities beyond the ordinary is derived from our early childhood experience of exploring the world through the pleasure-seeking body. A sober assessment of my mescalin vision leads me to the conclusion that even Lindsey's image of white fire is probably rooted, as an image, in some basic physiological experience, perhaps going back to early childhood erotic awareness of the world of light after coming out of the womb.

So it seems to me that philosophies which try to affirm the spirit by denying the body and physical nature are involved in the same kind of self-contradiction as the man who advocates decapitation as the cure for headache. If pain and physical adversity can sometimes be used – as they undoubtedly can – to achieve realisation of man's higher potentialities, this must always be in the context of a wider appreciation of man's unbreakable integrity as *embodied* spirit, and I personally think it will remain for most people the exception rather than the rule in the experimental quest for more abundant life. The matter was ideally summed up by Blake in *The Marriage of Heaven and Hell*, where he criticised the dualistic view contained in 'all Bibles and Sacred Codes' (I think he was going too far in saying all, but in view of the prevalence of the dualistic view in our culture the exaggeration was pardonable) as containing the following errors:

1. That man has two real existing principles, viz., a body and a soul.
2. That energy, called evil, is alone from the body; and that reason, called good, is alone from the soul.
3. That God will torment man in eternity for following his energies.

In contrast, Blake asserted the following contraries:

1. Man has no body distinct from his soul. For that called body is a portion of the soul discerned by the five senses, the chief inlets of soul in this age.
2. Energy is the only life, and is from the body; and reason is the bound and outward circumference of energy.
3. Energy is eternal delight.

The term 'eternal' here is not mere poetic conceit: Blake meant quite literally that by getting properly in touch with the life of the body man would discover the way towards realising the full spiritual potentialities of his life, going altogether beyond the ordinary limitations of time and space.

Blake was by no means starry-eyed or sentimental about nature or ordinary bodily life. On the contrary, he had his own elaborately worked-out doctrine of the Fall, drawing eclectically on many religious traditions, and his difference from the dualistic view is all the more striking for being cast in terms which were often derived from dualistic mythologies. For example, it was a key element in Blake's thinking that the world as we ordinarily perceive it *could* sometimes be usefully imagined as if it were the creation of an evil being or demiurge – a figure which Blake called Urizen the circumscriber, quite closely analogous to Lindsey's Crystalman – and part of this evil creation, or 'filmy woof' of illusion, was in Blake's view the human body as we ordinarily perceive it, 'the worm of sixty winters', not so very different from Lindsey's grinning mass of flesh. What Blake never countenanced for a moment, however, was the idea that we could achieve enlightenment by trying to deny ourselves pleasure from the body or physical nature; he was indeed very critical of any kind of tough discipline, as he wrote to his friend Linnell:

> No discipline will ever turn one man into another, even in the least particle, and such discipline I call presumption and folly. I have tried it too much not to know this, and am very sorry for all such who may be led to such ostentatious exertion against their eternal existence itself, because it is mental rebellion against the Holy Spirit, and fit only for a soldier of Satan to perform.

Blake's logic here was very simple, and has been confirmed up to the hilt by modern psychology, namely that you do not help yourself to be rid of an illusion by struggling against it in its own terms. The task is to see through it, and since man's real body in Blake's view was *not* the worm of sixty winters but 'a portion of the soul', then the more we get in touch with the real body the more likely is the illusion to be shattered; in the same way, since the real world is *not* the filmy woof with its 'globe rolling through voidness', the more we get real delight from nature the more likely we are to break out of our fallen, deluded state. Man's salvation to eternal life, Blake wrote, will come by an increase of sensual enjoyment. I personally see in this overtones of the Christian idea of the body and the whole of nature being ultimately changed, quite literally, into new spiritual forms in the process of general resurrection, but Blake's own expressions smack more of the eastern concept of the discovery, through change of consciousness, of the *dharma*-body as all nature is recognised as part of the life of God.

In either way of putting it, the immediate experimental implication is clear, and it is precisely the one which the modern human potential movement has drawn, namely that the root of man's alienation from his higher spiritual potentialities is in no sense in physical life, but rather in his *mind*, so that we are more likely to be liberated from our alienation by encountering the body in pleasure than by withdrawing from it in pain, although if pain comes our way we can always try to turn it to positive use. This, however, at once raises a further fundamental question: if simple physical pleasure can be sufficient to enable us to break out of our deluded condition, *why has the human mind remained so persistently deluded throughout most of human history*? Is it really enough, in other words, to ascribe man's fallen condition to simple error? This is why I have been at pains to emphasise throughout this section that the sense of the physical world as in some way inherently evil, a force that actually seduces us from enlightenment, can be, and clearly often has been, the reverse side of the coin of Buddhism's joyous cosmology. It seems to me that the idea that our alienation from our higher potentialities is simply a matter of our forgetting about them, or making a straightforward mistake about our true character, will stand up if, and only if, there is some kind of agency in the world outside us which blinds us, seduces us or drags us down, for otherwise surely the simple facts of life would have long ago been sufficient to correct the error, at least for large numbers of people. If we once conclude – as I believe we should, for the reasons I have given – that there is no such positively evil or anti-life element in the world of physical nature, then it seems to me to follow that man's persistence in alienation from his higher potentialities throughout history must imply that human beings *have voluntarily used those higher potentialities to create false ways of living in which the higher potentialities are denied*. In other words, I believe we are driven, if we reject the idea of *matter* as inherently evil, to look beyond the notion of the Fall as a mere error, to the other notion, found in the Biblical tradition, that man's fallen condition is itself the *result* of some kind of sin, as well as being the cause of the ordinary sins we continually commit in our frenzied attempts to escape existential alienation, through burying ourselves in ideology or sensual indulgence.

This is no mere academic point – at least, not if we are looking at the matter from an experimental/humanist point of view. From the traditional viewpoint the idea of human beings using their higher potentialities to deny the spirit is just one more consideration leading to the belief that we all need to give ourselves over to obedience to some higher authority. From the experimental/humanist point of view, on the other hand, we are concerned with precisely *how* human beings are to try to break out of their false ways of living here and now, and from this point of view the idea of original sin has an immediate practical implication, namely, *that mere technique is not going to be enough, since we are not concerned with simple error.* Techniques – of meditation, sensory awakening, creative use of pain or whatever – are obviously of the highest importance, and I believe Michael Murphy is right in saying that mind-opening drugs like L.S.D. and mescalin have done the human race great service in jerking people into new awareness of the fact that there is more in life than they had hitherto considered possible. I cannot myself resist the conclusion, however, that since such efforts towards enlightenment have been going on throughout history (even mind-opening drugs have been known to most civilisations in the form of sacred mushrooms, peyote, hashish and the like), the race would have made far more progress towards enlightenment than it has done had there not been something else going wrong to drag people back into their illusions again. It was in an attempt to diagnose *this*, I believe, that the world's great myths of Original Sin arose.

Indeed, this could be another way of looking at the whole battery of dualistic cosmologies. I said earlier that these could be interpreted as assertions, not of what the physical world in general and the human body in particular are really like in themselves, but of how they appear to our deluded minds – but this is of course logically and psychologically equivalent to saying that the evil being who is supposed to be the creator of this delusory reality is actually *inside* our minds, an aspect of our own creative potentiality. This was quite explicitly Blake's view when he borrowed the idea of the evil demiurge in order to envisage Urizen the circumscriber weaving the filmy woof of nature-as-we-ordinarily-perceive-it, including the worm of sixty winters: Urizen, for Blake, was one aspect of 'the divine body, human imagination', and Blake's Fall-doctrine is precisely an account of how man – the Giant Albion – allows this one aspect of himself to mislead him and bind him into a state of illusion, misery and sin. I wonder whether the dualistic mythologies may not perhaps all have arisen in this way, and afterwards slipped over into the conclusion (as I see it, a false conclusion) that the part of man which misleads him is the physical part, which would of course at once imply that there is something evil in all physical nature (since man's physical body is evidently closely akin to the rest of physical nature, and was recognised as such long before the modern idea of evolution arose to drive the point home). Blake quite deliberately resisted slipping over into this conclusion, by asserting soundly that Urizen was *not* the physical side of man (Blake created another figure named Urthona to represent that), but was much more like man's intellect or reason. Some critics even suggest that the name Urizen is actually a pun on 'Your reason', rather as Lindsey's name Maskull may be a pun on 'my skull': certainly Urizen's main functions are described as the drawing of lines and boundaries, which are normally associated with reason. Here Blake seems to be leaning much more on the Biblical than the eastern, Greek or Nordic religious traditions, for the majority of Hebrew commentators linked the figure of Satan (and hence the serpent in the Adam and Eve story) not with the human *body* but with what they called the *yetzer haragh*, or *evil imagination*, and in this they have been followed by the majority of Christian commentators, in spite of Christendom's overall bias against physical nature in general and sex in particular.

Perhaps my Buddhist friend was trying to get at this when she suggested that the redemption of human life has to start 'from the other end', from a change in the human spirit, but if she was, then she seems to me to have drawn a completely unnecessary and indeed wrong conclusion in thinking that we should let the body go hang. If the source of human alienation is in the mind or spirit, then the body and the physical environment can provide us with counterweights against it, and this, it seems to me, is what both Blake and the modern human potential movement are getting at; it also seems to me to be what happens with mind-opening drugs. But such counterweights will not be enough, unless we can come to understand just where it is that the human mind or spirit goes wrong, and what can be done to set things right at *that* level. On this question it seems to me that the Biblical Fall-story, the story of Adam and Eve, contains an enormously valuable insight which is echoed, though only much less clearly, in some other Fall-stories and which even Blake only picked up indirectly. It is moreover an insight which gears in with some of the most important findings of modern depth-psychology, although only one psychologist I know of has come anywhere near articulating it clearly, and that is Frederick Perls, the wild, eccentric analyst who abandoned professional psychotherapy in favour of the human potential movement's much more broadly-based attempt to help ordinary people find their way out of the net of mankind's alienated world.

Won't somebody show me an original sin? *And what about morality?*

The fashion for interpreting the story of Adam and Eve as a literal or semi-literal statement about the ancestors of the human race is, as I said earlier, a relatively modern one, and this is something which fundamentalists should realise if they are prepared to be honest. Prior to the Middle Ages, literalism of this sort was practically unknown in any field of discourse, in that stories from the past and even accounts of the lives of animals or of the movements of the stars were always taken primarily as parables of human life in the here-and-now even when they were believed to be literally true as well, and in any conflict it was the literal meaning that had to give way to the parabolic rather than vice versa. Bestiaries and history books alike were constructed on this principle, so it was in no way a contradiction for theologians to assert that the Bible was a true account of things that actually occurred, and at the same time to take it for granted that the main value of its stories lay in providing moral tales of various sorts for the illumination of life in every age. In this, St Augustine's view of the story of Adam's fall was typical. He did not question its historicity, but he also took it for granted that it was a parabolic statement applicable to all human beings at all times and in all places: 'We were all in that one man, when we all were that one man.' Other theologians with more sense of history recognised quite explicitly that if the story were taken only in a literal sense it would imply a poor view of God, as a creator prepared to allow the whole race to be disadvantaged by some mistake or misdemeanour of their ancestors. They accordingly insisted on a mystical interpretation with reference to a Fall undergone by every individual soul, and some of them tried to make metaphysical sense of this idea by positing the pre-existence of souls in a heavenly Eden, from which some have fallen through an original sin and so been born into this world for purposes of expiation.

Fundamentalism as we know it today, which makes the Pope hesitant about allowing Catholics to go too far in their acceptance of the idea of evolution, and made it possible as recently as 1925 for an American Presidential Candidate to prosecute a schoolteacher in a Southern state for teaching his pupils about Darwin, is a product of the modern period when people were beginning to abandon the traditional outlook and ask for experimental descriptions of the world. This led many religious people into the fallacy of thinking that if their doctrines were to continue to have the authority of truth, they must be upheld as literal statements of an historical or scientific type, and this was responsible for the misguided attempts of both Catholic and Protestant authorities alike to hold back the new thinking even to the point of trying to deny concrete evidence. The result was of course to discredit religion completely in the eyes of vast numbers of people – as Erasmus warned: 'By identifying the new learning with heresy,' he wrote, 'you make orthodoxy synonymous with ignorance.' The more liberal-minded religious leaders who tried to say that some elements of the

Bible might be parables rather than statements about history or descriptions of physical facts, seemed as if they were merely trying to save face in defeat, when in reality they were returning to the mainstream tradition of Biblical interpretation, both Hebrew and Christian alike.

It is a tribute to the psychological power of the Adam and Eve story that it has continued to fascinate many people who have completely abandoned all ordinary adherence to religion: it has been the subject of countless reinterpretations both by artists and by psychologists in the past two centuries. The irony is that such people have often been infected by the fundamentalist error even in the process of rejecting it, in that although they have treated the story as an allegory rather than as literal truth, they have still taken it as an *historical* allegory rather than a timeless parable. For example, the most popular interpretation of it as a myth depicting the evolutionary transition from unselfconscious animal life to selfconscious human life, bringing a sense of guilt and shame about sexual and other actions which animals do without question. There is also a psychological version of this interpretation which treats the story as a symbolic picture of every individual's transition from childhood innocence to a sense of responsibility, a transition which some people place at puberty but others, under the influence of Freud, place at the time of the Oedipus conflict, and still others trace right back to the 'fall' out of the womb into independent existence. None of these interpretations seem to me even to begin to do justice to the story itself, for all these transitions are *stages of growth* with unpleasant accompaniments, or what are sometimes called 'falls upwards', and this is palpably not the tone of the Adam and Eve story at all. True, the story as we have it has passed through many generations of editing by the guardians of traditional religion, who were naturally inclined to treat it as an account of a 'fall downwards' because the traditional outlook inevitably sees man as fallen out of harmony with a Grand Universal Design, but it seems to me that if a non-traditionalist interpreter makes this a reason for ignoring the story's whole flavour he might as well dispense with it altogether. One general rule that has emerged from modern psychological studies of myth and legend is that when a story has an 'archetypal' character expressing some deep psychological truth, as the Adam and Eve story certainly seems to have, then its essential flavour has a way of persisting irrespective of widely different conscious intentions on the part of those who tell and retell it.

So although the kind of insight I think it is worth looking for in the story is experiential rather than traditionalist, I also think that to do the story justice at all it should be approached in the basic *spirit* of the traditional religious interpreters who took it as a parable about the way human beings in general come to live in a 'fallen' way (that is to say, at an altogether lower level than they have it in them to do). This approach seems to me entirely in line with the way depth-psychologists have learned to look at the dramatic parables we all create in our minds every night – dreams.

Perhaps one of the most significant developments of our century has been the reinstatement, at a new level of understanding, of the ancient religious idea that these spontaneous nightly products of the mind can be useful in helping people achieve greater insight into life's problems. In the first flush of the new scientific era this whole notion was dismissed as mere superstition, all tied up with the idea of spirit-communications coming from other worlds behind the scenes, and dreams were explained away as mere fragments of nonsense triggered off by overeating or creaking doors. The credit for rescuing the baby from the bathwater of superstition in this case goes to Freud, who recognised that different people weave similar meaningless fragments into their own particular dream-dramas, and went on to show how the themes that emerge offer important clues to problems which have been thrust out of consciousness for one reason or another in waking life. Freud's own theory of dream-interpretation, however, was mainly concerned with wishes and conflicts which he believed to have survived under the surface of the mind from childhood, and more modern research has shown that this is a quite inadequate view of what dreams can tell us about ourselves. Since 1953, when American workers discovered that we all have long periods of dreaming at regular intervals every night, accompanied by rapid movements of the eyeballs under the closed lids which make it possible for researchers to know just when to wake someone up to be more or less sure of getting a dream recalled, a vast amount of new information has come to light which vindicates Freud's basic insight about the value of dreams but demands a much broader approach to understanding their meaning. One of the best popular summaries of this new view is given by Ann Faraday, a pioneer British experimental dream researcher, in her book *Dreampower*, and her main conclusion is that dreams reflect some aspect of the dreamer's total life-situation *in the present moment*, bringing in the buried conflicts of childhood only as and when they have immediate present significance and only as one amongst a whole host of significant factors. She remarks that this principle of dream-interpretation was originally suggested by Jung long before all the modern knowledge became available. It was Jung's achievement also to show on a really large scale what Freud had started to show in his famous treatment of the Oedipus story, namely that the world's great myths, legends and fairy tales can be treated as 'general dreams', reflecting the perennial problems of humanity as a whole in the same kind of way that ordinary dreams reflect the problems of the individual dreamer.

If the Adam and Eve story is looked at in this experimental or psychological way, it becomes possible to make sense of one of its features which has always caused trouble to traditional interpreters, even when their approach was parabolic rather than literalistic, namely the apparently childish behaviour of God after the Fall. Humanist criticism of the outlook of the Bible has long been summed up in the protest that a God who put temptation in his creatures' way and then punished them for succumbing to it would be an inhuman monster rather than a loving divine Father, but careful study of the story without theological (or anti-theological) assumptions reveals that God is shown acting like this only *after* Adam and Eve have fallen. Prior to their fall, God's character appears quite different – a numinous presence freely accessible to the human beings, telling them their destiny is to have dominion over nature. If the story is looked at like a dream, what this means is that man's alienation from his own higher potentialities makes him *see* God as a petulant, arbitrary tyrant 'out there' instead of experiencing the divine as a creative power inspiring human beings from within to undertake their own creative adventures. In other words, *the story depicts conformist religion as one of the main results of human alienation* – something which other Fall-stories assert directly, as I said in the section on the Fall, and which the Hebrew prophets continually got themselves into trouble for asserting when they turned the accusation of conformism on their countrymen. It is in this respect that I believe Freud's feeling of kinship with the prophets of his race had a more substantial basis than he himself realised. Accepting the common identification of religion with the traditional outlook, his diagnosis of religion as the universal neurosis of humanity amounted in effect to precisely the same diagnosis which I find in the Adam and Eve story.

This brings out a second feature which escapes notice in most conventional interpretations of the story, namely that although God after the Fall is shown getting worried, like a decrepit monarch, about human beings having access to the Tree of Life, they are by implication positively invited to help themselves to it beforehand. 'Of every tree in the garden ye may freely eat . . .' This seems to me to mean that if the story is taken seriously it cannot be read as describing a simple pastoral couple living a near-animal life in an ordinary earthly park. In fact it envisages Adam and Eve before the Fall as creatures who actually do exercise dominion over nature, and anyone with any experience of gardening will know that this is a long way from the ordinary realities of pastoral life. It makes sense only if the intention is to depict man not as he has ever been (as far as we can tell) on the earth, *but in his full potential*, which I suppose was another of the things the Hebrew and Christian scholars were trying to get at who interpreted the Garden of Eden as a heavenly realm in which human souls pre-existed before birth. I cannot myself accept this view, because I cannot see that it makes sense to speak of the soul pre-existing birth if it has no memory of doing so. What the story seems to me to be describing is *the full 'heavenly' potential human beings would have if they did not retreat into alienation*, and the point is underlined by the statement that God before the Fall invites Adam to give his own names to the animals. In ancient thought, the name of a thing was considered to be much more than a mere label: it was believed to have a magical significance as determining the very essence, shape and character of the thing, so God's invitation to Adam must be read as implying that man is made capable of determining what shape the world and everything in it shall have, and is given the responsibility for making this determination. In other words, the story seems to me to assert precisely the view of the universe which I associated, in the section on God, with the Hebrew-Christian idea of the Creator, and which I believe is implied by the whole experimental-humanist outlook without most people realising it, namely that nature is neither evil nor even, in any purely static sense, good, but *totally open-ended*, a Great Opportunity rather than any kind of Great System. If man were to live up to his full potentiality, the story suggests, he would have an enormous range of freedom open to him, including access to the Tree of Life, which I take to mean freedom to transform ordinary biological existence into a kind of life which transcends death.

In fact the down-to-earth, humanistic character of the Adam and Eve story does not in the least imply any lesser view of human potentialities than that taken by the more cosmic Fall-myths of most other religious traditions, as I emphasised right at the outset of my discussion of Fall-ideas. What it does bring out, by portraying human beings as biological creatures being inspired to a divine future rather than as separated fragments of a divine being that has descended into matter, is the positive thought that man's spiritual potentialities are realised through, and not in spite of, individual personal activity in the natural world. I do not think this idea is necessarily foreign to religious traditions with 'cosmic' Fall-myths, for many of them will be found to include assertions that re-integration of souls into the divine unity does not mean loss of the souls' individuality as such, but only of their unenlightened egoistic separateness. The point is actually made explicitly in those Fall-myths which depict the divine being's 'descent into matter' as a positive act undertaken to bring a new kind of creation into existence, characterised by individualised centres of consciousness. (This is the version of the Hindu Fall-idea made popular in the west by the Theosophical movement.) In the Biblical Fall-story, however, the central virtue of what Jung calls individuation and the existentialists call authentic existence is doubly underlined by the fact that life without (or 'prior to') alienation is depicted not merely as a life of individualised personal existence (to pick up Jung's expression) but as a life of *interrelationship between individuals*. Although theological interpretation often ignores this fact, and speaks of 'the sin of Adam' as if Eve were a mere incidental source of temptation, the story itself places the relationship between the two right at the centre of the action, both in describing the divine creative action ('Male and female created He them . . . in His own image') and in spelling out the character of alienation.

The story's diagnosis here seems to me to link up directly with the main theme of the encounter movement, for it suggests that the most important single characteristic of man's divine potentiality is that it involves interrelationship at a level of complete openness. This, Hebrew scholars agree, is the essential significance of Adam and Eve's nakedness; sexual innocence has nothing to do with it, except insofar as complete openness – lack of any 'cover up', lack of pretence, lack of what the psychologists call 'defences' – does imply a level of innocent frankness about sexuality as well as everything else. And the scholars' verdict on this point directly echoes what psychologists have now learned about the meaning of nudity in dreams – it very rarely has much to do with sex, but is concerned rather with vulnerability and unprotectedness. On the other hand the story undoubtedly does seem to imply that this kind of completely open relationship between people would be innocent of sexuality as we ordinarily know it, since ordinary sex and childbirth are quite pointedly remarked on as consequences of Adam and Eve's Fall, and this is of course the aspect of the tale which has attracted more comment all down the ages than any other, including what must now be many millions of jokes. To me this is yet another clear indication that the story is not meant to be an account of primitive pastoral innocence, for this is certainly not without sex. The true implication seems to me to be that man's potentiality for transforming ordinary biological existence *includes the power to transcend ordinary reproductive sex* – an idea towards which as I see it all the world's religions have been groping in their emphasis on the virtues of chastity and celibacy, although most of them have made the mistake of getting muddled up with a condemnatory, repressive attitude to sexuality as such, which I believe involves psychological self-contradiction, as I indicated in the previous section.

The almost universal sense, in all societies that have left any records throughout human history, that sexuality constitutes a very special problem for human beings, and seems to have gone wrong somewhere even from the point of view of the simplest cultures, is rooted in the paradox that our species has always had one of the lowest infant mortality rates in the animal kingdom, combined with probably the highest level of sexual desire. (Man is 'the sexiest primate of them all', as Desmond Morris puts it in *The Naked Ape*.) It seems to have been one of the basic objects of religion in all societies to find ways of resolving this paradox by directing sexuality towards a relational as well as a reproductive function, but the overriding bias towards the traditional outlook has meant that the relational role of sex, which is specifically human, has almost invariably been taken to be secondary to the reproductive, which the human species shares with the rest of the natural universe. The general tendency has been to treat erotic love as ideally a cement for family life, and although most religions have had the proviso that some people have a special vocation to devote themselves to the pursuit of higher human potentialities beyond the limits of ordinary nest-building domesticity, this has usually been assumed to involve the total denial of sexuality. To put the point in another way, it has been taken for granted under the traditional outlook that reproduction must be the essential purpose of sexuality as such, because it seemed to serve this purpose in the Grand Design of the natural world, and so those who attempted to redirect their psychological energies to the pursuit of non-biological ends were expected not only to deny themselves sexual intercourse (which carried the risk of parenthood) but also to deny all erotic feelings. This generally repressive attitude towards eroticism has sometimes even been justified by appeal to the Adam and Eve story on the ground that this was supposed to show the wickedness of sex, although the story itself actually says nothing of the kind, as even the sex-obsessed St Augustine was compelled to admit.

With the rise of the modern outlook there was a considerable reaction against traditional religious taboos on sexuality, but the general bias in favour of the reproductive function has tended to persist even in the thinking of professed humanists, with the result that Freud, for example, took it for granted that the general diffusion of erotic energy all over the body in early childhood marks a 'perverse' state of affairs out of which the infant has to grow to achieve a 'normal' concentration of energy in the reproductive organs. The same bias causes even permissive social moralists to think that sexual intercourse in the family ought to be the norm for erotic expression, even if extra-marital sex is no longer regarded as mortal sin: the fact that fertile family life now represents the biggest hazard to the future of the human race is assumed by almost everyone except the Pope to be simply a challenge to use better birth control methods within the family. It is only in very recent times that voices have begun to be raised urging the possibility that reproductive sex may not be the proper norm for human eroticism. It is an interesting if somewhat ironic fact that we are now witnessing the emergence of experiments in the possible re-direction of sexuality towards mystical and religious goals amongst that very section of the younger generation which has evoked most shocked protest from the official guardians of religion, the young people who have used contraceptives to practise 'free sex'. Some of them have no doubt been inspired by having experiences similar to the one I had when I was taking part in the mescalin research, when it seemed clear that ordinary sex was just one special aspect (and usually, in our society, a very pale, watered-down aspect at that) of a much more general, much more powerful erotic energy which is also profoundly spiritual. Other young people, however, seem to have arrived at the same conclusion without benefit of drugs, simply by giving themselves the chance to find out what happens if erotic openness to others is not held back by the kind of taboos that traditionally (and perhaps even wisely) surround ordinary sex in the family.

This experimentation, far from bringing about the relapse into animality and ever-spreading promiscuity against which so many moralists felt compelled to warn us when the Pill was introduced, seems actually to be leading a not inconsiderable number of people in precisely the opposite direction, towards a realisation that erotic affection for, and appreciation of, others can often be better expressed by simple touching and looking than by sexual intercourse. Of course, the experiment of 'free sex' has often led to mistakes and unhappiness, but no more often, in my experience, than the so-called normal relationships of more traditional social patterns, and meanwhile something new is emerging which for all its frequent naïvety seems to me to be of great religious interest. For unless some such redirection of sexuality is possible for human beings, in which the relational function of eroticism actually takes precedence over the reproductive function, mankind seems to be faced with a hopeless ethical dilemma, in which our most powerful moral instinct, the instinct to value the lives of individuals (which inevitably leads to efforts to prevent children dying and to prevent people from decaying in old age by every means in our power) is bound to lead to racial disaster through overpopulation of the planet. Contraceptive devices seem to me to be no more than stop-gaps in this situation, albeit vitally necessary ones at the present stage of human development. If, as seems likely, we are already within

sight of the technical possibility of enabling people to live in youthful
vigour for a century or more, and if, as Bernard Shaw emphasised in
Back to Methuselah, there is every indication that human beings need
these extra years to acquire the wisdom necessary for sensible living,
then the pistol of evolution is at our heads: we must either abandon
completely the ethical ideals connected with the valuing of individual
personality, or take up the challenge of finding a wholly new approach,
as a species, to the business of reproduction. I think Shaw was right
in seeing this as precisely the challenge with which all the great
religions have wrestled in their notions of spiritualising human life,
and I see this challenge set out directly in the imagery of the Adam and
Eve story, with its suggestion that mankind's higher potentialities
point towards life beyond both reproductive sex *and* death.

Looked at in this light, the attempts by the Pope and some other
religious leaders to restrict the use of contraceptive devices might be
described as doing the wrong thing for the right reason. Their claim
that the solution to the population problem lies in human beings
learning to control their sexual desires is actually based on genuine
religious insight; their error lies in thinking that such control can be
achieved by the repression of eroticism on any wide scale. (Perhaps
some people do reach the transcendence of sexuality through celibacy
and chastity, but to erect the possibility into a general principle seems
to me to imply taking the dualistic view of physical life as inherently
anti-spiritual, which Christian theologians would theoretically deny,
and which I believe can now be demonstrated empirically to involve
psychological self-contradiction.) In the event, as I have said, the
growing use of contraceptives, socially necessary if the world is not
to be choked by what an Elizabethan dramatist called 'plurisy o' people',
seems actually to be bringing about a lowering of sexual tension in
western society, where repressive moralism in the past served only to
heighten it. This new social experiment has found its spokesmen in
psychological critics of society like Herbert Marcuse and, most particularly, the American writer Norman O. Brown, who have concluded
that the real evidence both of human biology and of psychology points
to precisely the reverse view of sexuality to that taken by Freud. The
concentration of eroticism into the reproductive organs is really, they
contend, a symptom of the alienated character of mankind's traditional
patterns of social organisation: the overcoming of alienation would
lead people to become as little children, with a general, diffuse 'erotic
exuberance' emanating from the whole body towards all kinds of other
people and things.

This is, of course, a vision of ultimate possibilities – Brown in
particular links it explicitly, in his book *Life Against Death*, with the

M

Christian idea of the resurrection of physical nature – and its implications for practical social life in the more immediate future still have to be worked out. I personally would doubt whether any developments along these lines will ever detract from the need of many human beings to pair off in stable relationships, nor, in the foreseeable future, to anything like the total abolition of parenthood, but I do think it is almost certain that radical changes are likely to take place in the traditional patterns of family life – if for no other reason, because their terrible record in terms of the production of neurosis in parents and children alike is becoming clear. And here too the challenge seems to me to have been spelt out in a remarkable fashion long ago in the Adam and Eve story, which quite explicitly shows family life as we ordinarily know it as a disastrous consequence of human beings' alienation from their higher potentialities. The basic consequence of alienation, the story suggests, is loss of openness, the wish to 'cover up' – precisely the characteristic which, in the view of most modern psychologists, produces the neurosis-generating tensions in relationships generally and family relationships in particular, as people hide behind various social roles and try to live up to each others' expectations. The result, the story tells us, is a world where 'God' is assumed to require human beings to conform to roles appropriate to sub-human nature – the male as breadwinner, the female as child-rearer – and out of it all comes a family life in which ordinary competitive and hunting instincts are twisted into the murderous jealousy of Cain for Abel, far worse than anything that occurs in other species.

So, to sum up, the Adam and Eve story as I see it describes, in terms of a drama, a choice which has faced the human race from the beginning of its history and faces every individual at every moment of time. On the one hand is the possibility of creative adventure and growth, of experimenting (even if only in the first place to a very humble degree) to transform ordinary 'natural' life – that is to say, the life we inherit from the past – in accordance with our spiritual potentialities, with the promise whispered inside us by the voice of creative inspiration that there are no *a priori* limits to the extent to which such experiment might succeed in realising our spiritual aspirations. Just what the creative challenges are in practice for any individual or any society at any given time is something only they can determine, and in the very nature of the case only the actual carrying out of the experiment of creative adventure will reveal what the immediate practicalities are. The only absolutely essential preconditions of the experiment are that individuals should make the attempt to relate openly to each other in direct personal encounters, and that they should be prepared to take full responsibility for the consequences of the things they do – which conditions, taken together, seem to me to imply that all wider social groupings of human beings must always be kept entirely flexible, or, to borrow the terminology of Jesus, that social organisations and rules should be made for people, never vice versa.

Over against this creative possibility, the story sets the alternative of becoming alienated from spiritual potential by accepting the patterns of the past as divinely ordained, sacrosanct or in principle unalterable. The fact that, right from the beginning of the life of our species, the new creative animal, man, seems to have chosen to cop out of responsibility for his own creativeness in just this fashion means that every individual human being in every age is born into an alienated situation and grows up learning habits of alienation right from the womb – he is 'born into sin', to adapt the notorious phrase of the Christian baptism service. Modern psychology has brought out just how much this means in terms of the distortion of ordinary biological instincts into anxiety-dominated forms which not only lead to inhuman behaviour far nastier than anything seen elsewhere in the animal kingdom, but also impose neurotic conditions on the next generation of children in their turn. Yet it is of the essence of the human situation that every individual is still free to choose how he will deal with this entail of the past: for example, the mere fact that psychologists can discover how enormously we are determined by our infancy is itself an indication that we are not totally determined by it. At countless stages in every individual's life and in every society's life the age-old choice re-presents itself, whether to carry on with the cop-out by accepting the entail of the past as unalterable, or whether to take the risk of trying to make a change in the direction of some creative transformation of the situation. This, as I see it, is what the Adam and Eve story is getting at when it shows the couple being warned, by the same creative inspiration that urges them to have dominion over nature, that there is one choice they cannot make without passing up the whole opportunity of transforming biological existence – there is one tree in the garden whose fruit they must not eat 'or ye shall surely die'. This is no arbitrary prohibition, but the simple statement that if we choose the continuance of the cop-out we are preferring death to life.

Why should we choose it? This is the heart of the story's diagnosis, for it gives the fatal tree a name – 'the tree of knowledge of good and evil'. It has been a puzzle to traditionalist interpreters all down the ages, because it seems to suggest that God would have preferred human beings not to know right from wrong, which is almost a contradiction in terms for the traditional outlook, whose whole essence is the conviction that human beings are in grave danger until they *do* know what is right (i.e. in accordance with the divine plan) and what is wrong (i.e. out of harmony with it). So traditionalist interpreters have been reduced either to making the story vacuous by saying that it simply means 'sin is doing wrong knowingly', which says nothing, or else to making God the kind of monster who would set human beings a pure test of obedience with no meaning at all. If the story is approached from the experimental standpoint, however, a much more interesting interpretation becomes possible. What the story actually says is that human beings are tempted by a serpentine subtlety to go against the warning of their own inner creative inspiration by trying to '*be as gods, knowing good and evil*', which seems to me to mean quite plainly that the fundamental choice of death against life is directly bound up with *the wish to judge even when experiment gives us clear warning that the act of judging means cutting off creative initiative both in ourselves and others*. In other words, the one really original sin we can commit – original in the sense that it re-originates the whole alienated structure of life at points where creative initiative could be used to break out of it and change it even if only by ever so little – is deliberately to reject the option of change, growth or reform, deliberately to pass up the chance of greater freedom, health and happiness, *in favour of the sterile luxury of moralising about the situation as it is*.

This is a diagnosis with truly revolutionary implications both for individual life and for society as a whole, for it means that one of our very highest and most distinctively human faculties, the moral faculty, the capacity for taking responsibility for choosing between the alternative possibilities which are set before us by imagination, is being fundamentally misused. I think we see this happening in individual life whenever a quarrel is prolonged by one or both of the partners 'making a moral issue out of it' long after the point where a simple personal admission of hurt pride would have made it up, and it is a common observation amongst psychotherapists that people often cling on to neurotic suffering out of a perverse wish to enjoy the moral superiority of martyrdom. What is actually happening in such cases – and in all cases of moralising – is that morality is being used to pass up responsibility instead of to take it. The husband who makes a moral issue out of a quarrel, for example, is saying that it is not *his* decision that the relationship should remain broken, not a matter of what he personally feels – it is his wife's responsibility, for breaking whatever moral principle he claims to be appealing to. In the same way the neurotic who takes a moral stance is saying that it is not his responsibility that people dislike him, since he is merely standing up for some vital moral principle which forces him to act in this self-destructive fashion. In other words, moralising is the most fundamental perversion of creative freedom against itself, a usurpation of the role of God in the sense that the individual who moralises is in effect putting himself in the position of being able to pronounce whether or not someone is entitled to enjoy life.

Moreover if we take this idea as seriously as the Adam and Eve story seems to me plainly to suggest, the conclusion is that *the whole traditionalist approach to morality which has governed social life from the beginning of history, is founded on a literally diabolical lie,* which modern psychology seems to me to have been on the brink of unmasking ever since Freud discovered that society's moral suppression of supposedly nasty, destructive or anti-social impulses in people actually makes them more nasty and destructive than ever, by turning them back on themselves and causing them to be exaggerated and perverted by anxiety. Freud himself was so impressed by this apparent self-contradiction at the heart of life that he was driven to speculate that the moralising impulse in human beings – the super-ego, as he called it – was directly connected with a fundamental destructive force in the psyche, something like a wish for death. Most subsequent psychological theorists have shied away from this insight: they have allowed legitimate scepticism about the notion of an inbuilt, biologically based 'death instinct' to blind them to the facts which Freud was trying to express when he put the idea forward. Only a handful of Freud's more way-out followers, notably the eccentric Wilhelm Reich, allowed themselves to ask the obvious question which even Freud had not seriously raised, whether most human impulses need be nasty, destructive and anti-social at all apart from the anxiety generated by moral suppression. It has taken the new perspective of the human potential movement, with its attempt to transfer the insights of depth-psychology out of the clinic and consulting-room into the market place, to bring this fundamental questioning of the traditionalist view of morality really out into the open, probably helped, I suspect, by the fact that many psychologists in this movement have sought to augment their professional scientific thinking by seeking insights buried in the world's great religions. The man who came nearest to nailing the lie at the heart of traditionalist morality explicitly, in almost exactly the same terms as I find in the Adam and Eve story, was Frederick Perls (known to his friends as Fritz) who worked for several years at Esalen until his death in 1969.

Because he worked mainly with 'normal' people wanting more abundant life rather than with people who were especially mentally ill, Perls was less inclined than most psychotherapists to consider the problem of moralistic suppression of impulses as a special phenomenon connected with extreme neurotic guilt. He came, on the contrary, to see it as the most fundamental of all human problems, but it was typical of him that he chose to describe it in pop language rather than in high-flown technical terminology: instead of talking as Freud had done about the Id being repressed by the Super-ego, he said he found all human beings divided against themselves by an inner 'top dog' which continually tries to suppress a large part of the personality, the 'underdog'. Different people in different societies have widely varying versions of this conflict, derived largely (but not, Perls insisted, by any means wholly) from their childhood experience of parental discipline, but the basic self-division seems universal, and its principal effect, Perls found, is actually to *make* the underdog part of the personality nasty, destructive and underhand, for insofar as an individual succeeds in overcoming the conflict, the underdog impulses turn out to be of positive value in the total life of the mature person. For example, Perls found that many people in our society have suppressed aggressive impulses which 'top dog' tells them are thoroughly bad and which indeed are very nasty on the occasions when 'top dog's' control relaxes and they break out – usually when they have some socially-approved form of outlet in war, industrial competition, the disciplining of subordinates or the persecution of some disapproved-of minority. If, however, an individual can be persuaded to bring his internal conflict out into the open – for example, by acting out a dream as a drama in which the different dream-characters represent different elements in the personality – and if he can be persuaded to allow underdog to claim its right to exist, he will discover, Perls maintained, that his aggressive impulses are not really bloodthirsty in themselves at all: they are simply natural impulses towards self-preservation which *in their undistorted form* threaten to do serious harm to no one – a little shouting or a quick blow, perhaps, but no more – while their driving energy is actually a very positive part of the individual's healthy existence. The really fundamental trouble, Perls found, is that when people are brought to see this they very often choose to go on repressing their 'underdogs', with all the disastrous consequences that are implied, including personal unfulfilment, *because they need to be hard on themselves in order to enjoy the 'godlike' privilege of passing judgements on others*. Perls called this the 'self-torture game', which he believed had to be consciously renounced before any progress towards psychological growth could be made.

Although Perls had no direct contact with orthodox religion, his ideas took on definitely mystical overtones from his repeated discovery that if the personality *did* accept integration beyond the conflict of the self-torture game, a release of psychic energy seemed to take place on such a scale as to suggest something transcendental. Earlier, when Wilhelm Reich had arrived (albeit in much less clear terms) at an essentially similar diagnosis of the human situation, he had actually used the Christian term 'original sin' to describe the self-torture game, and I prefer this term because it serves to hint, as Perls' does not, at the sinister implication – that we are all in one way or another conniving, in ordinary society, at a duplicity which, as I have said, seems literally diabolical, namely the perpetuation of 'immorality' in order to justify moralising. This insight seems to me the fundamental point of that remarkable modern parable, George Orwell's *1984*. It has meaning at more than one level, but its deepest level seems to me to be a diagnosis of a 'double-think' at the heart of all traditionalist social life, not just of life in totalitarian states. He portrays a state of repression in which people continually rebel because the repression grinds them down to desperation point, and he shows such rebellion being positively encouraged by the character O'Brien who is really the chief torturer, *because it gives him the excuse to maintain his regime of torture*. Taken at this level, I do not think O'Brien's motivation should be seen as literal sadism: his famous declaration of the truth that cruelty and torture are absolutes, ends in themselves, would certainly not be true of ordinary sadism, which is a neurotic disease probably produced by extreme deprivation in childhood – and in any case, literal sadism seeks no excuse. I believe the reference is to what I in an earlier essay (written at about the same time as Perls was developing his ideas, but before I had ever heard of him) called *moral sadism*, the desire to sit in the seat of the scornful and pronounce what others ought to do if they are to be entitled to enjoy life.*

I linked moral sadism quite explicitly with Freud's 'death wish' on the one hand – for the essay was a contribution to the theory of psycho-analysis – and on the other with the temptation of the serpent in the Adam and Eve story to 'be as gods, knowing good and evil', and I pointed out that the story ends with the couple seeing God as precisely an embodiment of this moralising attitude, the Great Moraliser who underwrites their own morality-bound existence which breeds Cain. I believe it may have been this ancient Hebrew insight, rather than a tendency to dualism, which in the first place led the writers of the story of Jesus to depict him as referring to Satan rather than God as the ruler of this world (although dualistic feelings about the inherent evil of nature undoubtedly crept into the New Testament later). Certainly this was the view of Blake, who more than any other writer in history seems to me to catch the essential paradoxical flavour of the personality of Jesus as we read of it in the Gospels. In his famous poem 'The Everlasting Gospel' he wrote:

* *Psychoanalysis Observed*, ed. Charles Rycroft (Constable, 1966).

> If moral virtue was Christianity
> Christ's pretensions were all vanity

and in his prophetic books, written directly under the influence of the
inspiration of Jesus as he saw him, he depicted Urizen the circumscriber
(surely a remarkably accurate image of the moralising impulse) creating
a world in which people were led to worship Urizen himself – or, as
Blake put it elsewhere, to worship Satan, the moralising accuser, under
the name of God. Jesus's continued attacks on Pharisaism were not,
in Blake's view, an obsessive concern with the special vice of a small
section of the population, but a recognition of the fundamental
character of the world's evil, summed up in the lines

> The Accuser, holy God of all
> This Pharisaic worldly ball . . .

This was the essential point Dietrich Bonhoeffer was making, I believe,
when he said that the churches whose evangelism consisted of trying to
make people feel guilty, weak and in need of divine help were following
the spirit of Nazism rather than the spirit of Jesus. This particular
insight of Bonhoeffer's serves incidentally to bring out the other side
of the diabolical lie at the heart of traditionalist morality, namely the
fact that it never actually succeeds even in doing what it claims to do:
given that human beings in ordinary life do have destructive and cruel
impulses, the attempt to suppress these in the interests of social
cohesion merely leads to their finding new outlets in group aggression,
group violence and group cruelty whose consequences are far worse
than even the nastiest individual impulses would ever be in all but the
most extreme psychopaths. This has always been true, as prophetic
figures like Jesus and Blake have always known, but today the progress
of technology has made the truth almost inescapable, as I said in
Chapter Six and brought out again in this chapter in discussing the
existentialist case against ideology. Today, there is no doubt at all that
the greatest threats to human life come, not from individual delinquency, but from people with high moral belief in the virtues of
Communism or western Christian civilisation, while tomorrow the
world faces even greater danger from those who believe in the moral
sanctity of the breeding family.

It is because this diagnosis of traditionalist religion and morality
resonates both with my own personal experience and with everything
I know in psychology and sociology, that I regard the rise of the
humanistic outlook over the past few centuries, with its concomitant
trend towards more 'permissive' forms of morality, as not just *an*

advance for the human race, but actually the most important advance that has ever taken place or could have taken place. I think Bonhoeffer was absolutely right in describing it as mankind's coming of age, and I would also go along with him in seeing it as a fulfilment rather than a denial of the spirit of the founder of Christianity, although organised Christianity has shown remarkably little of this spirit and has mostly tried to resist the new trends. Of course, there will be many people who will disagree with me in this diagnosis in various ways, and not all of them dyed-in-the-wool traditionalists, but I am sure there is sufficient evidence in its favour to make it an essential line of thought to be taken into account in any serious discussion of what we should tell the children, not only about religion but even about morality. For this reason I would urge that any teaching or discussion about religion should postpone most consideration of moral questions until after there has been an opportunity to explore the general issues about human nature with which I have been dealing in this and the two previous sections. I do not think there is much likelihood that many modern children will allow parents or teachers to get away with purely dogmatic inculcation of moral ideas, any more than with religious dogmatism, but they have a right to expect an honest statement of where parents or teachers themselves stand, and some explanation of the reasons for and against various moral options. In this context it is of paramount importance both to understand traditional moral ideas about various major human topics and also to consider fully the objections that can be raised against them from the kinds of considera- tion I have been discussing. Above all, it is essential to give full consideration to the possibility, which I have raised in conjunction with the Hebrew-Christian Fall-story, but which could also be raised on purely psychological grounds, that in ordinary experience some- thing goes very wrong with the moral impulse itself.

To take a specific example, in any discussion of religion and morality in our culture it is essential to consider the traditional Christian view that the true purpose of sex, from which individuals and society deviate only at their peril, is to express and fructify monogamous marital love, but in considering this it is as important for its pro- ponents as well as its opponents to be fully aware of the difficulties it involves. In the first place, it is essential for all alike to acknowledge, as I emphasised earlier in a different context, that arguments about this or any other view of sex being 'natural' to man are purely and simply nonsense, since human arrangements are never natural. Secondly, it is necessary to recognise just how many widely different opinions about sex there have been in the history of Christian thought, and how much of what has passed for Christian sexual morality in the past was bound up with dualistic feelings of disgust for all bodily functions which few Christians today would countenance. A book like W. G. Cole's *Sex in Christianity and Psychoanalysis* is a useful eye-opener here. These, however, are only preliminary considerations. Much more fundamental is a really honest examination of the evidence concerning the actual effects of monogamous family life on the health and happiness of individuals, both adults and children, coupled with an equally honest estimate of what we know, and what we can reasonably speculate, about alternative possibilities. In this it is necessary to recognise that the most important opposition is not between the Christian view of the purpose of sex and such alternatives as the polygamous views associated with some other religious traditions, but rather between *all* traditionalist ideas and the experimental/humanist view that there is no such thing as an inbuilt purpose of sex or anything else. On the humanist view all possibilities are open to trial, subject to the fundamental constraint that by definition people should try to avoid allowing their own creative self-expression to suppress the creative self-expression of others: beyond that, the only criterion for evaluating any patterns of behaviour is the experimental one of determining in practice how they stand in relation to alternative patterns in promoting creative personal fulfilment for those involved. Traditionalists will of course see such an approach as highly dangerous, and their fears must be seriously considered, but they must not be allowed to get away with dishonest arguments about the supposed ill-effects of free sex, or abortion, or childless marriages, or bottle feeding, or unisex, when there is so little evidence of the positive value of normal monogamous marriage. Most important of all, however, anyone who sets out to lay down the law about the 'proper' purpose of sex or anything else must in everyone's interests, including his own, be asked to face honestly what this is 'doing for him' personally as far as his own feelings are concerned, and in discussing this, the question must at least be raised whether he may possibly be taking up his position, even perhaps at the cost of accepting limitations on his own behaviour, because he enjoys being able to lay down the law for the rest of the world.

At the same time, by setting the discussion of morality in this highly personal context it will be made obvious that humanistic and permissive approaches to morality are also 'doing something' for their proponents, and this should serve to bring out the fact that if these approaches are taken at all seriously they are *more* demanding than the traditionalist approach, not less, as traditionalists often try to make out. For to be permissive means accepting total personal responsibility for every decision you take, instead of trying to refer it to some supposedly external standard of right and wrong. If a superior in some organisation needs to reprimand an employee for going against the organisation's current rules and regulations, for instance, he must, in a humanist/permissive morality, take full personal responsibility for saying to the employee that he, the superior, John Doe, 47, married with two children and earning £4,000 a year, *wants* to place more value on the rules of the organisation than on the future fate of this particular employee. Considerations about what would happen to the organisation if everybody did what this particular employee had done are, on a truly humanist view, relevant only at a secondary level: the decision finally comes back to a personal one about what John Doe as a man most wants out of life in this particular confrontation, and he cannot appeal to abstract principles without copping-out of his personal responsibility. In the same way, a husband confronted with his wife having an affair with another man and then asking for a reconciliation has to take responsibility for saying that she has hurt him so much that he would prefer to sever the relationship rather than go on: to try to maintain that she alone is responsible for severing it because she has broken the working rules of fidelity on which most marriages are based is to cop-out. Yet again, the soldier who kills someone in war must, on a humanist permissive basis, accept personal responsibility for the fact that he, Richard Doe, 20, prefers to put a bullet in someone's head than risk giving up his way of life in the country that sent him to war: to appeal to general considerations of patriotism, or even to the belief in the ultimate rightness of his country's cause, is to cop-out. In my experience many people who take up a humanist or permissive stance mainly in order to criticise traditionalist morality have never really faced up to these considerations, and I find from many discussions that when people come to think about these things seriously they are brought face to face with existential problems which lead on beyond morality to religion – that is to say, to questions about the sense of existential alienation, about man's relationship to nature and about the meaning of creativity such as I have been discussing in the earlier sections of this chapter.

As I see it, in the light of the diagnosis of the human situation which I believe to be contained in the Adam and Eve story, the real purpose of permissiveness is not to take the moral fibre out of life but to restore morality to its positive function as a striving towards life more abundant, towards the realisation of human potentialities; instead of allowing it to cut us off from the very creative freedom that makes moral striving possible in the first place. And this therapeutic function of permissiveness is possible, it seems to me, *if and only if we deliberately set out to introduce into life some dynamic process to compensate for our continual lapses into the original sin of moral sadism*. It is not enough merely to recognise the good sense of Jesus's injunction 'Judge not': the very fact that the world is as inhuman as it is derives, on my diagnosis, from the fact that we all again and again freely choose to go against this injunction even when the inner voice of creative inspiration gives us clear warning that to do so is to kill the spirit. The only ultimate remedy for this situation is to make a positive extra effort, in our saner moments, to go beyond mere 'non-judging' to the point of actually *reversing* the process of the Fall by deliberately accepting some of the burden of other people's 'sins' even when we would have every ground for rejecting them. In other words, if the permissive society is really to succeed it has to be based at its heart on some people's acceptance of a positive dynamic of *forgiveness*.

The word forgiveness is a difficult one because it carries overtones of unctuous self-righteousness, of saying 'of course you have behaved very badly, but in my godlike magnanimity I will let you off this once provided you are truly sorry,' which is probably the worst of all forms of moral sadism. Blake, who saw forgiveness as the essence of Christianity, the way back through the gates of paradise, was at great pains to denounce this bogus forgiveness in no uncertain terms:

Doth Jehovah forgive a debt only on condition that it shall
Be payed? Doth he forgive pollution only on condition of purity?
That debt is not forgiven! That pollution is not forgiven!
Such is the forgiveness of the gods, the moral virtues of the
    heathen
Whose tender mercies are cruelty. But Jehovah's salvation
Is without money and without price, in the continual forgiveness
    of sins
In perpetual mutual sacrifice in great eternity.

The operative word here is 'mutual', for it serves to counteract the other misleading association which the word 'forgiveness' has acquired for many people today, the idea that to be forgiving implies allowing yourself to become a doormat. To be genuine, permissiveness must include permitting yourself to express your needs as well as allowing others to express theirs, and this includes the expression of hurt or anger towards others who let you down or exploit you in some way. Anyone who fails to express such feelings is hiding behind just as big a fig-leaf of defensive pretence as people who resort to more obvious forms of emotional dishonesty, and the probability is that he is indulging in the subtle form of moral sadism which consists of exercising the silent reproach of martyrdom. It is quite certain that he will be building up a great deal of unconscious or even half-conscious resentment, which sooner or later will lead to a far worse explosion than would have occurred if the hurt or anger had been expressed straightforwardly in the first place.

The essential (though often unarticulated) principle of permissive morality is that so long as personal needs and feelings are expressed openly and not repressed or 'frozen' into hard attitudes by moralising, they will always sooner or later be governed by the overriding basic need to love and be loved, which given time and a little creative initiative will modify even the most selfish, aggressive, destructive or neurotic impulses. Real forgiveness means simply going out of your way to allow this therapeutic process to happen, and in this sense anyone who devotes part of his time and energy to the kind of emotional education work that goes on in the human potential movement, or in more professional forms of psychotherapy, is contributing to the dynamic of forgiveness in society. So equally is anyone who devotes time and energy to genuine efforts to achieve greater humanity in society at the organisational or political levels, although in all such work – even psychotherapeutic work – there is constant need, on my diagnosis, to struggle against the temptation to ideological moralising if the work is not to do more harm than good. (The danger of such moralising in politics is obvious enough: it is less obvious in the field of psychotherapy, though in recent years more and more writers have been calling attention to the way Freudian theory has become a new kind of moral sadism, particularly where it makes women feel guilty about being anything other than breeding animals. And I find that even in the encounter movement there is a constant danger of a new encounter ideology developing in which, for example, women who do not look after their own children are frowned upon!) At the more personal level, forgiveness means going out of your way to give other people who have offended against you in some way a chance to put things right if they want to, provided you do no fundamental violence to yourself in the process. Jesus is supposed to have allowed physical violence to be done to himself to this end, and to have told his followers to do so, forgiving unto seventy times seven, but I believe that if this is not to become yet another form of morally sadistic demand on people it must be qualified by the disclaimer that only the individual can judge for himself how much hurt he can stand in any situation before he exercises his right to do his own thing by pulling out. The really important point is to recognise the danger of moralising hurt feelings: beyond that, forgiveness at the personal level should I think have about it the simple lightness so well captured by Shakespeare in some of his last plays. The line that expresses it for me is that given to Paulina in *The Winter's Tale* when she suddenly sees the folly of continuing to castigate the king for what his jealous rage has done to his wife and son:

> What's done, and what's past help, should be past grief.

I personally believe the establishment of the dynamic of forgiveness in society is of the highest importance even from a purely secular humanist point of view, and an interesting point for debate in any group of adults or older children discussing religion is how far along these lines secular humanists would be prepared to go on general psychological grounds, without benefit of the idea of Original Sin or the religious concept of forgiveness as the key factor in man's atonement, or at-one-ment, with the supernatural. It is also an interesting question for exploration, how far the ideas I have been discussing are to be found in the world's other major religious traditions apart from those derived from the Bible. I certainly think I can detect hints of the key idea in some Hindu and Buddhist teachings about the need for compassion and about the ultimate goal of life being 'beyond good and evil', though I do not myself find the same emphasis on the life-denying character of moralisation anywhere outside the Biblical tradition. The main body of eastern religious thought seems to me to treat compassion as just one factor in enlightenment, whereas I would see it, on my diagnosis, as the crucial factor without which all other efforts at enlightenment – by the creative use of pain, by meditation, by the heightened awareness of the body or whatever – will simply be undone again. In this sense I personally find it interesting that it was in the west, in the wake of the Judao-Christian religious tradition, that there occurred the major revolution in outlook which has formed the main theme of this book, whereby the experimental/humanist attitude to life began to emerge on a major scale for the first time in history, and led, in our own day, to the first major development of permissive moralities and experimental therapeutic disciplines. I think it is probably fair to say that some far eastern cultures, particularly perhaps in India, have for many thousands of years had a much more permissive general atmosphere than has been found in the ideology-ridden tribalism of the west for most of recorded history, yet for all that the new development in the west over the past few centuries is still a remarkable phenomenon, inasmuch as it is the first major break with the traditional outlook that has ever taken place. It is for that reason, and that reason alone, that I personally am inclined to wonder if there may not be some experimental truth behind the claim of the Christian religious tradition to enshrine something more than general religious wisdom, something more like a new breakthrough in the psychological life of the whole species, the birth of a 'new Adam'. In any case, this claim is certainly a major question which must be dealt with in any teaching or discussion of religion in the western world, and probably any other part of the world too nowadays considering the universal influence of western civilisation.

Are we saved? *Or was Jesus just a mushroom?*

Convinced Christians may consider that the question of Jesus Christ and his significance ought to be raised at the beginning rather than the end of a course of teaching or discussion about religion, but I think this would be doing a disservice to their own position as well as being discourteous by implication to people of other faiths or none. In the modern world Christians are probably more prone than any other group to bring discredit on themselves by thrusting their ideas forward as uniquely superior when they are in fact common to many pagan religions and have moreover often been subject to such widely varying interpretations within Christendom as to be virtually meaningless. I have already mentioned, for example, how Christians are wont to claim that theirs is a uniquely life-affirming faith with regard to nature, the body and sex, in contrast to the Gnostic religions which called the body the tomb of the soul or the eastern religions which dismiss the physical world as *maya*; while at the very same time the proponents of eastern religions are making the identical claim on their own behalf by contrast with Christianity, which they see as puritanical, dualistic and world-hating. In the same way, it is still a common point of popular Christian teaching in Britain that Jesus brought a 'gospel' or 'good news' of love and forgiveness to a Judaism which had hitherto been rigidly legalistic, although in fact it has long been demonstrated by Jewish scholars (notably in recent times by C. G. Montefiori's *The Synoptic Gospels* and Hugh J. Schonfield's *The Passover Plot*) that the teaching of Jesus contained nothing that had not been present in Rabbinical Judaism for centuries. Eastern scholars have made the same point about their own ethical traditions, while on the negative side, a glance at history will show that Christendom could give points to any other religion when it comes to legalistic morality. Religious 'one-upmanship' is almost always based on ignorance, or on giving your own religion the benefit of a sympathetic inside view while looking at all others critically from outside, and in the modern world it is becoming less and less easy to get away with this. Hence in my view the only sensible approach to religious teaching today is to survey the whole global religious scene and its basic ideas, including the ideas of irreligious humanism, before going on to look in detail at the special claims of Christianity or any other particular religion.

Moreover the effect of doing this is in my experience to raise questions about even the more fundamental claims of Christians to a unique faith. For instance, one very common claim of evangelical Christians is that Christ alone offers direct personal salvation to every individual, where all the other religions offer only teachings about general ways of salvation. I have to confess right away that I personally do not know what 'a personal experience of Christ as saviour' means, and neither do the majority of people in most of the groups with whom I have discussed religion, including most Christians, but I am prepared to believe that it is a vital experience for some, and I think religious education must include the opportunity for such people to try to convey, by any means in their power, what the experience is like, how exactly they came by it and precisely what it has done for them in practical terms. It will be a help rather than a hindrance for them to do this against a background of more general understanding of religious issues such as I have tried to convey in the earlier parts of this book, since this will make it possible for them to relate their own use of terms like 'God', 'sin', 'salvation' and 'forgiveness' to other people's usage. The really important questions they will have to face in doing this, however, are not theological or philosophical ones but questions concerning the extent to which other people have had similar experiences to their own 'salvation experience' without associating them with Christ. Thus it is just not good enough for them to say they have known Christ as personal saviour in contrast to Buddha who was only a teacher, when anyone who has been to India knows there is (or at any rate used to be) a Young Men's Buddhist Association there with a special Y.M.B.A. hymn book containing the hymn 'How sweet the name of Buddha sounds, In a believer's ear.' It would be a mistake for anyone to try to put the Evangelical Christian's experience down by calling it hysterical imagination or a projection of the long-lost love of his parents, but by the same token he cannot be allowed to put down the experience of anyone else who claims to be in contact with the spirit of Buddha, or the Lord Krishna, or any other spiritual power bringing peace of mind or guidance or a sense of forgiveness of past wrongs. And if he does not put such experiences down, he must face seriously the question of whether his own experience is really so unique to Christianity as he has hitherto believed, and indeed whether it really has very much at all to do with the historical character called Jesus of Nazareth.

The same questions arise in relation to the more general claim of Christian theologians, that Jesus was the final and complete revelation of God because he actually incarnated the divine life in human form. In my experience a great deal of time is wasted during religious discussions in arguing about whether this claim is true or not – for example, in arguing about whether or not Jesus was asserting his divinity when he said he could exercise the divine prerogative of forgiving sins – when the most important point to establish is what the claim actually means to those who make it. If for instance they take it to mean that Jesus provided some kind of model of ideal human behaviour, then they must in honesty admit that the model is pretty useless unless the fragmentary and often apparently contradictory accounts we have in the Gospels are filled out with theological assumptions that do not derive from the Gospels at all. No Christian as far as I know has ever maintained that ideal behaviour means becoming a wandering celibate teacher with twelve disciples who works miracles. What they mean is that Jesus embodied the perfect *spirit* of human behaviour, the spirit of total unconditional love, but as I argued in Chapter Seven, the Gospel portraits show hardly any signs of such a spirit, since they give no picture of the person of Jesus in depth at all. The idea of total unconditional love is imported into the Gospel portrait from subsequent theological interpretation which sees Jesus as the divine saviour being sacrificed for others. There is an exact parallel to this in Buddhism, where it came to be believed after Buddha's death that he was a unique manifestation of the divine Nirvana-principle who, having attained bliss in his own life, made an act of loving sacrifice in returning to ordinary life, with all its suffering, in order to enable others to follow him – and in both Christianity and Buddhism alike there have been as many different interpretations of what the supposed revelation of the ideal life amounts to as there have been sects, which is a great many.

If issues like these are discussed openly and honestly, encounter-fashion, it soon emerges that most people who put up claims about the uniqueness of Jesus are really simply claiming, indirectly, that the theological tradition they favour has divine authority – which is fair enough so long as they appreciate what they are up to, and recognise that their view of Jesus depends upon acceptance of the authority of their tradition, not vice versa. The Roman Catholic is quite explicitly concerned to argue that because Jesus was the unique incarnation of God, salvation is to be found only in membership of the new 'body of Christ', the sacramental Church which Jesus founded – but those who do not already accept the authority of the Roman Catholic Church will not be in the least impressed by the evidence that Jesus founded a definite organised Church based on St Peter, nor will they see any necessity to equate the Roman Catholic Church with the *ekklesia*, the fellowship of Christians, described in the New Testament. The evangelical who disputes with Roman Catholics on these points, however, is in precisely the same logical position as they are once he goes beyond his personal experience of being saved to maintain that salvation is only to be had through 'believing in the Lord Jesus'. His own personal experience of Jesus as saviour cannot possibly justify such a claim, for no experience can prove a negative: in making the claim he is in fact accepting the authority of a particular religious tradition, and to those who have not accepted it his experience will prove nothing beyond the fact that *he* has found happiness in something which *he* calls 'meeting Jesus'.

Here once again we come up against the crucial point that has been my central concern throughout this book, namely that claims to authority cannot rest on the evidence of either personal experience or of history, since in the nature of the case the whole point of authority is that it sets out to provide a truth against which evidence from experience or history can be judged as reliable or unreliable, genuine or bogus. Thus if either Catholic or evangelical stick to their claims about the uniqueness of Christ, they are compelled to say that people whose experience seems to contradict their claims are in some way deceived. The Catholic who obeys all the rules of the Church yet remains in spiritual misery has to be consoled that he is really saved although God in His wisdom does not allow him to know it. The agnostic who has called on the name of Jesus without getting any experience of salvation has to be explained away as somehow not sincere in his call, however sincere he feels himself to be. On the other side of the coin, the Hindu who experiences *samadhi* without knowing about Christ, or the agnostic who has an inner experience of liberation which he explains on Jungian lines, have either to be told that their experience is in some way not the genuine article of salvation, or else that it really is Christ coming to them *incognito* (which is just as much a denial of what they actually experienced as an outright dismissal would be). And by the same principle, neither Catholic nor evangelical will accept the validity of the other's interpretation of the evidence of the Gospels about Jesus, and neither of them has any difficulty in finding reason for rejecting the arguments of sceptics who dispute the idea of Jesus's divinity, or consider that the accounts we have of him are largely fictional, or explain him away as a code name for the sacred mushroom that gives mystical ecstasy. As I emphasised earlier, in the context of the 'science and religion' question, anyone who finds the authority of his religion seriously affected by the evidence of experience or history must have been starting to have doubts about it already, for otherwise he would simply find a way to fit the evidence to his beliefs, as the Azande chiefs did – and this holds good as much for the various Christian traditions' beliefs about Jesus as for any other beliefs.

In the modern world even the most convinced Christians have begun to have doubts to some degree, because the traditional outlook, which is the fundamental basis of all authority, is no longer universally taken for granted; and a substantial part of any serious religious education must consist of considering how Christians of various traditions come to terms with these doubts (as well of course as the major non-Christian traditions). In considering this, it is important for everyone concerned to be clear that if any kind of traditional-style Christian belief is to be retained, considerations about personal salvation-experience or historical evidence related to Jesus will ultimately be subordinate to the question of whether this tradition or that (Catholic, Orthodox, Anglican, Methodist, Evangelical, Coptic or whatever) *taken as a whole* seems to offer the most trustworthy authority for guiding people's lives. Anyone who is prepared to consider either personal salvation-experience or historical evidence related to Jesus *seriously in its own right* is by implication taking up the experimental standpoint whether he knows it or not; *and from that standpoint there can be no such thing as a unique once-for-all revelation and no such thing as an authority that is not open to question, neither in Jesus nor anywhere else.* However important Jesus may have been in the history of mankind, however special his relationship may have been to God, the most that can ever be said of him from the experimental point of view is that certain traditions associated with his name seem interesting in offering a basis for experiment in the enhancement of life. The Gospel stories themselves are, after all, no more than traditions associated with the name of Jesus in Christian history, and although they may be considered to have a special significance there is no reason in principle, from an experimental point of view, why mystical traditions about Jesus should not be interesting too if Jesus is interesting at all. And even if someone finds the recorded life or teaching of Jesus, or some mystical tradition about Jesus, more significant than anything else he has ever come across, the value will still lie, from the experimental point of view, in the practical results of following out this interest in some kind of life-experiment, and this means Jesus remains always open to question, always subject to the possibility of being improved upon.

I find this conclusion disturbs many Christians even today far more than any other doubt that may be expressed about religion. No one in most western countries take much notice at atheists' denials of God, but there is still a stir when anyone challenges the authority of Jesus on any notable public platform – when John Lennon says that the Beatles are better known, or when an Anglican divine suggests that

Jesus may have been homosexual, or when Dr Hugh Schonfield publishes a book suggesting that the resurrection was deliberately faked by Jesus himself, or when John Allegro puts forward his 'sacred mushroom' theory. A distinguished editor once remarked to me that in the interests of free speech he was prepared to publish an article by a psychiatrist arguing, from a detailed analysis of the Gospel accounts of the days before the Crucifixion, that Jesus was suffering from a psychotic breakdown – 'although decent people will be disgusted that anyone should consider such an idea,' the editor added, as if it were absolutely obvious. In my experience many parents and teachers have feelings like this even though they have never themselves had anything remotely like a personal salvation-experience connected with Jesus, nor any real knowledge of the Bible, nor even any close relationship to any brand of organised Christianity. I use this deliberately as a talking-point in most of my own discussions about Christianity, and I begin by putting what I would consider the basic humanist question, 'Why is it of any serious interest to you personally *what* Jesus may or may not have said or done? If you believe that certain standards of behaviour are good, either with or without religious reasons, why can't these standards rest on their own merits irrespective of what Jesus may or may not have been like?'

My mother would have had an absolutely clear answer to this: she believed that the story of the miracles, and especially of the Resurrection, proved that God Himself has given us a direct supernatural lesson in how to behave which we ignored at our eternal peril – and she really believed that if the mass of people ever seriously came to doubt that Jesus rose from the dead, they would at once think there was no longer any reason for good behaviour and would rush out and start raping, pillaging and murdering. This theme was quite seriously put forward in a popular novel called *When It Was Dark* just around the time of the First World War, and my mother solemnly quoted this to me when I first began to express doubts about the truth of Christianity; she just did not know that hosts of people all around her, whose behaviour was exemplary, had long since ceased to believe in the supernatural authority of Christianity in *that* sense, to say nothing of equally exemplary behaviour shown by millions of adherents of other religions who had never heard of Jesus. (She was prepared to admit, as a concession, that some Jews, Arabs and Hindus could be 'just as good as us', but the majority of them in her mind were grouped together in a vast blur labelled 'savages'.) It also never seemed to have occurred to her that neither she nor most of the other people we knew had ever been seriously tempted to rape, pillage or murder; she took it for granted that this was because Christian influence controlled their lives, although she had never had any personal salvation-experience. She just did not ask why Jesus's teaching had influenced her and her friends but not the drunkards who beat up their families on Saturday nights, considering that the lesson of Jesus's supernatural authority was equally available to all alike. It did not occur to her either to ask why the story of Jesus was supposed to impress people when other miraculous stories about, say, the Greek gods did not: she just accepted, more or less without question, that 'truth' was what 'they' – the authorities of church and school, the *Family Herald* and the *Daily Mail* – taught. I suppose there are parts of the world where people still think like this, but they cannot be very common any more, and I have never come across anyone who holds anything like these views in the past thirty years – but without this kind of thinking, how does the name of Jesus give any added authority to 'decent behaviour' or anything else? Yet there is no doubt that many people still feel that it does, including, as I have said, many who have little or no formal Christian belief. I find it most instructive to get both adults and older children to talk about this as openly and honestly as they can.

What invariably emerges is that many of those present, even some who call themselves agnostics, atheists or humanists, have somewhere in their lives acquired a feeling that the figure of Jesus represents an ultimate personal authority for living, although usually they cannot say exactly when or how they came by it. It also emerges, however, that there is little agreement about just what kind of character Jesus is supposed to have had. One person sees him as a guarantor of commercial honesty, another as a communistic prophet who scourged the moneylenders for exploiting the poor. One sees him as an upholder of the sanctity of marriage, another as the detached mystic who urged men with a serious concern for God to cut off ruthlessly from the family in order to follow a vision not of this world. To some people he is an exemplar of the kind of self-sacrifice which always puts others first, to others a balanced preacher of proper self-love alongside love of neighbour. To some he is an ascetic, to others a warm human creature who could draw from his enemies the charge of being a gluttonous man and a wine-bibber. In a large heterogeneous group of people most of these views, and perhaps more, will emerge spontaneously, and it will soon become obvious that arguments about which view of Jesus is correct are completely beside the point. In a smaller or more homogeneous group this may not be quite so obvious, in which case it seems to me to be an essential part of the duty of the group leader to make it absolutely clear, probably by reference to literature, that this wide diversity of views does exist, and that *every* such view can be supported with arguments from the evidence of the

Gospels, even though some views may perhaps be able to produce more evidence in their favour than others. The only sensible course, in face of this situation, is for people to try to trace back as honestly as they can just how they came by the values they associate in their minds with the figure of Jesus, and then to ask themselves whether they do or do not consider that they were at this point in touch with some tradition which commands authority *in its own right* for the guidance of people's lives. If they do, or if in the course of discussion they come to believe someone else has such a tradition, then it is of course their privilege to give themselves over to its authority, but they should be clear, as I said earlier, what it is they are about: they have no right to say 'I believe in the values of Jesus' – they can only say 'I believe in the values of the Roman Catholic Church', or the Evangelical Christian tradition, or British Public School Christianity, or the Nonconformist Conscience, or the American Way of Life, or whatever. Anyone who is not prepared to give himself over to such a tradition must, it seems to me, admit that his interpretation of Jesus is essentially a private one which accordingly adds nothing to his own self-chosen values except the *mana* which in our culture still attaches to the name of Jesus – and *that* means he must face the charge that he is using the name to escape from taking responsibility for his values himself.

Indeed, I think it an important part of religious education today to ask *all* those who claim to derive their values from Jesus to face this possibility, including those who accept the logic of the traditional outlook. A useful exercise for exploring this issue is to ask people – not just believers, but atheists and agnostics too – to conduct an imaginary dialogue with Jesus after the fashion recommended by Fritz Perls for bringing out the personal meaning of the characters who appear in our dreams: the individual who conducts the dialogue plays both parts, moving from one chair to another as he does so and answering himself as he thinks Jesus would do. Of course, anyone who feels such a procedure would be blasphemous, or too intimate a matter to be undertaken in public, must be allowed the right to contract out, but for those who are prepared to do it the results can be very illuminating. One common conclusion is that 'Jesus' emerges as a sterner version of the voice of the individual's parents or other authority-figures of his childhood. For me personally (and I know I am by no means untypical in this) 'Jesus' began by making fairly reasonable comments on my life from the point of view of my conscience, but became more and more reproachful as the dialogue went on, eventually making it clear that 'he' was not interested in getting me to abide by any specific moral principles, but simply in making me feel I had no right to a moment's enjoyment so long as anyone anywhere in the world was worse off than me. In this, 'Jesus' was simply putting into words the message I had taken in as a child from my father, whose whole role in life has always been that of the long-suffering servant who never thinks of himself, always puts others first and is constantly reproaching everyone in any position of even minor wealth or power for oppressing the underdog. As I grew up my rational mind came to see my father in perspective, to recognise that he usually managed to find ways of doing what he really wanted to do and normally used his much-vaunted moral principles as an excuse for not venturing on things he was afraid of: I also came to see his more human side, and in particular the sense of humour which frequently broke through the mask of long-faced goodness and made him a nice man rather than a Pharisee. Inside, however, my childish mind had swallowed his moral attitude whole and exaggerated it even beyond the furthest points to which he took it, associating the constant demand for self-abnegation and service with a figure of Jesus gazing down at me in silent reproach from the cross whenever I allowed myself to enjoy anything. I do not think I ever consciously held such a view of Jesus – on the contrary, during adolescence I adopted H. G. Wells' view of Jesus as a kind of humanistic revolutionary, as an integral part of the process of breaking away from my family in general and my mother's fear-dominated religion in particular, and my conscious view of Jesus remained of this general character for most of my life. Underneath it, however, the old reproachful Jesus still lurked, and it is only quite recently that I have really begun to break free of the influence of this baleful inner 'top dog' (as Perls would call it) who did not make me one whit more generous or charitable a person in any real sense, but simply ensured that I felt constantly guilty at any sniff of rest or fun and hence that the lives of those around me were made miserable as well as my own.

My use of an alternative vision of Jesus to oppose the stifling 'Christian' demands made on me by my parents is also, I find, a fairly common phenomenon. In fact this is the other main conclusion to emerge when people have Jesus-dialogues in my groups – 'Jesus' often turns out to be a kind of *alternative* parent-figure whom they invoke against their real parents or against teachers and other flesh-and-blood authorities. One of the most interesting phenomena of our time is the way young Russian poets and writers, brought up under an atheist regime, find it useful to invoke Jesus in protest against the state's infringement of personal liberty, at the same time emphasising that Jesus shared the Communist Party's ideals of helping the poor against exploitation by the rich. In the west these same sayings of Jesus about the rich and the poor are a favourite weapon, even today, of the children of middle-class parents who want to reject what they see as the smugness of their home values. I have also heard Jesus's rebuke to Martha used by a girl to fend off her parents' demand that it was unfeminine to prefer an intellectual career to home life; his friendship with Mary Magdalene quoted to oppose narrow-mindedness about sex; and his remarks about hating father and mother invoked to rebut the parental complaint that children are ungrateful in not wanting to spend more time at home during adolescence. Under all these ally-Jesuses, however, I usually find, as I did in my own case, that another more punitive or reproachful figure is lurking from whom the ally-Jesus derives most of his energy. For example, one girl in a discussion group I conducted recently started out with Jesus as an ally telling her parents that they should not blame her for occasional outbursts of temper, because he said he came to bring not peace but a sword – but further dialogue revealed that underneath the ally lay another Jesus who constantly told her it was wrong to get too close to anyone, or to form affectional attachments, because duty to God must come first. She was able to wax indignant at her parents' demands for harmony and affection in the home only because she was at a deeper level reproaching herself every time she felt affection, and in the same way I was able to lecture my own parents about their conformist life-style only because I was at a deeper level driving myself constantly to work for some cause or other every time I felt like settling down to a little comfort. In other words, the name of Jesus turns out again and again to be a sign of the self-torture game, the game of turning the responsible statement 'I want' into the evasion of responsibility, 'We ought'. This, it seems to me, is what Blake was getting at when he said that Satan is often honoured not only under the name of God, but also under that of Jesus.

I cannot of course say dogmatically that people must necessarily always be falling into this trap when they have the feeling – with or without adherence to a formal Christian tradition – that Jesus in some way represents an ultimate personal authority for living, but I am sure it happens sufficiently often that the possibility must be honestly faced in any programme of religious education or discussion that is really serious. Only when the danger has been faced fairly and squarely is it possible to go on to discuss properly the obvious question of how the figure of Jesus came to acquire this sense of numinous authority throughout western civilisation – or to put the same question in another way, what is the significance of the fact that a major religious tradition has grown up around the story of a wandering teacher reared in the home of a Jewish carpenter in Nazareth around two thousand years ago? When traditionalist Christian apologists raise this question we should, I think, suspect that their motives may be ulterior. They are likely to be trying to argue, from the facts of Christian history, that Jesus must have been in some way so special to have started it all that he ought to be accepted as an authority, but the truth is that any argument along these lines is bogus for the reason I have already given, namely that there is no such thing as 'accepting Jesus as an authority': what it means is 'accepting a particular Christian tradition (Catholic, Evangelical or whatever) as an authority', and the only valid argument for doing this is a matter of judging the trustworthiness of *the tradition as a whole* for guiding life, the tradition's interpretation of Jesus being only a small part of this. If the question of the special significance of Christianity is raised from the experimental point of view, on the other hand, it is not a matter of trying to *prove* anything, or to put anything over, or to persuade anyone to accept anything. It is simply a common-sense matter of asking whether there is anything *particular* to be learned from the religious tradition that has shaped the destiny of western civilisation over the past two thousand years, or whether it was simply an historical accident that the story of the wandering Jewish teacher from Nazareth became the focus of the major religion in the west, comparable to the figure of Buddha in the major eastern religion and to other figures who are now of lesser importance on a world scale such as Krishna, Moses and Mohammed.

In discussing this, it is important to be clear about what kind of answer would be meaningful. It cannot have much to do with either the life or the teaching of Jesus as we have them recorded, since neither are very special – the teachings find echoes in all the major religions and are derived directly from Judaism, while there are plenty of other stories of martyrs who worked miracles, including some who were even supposed to have miraculous births and to rise from the dead. The influence of the recorded story of Jesus on our civilisation is the problem, not the answer: why was it that this particular story rather than another gained such a hold? The answer must have something to do with the religious experience of the early Christian community, which they expressed by saying that the wandering teacher from Nazareth had been a decisive intervention of divine power in human history, inaugurating a new age wherein a new kind of salvation had become possible. I do not think it is possible for us to know anything now about the historical basis for their assertion, since there is little doubt that the story of Jesus has been enormously elaborated with quotations and allusions to the Hebrew scriptures and possibly other religious writings: all we know is that these are the things the early Christians chose to say, in order to express their own religious convictions – convictions which proved so forceful in the Roman Empire at the time that they eventually became the basis for a new organised religion of major proportions. The significant question, therefore, is *whether those convictions represent an experience which could still be of special value today in people's religious quest,* in their efforts to realise their higher potentialities. It seems to me that it would be foolish for anyone brought up in western civilisation to ignore this question, however gloomy the record of organised Christianity may have been, and however many claims other religious traditions may have to our attention. There is no excuse for parochialism of any sort in a world that has been unified by modern communications, and which has such urgent need as ours has to find ways of improving the human quality of life, but it would be the height of folly to ignore the possibility that there is a treasure hidden under the mud in our own back garden – a treasure to whose existence the very blackness of the mud may bear paradoxical witness.

A key feature of the early Christians' religious message was that Jesus had fulfilled the ancient Hebrew hope of the Messiah, or divinely-inspired leader who would in some way save the whole world. It was in fact only because the early Christians did believe this, that the Hebrew scriptures came to be known throughout the civilised world instead of being the esoteric possession of the dispersed Jewish community and their few proselytes. An essential part of understanding what special significance, if any, there might be in Christianity, would therefore seem to be an appreciation in depth of the Jewish Messianic hope, with special reference to the way Hebraic ideas were understood in the religious communities of the Roman Empire in which Christianity first spread. Now there are many different ideas about this amongst Christian, Jewish and humanist scholars, but the one thing they all seem to have in common is that the Messiah was expected to inaugurate a new historical epoch in which the age-old alienation of man from God would be in some way overcome. The early Christians seem to have been convinced that this had actually happened, but in setting down their conviction they chose to record a story in which the Messiah himself was supposed to have described the principle of the new age as something like leaven, an influence working away in society in a way which would not be at all obvious until it suddenly became apparent, to everyone's surprise, that the whole life of society was somehow different. They also chose to record him as saying that no one could predict how long this process would take, and that in the interim many of the people who claimed most loudly to be his followers (saying 'Lord, Lord') would actually be the strongest opponents of the new spirit and of the leavening process.

My own personal evaluation of the significance of this stems from the views I have already outlined of the Hebrew notion of God and the diagnosis of human alienation contained in the Adam and Eve story. Anyone who has a different view of the significance of the Hebrew religious tradition will have a correspondingly different view of what the original Christian message was about, and will assess its personal value for him accordingly. As I see it, the idea of a new era in which the age-long alienation of man from God has been overcome must mean the end of mankind's (ultimately self-chosen) bondage to the traditional outlook, the outlook whereby the power of creativity, of self-transcendence, in human beings is evaded by assuming a Grand Design already in the world to which people are expected to conform – in other words, the end of idolatrous religion. It means an era in which people begin to accept the challenge of overcoming their subordination to biological nature, and with this the responsibility for organising social life on the basis of respect for personal creative initiative in every human being. And this could come about only by some kind of a breakthrough in bringing a dynamic of forgiveness into life at the personal level – which seems to me to be exactly what the early Christians were convinced had happened, although I do not think they themselves claimed to understand much about how it had happened, and we at this late date have little hope of finding out.

The most likely hypothesis, in my view, is that it had something to do with a real wandering teacher called Jesus (or Joshua) from Nazareth who in some way focused the Hebrew diagnosis of the human situation as no one had done before and brought the need for a dynamic of forgiveness into full consciousness, although exactly how he managed to pass it on to others, and what if anything it had to do with his early death, I am at a loss to say. It would not strike me as utterly absurd, however, to argue that the new dynamic could have come through something like a sacred mushroom, whose action the early Christians chose to personify in order to link it with the Hebrew idea of the Messiah: Dr Allegro's assumption that this would discredit Christianity if it were true seems to me to rest on a failure to appreciate the dramatic mind-opening effects which some drugs can have. In my own experience Michael Murphy of Esalen was right in claiming that they have changed many people's lives for the better, opening their eyes to the folly of many of this world's vanities: they might well, it seems to me, cause people to decide to have done with the self-torture game. My main reservation about Allegro's view comes from the fact that sacred mushrooms have been widely known all over the world for centuries but have never produced quite the dramatic effects which the early Christians seem to have experienced, bringing belief in an entirely new era whose spirit was symbolised by the idea of a literal resurrection from death. It seems to me that the explosion of early

Christianity – an explosion which often took grotesque forms and frequently became tied up with things that were a long way from the teachings attributed to Jesus – was such as to imply a breakthrough so remarkable that fanatically monotheistic Jews were driven to use language suggesting that the breakthrough-event (whatever it was) was more than just the fulfilment of the Messianic hope, was something like a new act of creation, a new manifestation (or incarnation) of the divine creative power in human life. But as I have said, I do not think we can say what it was, and it is only speculation on my part to say that it seems most likely to have been some unprecedented display of the dynamic of forgiveness on the part of a real wandering teacher from Nazareth: certainly no one is justified, in my view, in trying to construct anything like a doctrine of a divine act of atonement-through-supreme-self-sacrifice on the basis of the evidence we have. Such a doctrine must derive from subsequent Christian tradition, and while it is anyone's privilege to accept such a tradition, I must declare my own view that none of the Christian traditions I have come across begin to convince me that I ought to submit myself to their authority: in particular, most doctrines of atonement-through-sacrifice strike me as exercises in moral sadism.

What I think we *can* say is that there seems to have been *some* very remarkable religious experience at the back of the early Christian movement, and that it was undoubtedly in some way connected with a dynamic of forgiveness in personal life, since their official accounts in the Gospels of the Messiah's teaching give a great deal of emphasis to forgiveness – negatively in his attacks on Pharisaism and his various injunctions against judging, positively in the 'Lord's Prayer' and several parables – while their theological statements about the Messiah again and again associate him with the ancient Hebrew idea of the paschal lamb or scapegoat through which the ritual forgiveness of sins was sought. It may therefore be useful to study some of the early Christian writings, and notably those of the New Testament itself, for practical hints on ways in which the dynamic of forgiveness might work out, but in this I would not claim any necessary virtue for them as against other great religious writings. The really distinctive characteristic of Christianity, it seems to me, was the early Church's conviction that a new age *had begun*, although this has to be taken, as I have said, in the context of the idea of a leavening process whose precise mode and duration cannot be predicted, together with the notion that the people who are loudest in proclaiming their allegiance to the new dispensation would often turn out to be totally opposed to it. To me, this seems like a conviction that the new breakthrough had set in motion a release of creativity in society which would act as a chain-reaction, building up to produce changes which would increase man's transcendence over biological nature, humanise organisations and undermine idolatrous religion *in spite of the fact that the conservative forces of the world would do their best to take the new movement over and would to all appearances succeed in turning it into a new form of idolatrous religion.* And this in turn seems to me to link up in an uncanny fashion with Marx's notion that Christianity was in a literal sense the religion to end all organised religions; the religion which carried to the ends of the earth a message that sooner or later led many of those who heard it to turn against the whole traditional principle of organising life on a supposed divine plan, and to assert every man's right to make his own creative experiment in living.

I am not saying the early Christians were crypto-Marxists, nor that Marx was a crypto-Christian. I *do* think Marx may have had a more positive interest in the supernatural concerns of religion than is recog- nised by most of his interpreters; his wish to get rid of religion as the opium of the people is normally assumed to imply a totally naturalistic view of life, but there are numerous hints in his writings that he believed the creative faculty in man might turn out to have spiritual horizons undreamt of in most contemporary scientific philosophy once the alienation of economic exploitation had been overcome. For me, however, this is not good enough. However important the need for a more just social organisation may be in order to release man's creative energies, I do not think people who feel they are not contained between hat and boots can or should be content to devote themselves to social progress or revolution simply in the hope that their children's children will begin to explore new spiritual horizons – and on the practical level there is no doubt that Marx's followers have used his strictures against traditional religion to create a new materialistic dogmatism which is often as much a tyranny as the old religious dogmatisms ever were. To do real justice to man's humanity it seems to me essential, as I have affirmed repeatedly throughout this book, to give first priority to the inner dynamics of personal life, including its longings for transcendence, and to make social changes subservient at every point to this priority – and that was undoubtedly the view of the early Christians. Their first concern, as with all vital religious originators, was with the transcendent in the inner life, and it seems to me Jung is right in saying that when the image of Jesus came to acquire mystical value for them, it was fulfilling much the same psychological role as the image of Buddhahood or the Atman or the Diamond Body in eastern mystical traditions. The unusual factor in the early Christians' religion was that they took over and gave a new twist to the Jewish religious view that the individual's realisation of the transcendent is directly linked to the spiritual destiny of the race as a whole, as expressed in the idea of the creation of an earthly paradise in the future. Jesus was proclaimed as Messiah, with a quasi-political significance, *as well as* Saviour with mystical significance, and while he was reported as saying firmly that his kingdom did not derive purely from the social organisation of this world, he was also recorded as announcing the arrival of a new age in which the life of mankind on earth would begin to be leavened in ways whose spiritual significance might well not be seen until after the event.

It is in this sense that I see a real link between what I believe to have been the special religious experience of the early Christians, and Marx's view of the special role of Christianity in the history of mankind. The role of organised Christianity seems to me to have been an example of what Marx called the dialectical principle of social development (the principle whereby, to quote one of Marx's own illustrations, capitalists in the nineteenth century taught the proletariat to read so as to enable them to follow instructions for working machinery and doing accounts, and thereby made it possible for the first time for the workers to begin to realise just how they were being exploited).

For most of its history the Christian Church has behaved exactly like any other organised religion. It provided people with a pattern of social life based on obedience to rules (which were supposed to embody the Church's revelation of the divine plan underlying the universe) and it resolutely put down anyone who seemed to threaten the system either with ideas from outside (hence the banning of pagan writings for many centuries and such acts of vandalism as the destruction of the library at Alexandria) or with questioning from within (hence the unspeakable tortures inflicted on heretics). Inside this general structure of Christendom, the cultivation of the inner life was encouraged amongst special religious orders, whose disciplines seem to me, on any honest assessment, to have been at their best very much the same as the much older spiritual disciplines developed in the monasteries of the eastern religions for bringing about enlightenment, at their worst rigid rules for making the minds of devotees conform to the Church's supposedly revealed truth. In society as a whole, the Church's rules of conduct were perhaps more civilised – in the sense of paying at least token regard to considerations of justice, mercy and individual rights – than those of some of the world's more savage religions, but they were not in my own view much superior, if at all, to those of the other great world religion, Buddhism, or to those of the other religions deriving from the same stock as Christianity, namely Judaism and Islam; and in practice Christendom has been as prone as any other faith to blessing war, to encouraging exploitation and to urging the rigid subordination of sex to breeding.

Yet because all this was being done in the name of the 'Good news' of the early Christians (recorded in scriptures which had to be learned by all clergy and missionaries and could not be entirely kept from the general population in spite of normally being written in Latin), the Christian Church seems to have been instrumental in spreading the very thing which as an organisation it was most concerned to prevent – individual confidence, belief that mankind had entered a new age in which every individual man was expected to see himself as the vehicle of the divine creative power, in which rules were supposed to be made for men not men for rules, and in which the idolatrous worship of priesthood and temple should be overthrown. So the life of Christendom has been continually beset by upheavals of questioning and experiment. In the early centuries these may not have been noticeably different from the occasional outbreaks of prophetic individuals and groups that occur in all organised religious traditions. They began to assume quite unprecedented proportions in the later Middle Ages, however, leading first to the Reformation, then to the Renaissance, then to the scientific and industrial revolutions and the birth of democracy, and finally to the beginning of the first age the world has ever known in which the confidence necessary for the experimental-humanist outlook has spread to ordinary people. Because these developments were strenuously and often viciously opposed by the religious authorities crying 'Lord, Lord', many humanists in the eighteenth and nineteenth centuries were driven to deny Christianity altogether, and indeed often to repudiate all transcendental concerns; but I believe we totally misunderstand the forces at work in our civilisation if we allow this to obscure the fact that modern experimental-humanist culture is actually a direct, albeit dialectical, fulfilment of the development of Christendom from its beginnings in the early Christians' sense that a new era had begun in mankind's relations with the transcendent.

I would combine Marx's view of Christianity (as the religion to end all religions) with Freud's view of religion (or, I would say, the traditional outlook) as the universal neurosis of humanity, and say that I see Christianity as having been the means by which the human race has at last begun to escape from its age-old cop-out, although this has taken place in spite of rather than because of Christianity as an organised faith. I accordingly see the natural consummation of western civilisation in our own time not in the mass technology of Marxism or materialistic capitalism; not even in the triumphs of natural science or the insights of psychoanalysis (though neither of these should be underrated); but rather in the experimental spirit of the humanist west reaching out, through many of our young people and through the human potential movement, to the ancient religions of the east for clues to that most vital of all adventures, the exploration of inner space. Sociologists sometimes describe ours as the 'post-Christian' era. I accept this term in the sense that I see our world as one in which the new outbreak of religious energy which began with the early Christians has brought us to a stage where we can and should rise above the principle of belief or faith, including so-called Christian belief or faith. As I have affirmed at several points in this book, I am far from being naïvely optimistic about the future, but I am convinced that all the really important dangers now facing mankind spring from the surviving remnants of the traditional outlook which requires belief or faith (remembering here that materialism is a form of traditionalist belief), and that our hope lies in being more confident to experiment, not in any going back on the spirit of science or humanism. But I am also convinced that genuine experimental spirit both implies and moves towards transcendence, and involves a view of the universe which, because it is of its nature open-ended, cannot stop short of the concerns which have traditionally been called religious, concerns with the possibility of infinite creativity and the triumph of life and love over death. In pursuing these concerns we are likely to find experimental inspirations from all the world's great religious traditions, including Christianity. As I do this myself, the most important thing I find there is the conviction that the key factor in overcoming alienation from the transcendent, the essential foundation for maintaining the confidence for experimental adventure, is the dynamic of forgiveness or permissiveness which overcomes man's constant tendency to turn human transcendence against itself by the original sin of sitting in the seat of the scornful.

9: Looking forwards

It would be foolish to try to predict what form religion will take in the societies of the future, for even the most traditional religious organisations are becoming more and more convinced of the need for experimentation with new forms. The one thing that seems certain is that questioning about religion amongst the young will increase everywhere, probably even in societies that have officially abandoned religion, and that the general atmosphere of the modern world makes children dissatisfied (even if they are not always able to articulate the fact) with answers that are either glib or less than honest. It is therefore encumbent upon anyone who has any kind of care of the young, whether as a parent, as a teacher, or in less formal situations such as nurseries, clubs or churches, to put himself in a position where he can meet questioning seriously and honestly – which means being prepared, on a great many occasions, to say simply 'I honestly don't know – what do you think?' and then engage in whatever kind of conversation is appropriate to the age, interest and situation of the children concerned.

For the real challenge of children at any time, but most of all in a questioning era, is to make their adult guardians look to themselves and their own beliefs, feelings, experiences and puzzles. If we fail to do that, it does not make much difference what we *tell* the children – what they will *hear*, and what they may well learn, is evasion, dishonesty and sloppiness both of mind and feeling. Putting up any kind of false front to children is at best the short way to losing their respect, at worst a contamination of their souls – and this includes the unadmitted false front that consists in protesting too much in order to conceal doubts from yourself. If religion is a serious matter for the adult, even a tiny child will catch his feeling, and there is no need for him to think he has to back it up by a pretence of knowing the answers to all questions. If

o

the adult finds religious issues largely meaningless, this feeling too will come over no matter what he says, and it is sheerly pernicious to try to pretend otherwise 'for the sake of the child's moral education' or anything of that sort. But either way, we must face the fact that the children of whom we are guardians will meet other adults besides ourselves with different feelings, and even more important, will meet children from other homes where different feelings prevail, to say nothing of being exposed to other views of life on television. It is an integral part of our duty to the children in our charge to prepare them for this, or at very least to be prepared to meet their questions and confusions of feeling after the event, which means that no adult who has any kind of concern for children's religion can justify neglecting the effort to understand the beliefs and feelings of other people in our society as well as to be both honest and clear about his own.

The main objective of this book has been to provide a framework within which this can be done, but it is only a framework. I have tried to put the whole contemporary scene into what I hope is an intelligible and sensible perspective, but I cannot possibly claim to have done full justice to any views (and still less to any feelings) other than my own. I have given a few illustrations, in my outline course of religious discussion, of ways in which different views can be given the chance really to speak for themselves in a group. There is no substitute, however, for direct encounter with different points of view, at best in actual face-to-face meeting with people who hold them, at second best in their writings. It is just not good enough to read interpretations written by people who have never experienced the thing they are interpreting (although it may sometimes be a salutary exercise to read how alien interpreters see your own belief, whatever it is!). Far too many Christians in my experience are guilty of dismissing Buddhism and other eastern religions on the strength of some assessment of them they have read in a work of Christian apologetics, although there are plenty of good books written by Buddhists, and nowadays there are also many young people in most towns in western countries with at least a smattering of practical experience of eastern meditation, who would be only too willing to talk about it to any interested enquirer. Any parent or teacher who takes his responsibilities in the religious education of children seriously can seek out personal encounter with at least some people of markedly different outlook and experience from himself, and such encounter should if at all possible go beyond conversation to some attempt at shared experience: a Christian and an atheist should at least know what it is like to go to a Jewish synagogue, for example, and get something of the feel of what Jewish family ceremonial means to those who practise it; while no one should write off the more modern sects devoted to mystical concerns – theosophy, anthroposophy, Subud and so on – without attending some meetings for first-hand acquaintance with the people involved and what they are really up to.

In fact I would urge drawing the children themselves into this sort of practical encounter with different kinds of religious life where possible, so that they grow up vividly and personally aware of the diversity of human concern in this area of life. For small children, of course, any religious activity, *including the official one they are brought up in*, is taken in only at the pantomime level, and it is important for both parents and teachers (including official religious teachers) to be aware of this. Up to the age of about eleven or twelve, a visit to a church or synagogue, or to a Sunday School, or to school prayers, is like a visit to any other show, and it is quite useless to expect children to take it with any more solemnity, either in behaviour or in thinking about the meaning of what they hear and see. To say this is in no sense to put religious ceremonies down – on the contrary, there are few things that make more impact on a child than a show – but it is absurd to expect children under about eleven or twelve to be anything other than resentful if attendance at religious occasions is thrust on them as any kind of duty. So if there are to be regular compulsory religious classes or religious assemblies in a school, or if there are to be regular children's classes or services at churches for the children of parents who are themselves regular churchgoers, those who organise these activities must approach their task in a conscious spirit of showmanship, giving at least as much attention to holding the children's interest and getting them to participate creatively as with any other lesson or the organisation of a school play.

Teaching for this age-group should be almost wholly a matter of telling stories about people, with conscious recognition that the children will take every character they hear about, God included, in the same spirit as they take the characters of fairy-tales, adventure stories or science fiction. God will be understood as a kind of super-genie or super-power and there is no use expecting otherwise, so it will be a positive advantage, in finding good stories to capture the children's interest, to draw on all the world's religious traditions rather than just one and to treat them all alike *as* stories. If the children themselves raise questions about historical accuracy ('Did it really happen?') or theological reason ('*Why* did God do that?'), the teacher must be prepared to return an honest statement of his own views, which will of necessity almost always be of the form 'I don't really know, but I *think* . . . and some other people think . . . What do you think?' But unless the children themselves do raise these questions there is little point in the adult making an issue of them, for in this age-group the distinction between fiction and history has not yet been clearly formed in the mind except in matters affecting the child himself directly.

One practice which should be strenuously avoided in teaching young children about religion is that of using stories about the child Jesus (or for that matter the child Buddha) as a means of inculcating 'good behaviour' – for example, by telling fictional tales in which the young Jesus is said to have been diligent at his schoolwork or kind to his mother. This is the most blatant kind of projection, in which the adult puts up Jesus (or Buddha, or whoever) as the exemplar of the values he himself happens to approve of, in order to avoid taking responsibility for putting them over on the child himself. Such tales have absolutely no warrant from what we actually know of the lives of the great religious leaders, and in fact Blake drew precisely the opposite conclusion about Jesus from the evidence of the Bible:

> Was Jesus humble, and did he
> Give any proofs of humility?
> Boast of high things with humble tone
> And give with charity a stone?
> When but a child he ran away
> And left his parents in dismay;
> When they had wandered all day long
> These were the words upon his tongue:
> 'No earthly parents I confess,
> I am doing my Father's business.'
> . . .
>
>   . . .
>
> He left his father's trade to roam
> A wandering vagrant without home,
> And thus he others' labours stole
> That he might live above control.

Any parent who puts up the Little Lord Jesus as an example of good behaviour is likely – and thoroughly deserves – to have this Dropout Jesus quoted back at him when the child grows a little older. Meanwhile, however, in the years before the child's critical faculty has developed this far, the teaching may have done him real psychological harm by holding up babyhood as a kind of ideal when his real need is for the kind of vision which will inspire growth, development and independence. There is now wide agreement about the psychological evil of this kind of teaching even amongst psychologists who profess traditional kinds of faith, but popular practice in religious homes and Sunday schools does not seem to have caught up with it yet.

As far as the practical side of religion is concerned, I think parents should aim to take their young children with them on occasional exploratory trips to as many different kinds of religious observance as they can find; giving the whole business something of the excitement of visits to pantomime or cinema, although usually it will be sensible not to expect them to stay very long at any kind of service that lacks action capable of holding their attention. Regular attendance at any ceremony which is purely repetitious will merely make most children associate religion with boredom, so if there are to be regular 'school prayers' or Sunday School services they must of necessity be highly experimental with plenty of variety – and I believe it would be a sensible policy in this area also to introduce quite deliberately a whole range of different religious approaches. For example, a Buddhist might be invited to conduct a short meditation exercise at school assembly or Sunday School one day, a Muslim to conduct a brief Islamic ceremony on another, and so on, not forgetting the possibility of inviting an encounter group leader to come in one day and conduct a short session of purely secular sensitivity training, teaching the children how much we can all learn about ourselves and each other by looking and touching without words. On another day a psychotherapist might conduct a short session on dreams along the lines I shall be discussing in more detail shortly for use with older children and on yet another a humanist might conduct a short session of poetry and music.

In other words, I believe young children – that is to say, children up to the age of about eleven or twelve, for whom the faculty of general thinking has not yet developed – should be introduced to religion as a many-faceted aspect of human life, by being allowed to share, at their own level of experience, in their parents' and teachers' exploration of the phenomenon. If parents with definite religious convictions wish to go beyond this, to the extent of trying to pass something of the conviction on, there is one and only one way to do it, and that is by allowing the children to *share the experience* of the way religion affects their family's life. To teach the child to say special childish prayers will merely bring religion into discredit, when the child grows a little older and finds that it has been conned into an activity which from the adults' point of view is meaningless. The parent who believes in prayer must make a real effort to discover honestly what prayer actually does for *him*, and then try to put the child into the way of having the kind of same experience: if he cannot do that, it is better not to teach the child anything about prayer at all. The same applies to teachers in special religious schools, in Sunday Schools and in churches: it is quite wrong for them to ask any child to say prayers in a way that they themselves do not find personally meaningful. In ordinary schools I do not think teachers have any business asking children to say prayers at all, except insofar as they are giving them the experience of what it is like to take part in some standard form of religious service which is a feature of the adult world-scene, in which case the saying of prayers will be accepted naturally by the children as part of the total activity, just as if they were taking part in a play.

Prayers, hymns and readings from scripture are notorious sources of confusion in young children's minds because of their special language. I am sure I was nearly nine before I discovered that the hymn 'Onward, Christian soldiers' did not contain an obscure reference to doctors in a shower of tea ('One in hope and doctrine, one in charity'), and Ann Faraday, in her book *Dreampower*, tells how her daughter had learned the carol 'While shepherds watched their flocks by night, Horsey dead on the ground'. For this reason, parents and teachers should not merely allow, but positively encourage, the asking of questions after a young child has had any contact with a religious occasion, and the important principle in dealing with such questions is always to start by getting a real feeling for the child's own world-view and vocabulary, since unless his puzzles are discussed in these terms he will receive a dusty answer however hard the adult is trying. Thus if the child asks, 'Where is God?', it is absolutely useless saying 'God is all around us, rather like the air', or anything of that sort, for the child simply has not the capacity to think philosophically, and in his experience air just cannot do the kinds of thing he hears people saying God does, like loving and forgiving. The approach should be to begin by finding out what the child has recently heard about God to trigger off the question, and then to discover in what terms the child himself is capable of thinking about the issue: after that, the adult must try to convey, *in that vocabulary*, the essential meaning of the statement about God that originally puzzled the child.

A traditionalist Christian parent, for example, must face the possibility that the essential point of any statement he makes about God will be to convey the sense that the whole universe is a vast system running according to a divine plan, which we all have to trust irrespective of whether our experience seems to bear it out or not, in which case his objective must be to convey *this* to the child in whatever terms seem most appropriate to the child's own current world-view – a super-genie with magic telescopes, or a super-space-being with a cosmic computer, or whatever. A humanist parent, on the other hand, confronted with the question 'Where is God?' after his child has heard a clergyman praying for God to bring peace or heal the sick, will have to try to convey – again in terms of the child's own world-view – what he thinks the clergyman and other religious people believe about God's action in the world, and will then have to say something like, 'But I don't really believe there is any super-being who does that, because it doesn't seem to make any difference to what happens, whether people pray or not.' My own personal answer would have to be on humanist rather than traditionalist lines here, though I might add that while I do not believe in any super-being controlling nature, it does sometimes seem to me almost as if there were a super-being somewhere feeding good ideas into our minds to help *us* cope with problems (rather like the idea implied by the film *2001: a Space Odyssey*). In other words, I would use the science-fiction or fairy-tale language of the child to try to convey my own fundamental conviction that the creative faculty in us is capable of proving greater than the forces of nature even though we seem like very small creatures in face of the rest of the universe. I might also add that although I do not agree with the terms in which the clergyman prays for things, it does sometimes happen that if people stop striving to fight a headache, say, and just relax a little, there seem to be forces in us which will make things better, so that sometimes it might be useful to pray in the sense of trying to open the mind and quieten our inner panic.

There are no stock answers to this or any other question, because there are no stock children. A young child's questions are almost always highly personal, and the answers should always take the form of some kind of personal encounter, however brief, between that particular adult, whether parent or teacher, and that particular child. In fact the answer always *does* involve a personal encounter, whether we know it or not, for children catch feelings very quickly, and if the verbal answer to a question is either a platitude or a long involved piece of theology, the message the child will receive is indifference to its existence as a person, which is the reality of the encounter. The adult who wants to take his responsibilities seriously in answering young children's questions about religion must cultivate something of the capacity which psychotherapists call 'listening with the third ear', the art of tuning in emotionally to the child's actual meaning. Very often, for instance, a child's questions about God reflect not metaphysical curiosity but feelings about his relationship with his parents – or he may ask 'Why were the Roman soldiers so cruel to Jesus?' when what is really at the back of his head is a worry about the school authorities punishing him if he speaks his mind. On other occasions, questions are ways of probing the nature of the relationship between the child and the adult he is actually talking to: 'Does God punish naughty children?' may mean 'How much independence are you going to allow me?' The only really satisfactory answer to a young child's question is one which speaks both to his mental world-view *and to his real emotional concern* – and in trying to give such an answer, the adult must take into account that he is, at any rate for this particular moment of encounter, a figure of personal significance in the child's life, an emotional reality evoking either assent or rebellion as the child builds up his attitude to the world. The adult must accordingly take proper responsibility for the statements he makes, saying 'I think', 'I believe' and 'I feel' instead of hiding behind general assertions which really imply that no one has any right to any other opinion.

Encounter should still be the rule with older children, but as they get to ages where they begin to become capable of thinking in general terms, and have the beginnings of real settled identity, the emphasis should go over to *discussion* of religious questions, within the kind of framework I have outlined in the previous chapters. In the age-range from eleven to fourteen or fifteen the minds even of most intelligent children are of course unsophisticated, but it is fatal at this stage of life to underrate their capacities by over-simplifying or talking down on religious matters; and in fact the discussion of these matters is one of the most powerful ways of developing the capacity for general thought. The religious studies class which is given over to learning the journeys of St Paul is therefore a great wasted opportunity from the point of view of general education, as well as from the point of view of giving a respectable understanding of religion. Religious discussion may also be the spearhead for introducing the principle of open personal encounter into both schools and homes where for various reasons other opportunities for it may be rare, and this too would be valuable achievement in its own right.

At this stage parents and teachers acquire the additional responsibility to disabuse the children in their care of common misapprehensions which arise from the tendency of writers, broadcasters and preachers to go in for special pleading and to argue from ignorance both of facts and logic. One of my main aims throughout this book has been to expose some of the fallacies and *non sequiturs* which commonly bedevil religious discussions, the most important of which are:

1. The fallacy of thinking you understand a point of view different from your own when you have no direct experience of what it actually means in practice to people who hold it. (In particular, the fallacy of dismissing some religion, sect, or movement on the basis of what some outside observer or theoretical critic has written about it. This leads to such absurd situations as Christians and Buddhists each claiming that the other's religion is life-denying in its beliefs about sex, the body and nature.)
2. The fallacy of making judgements about trends in life without

realistic consideration of alternatives, e.g. of thinking that the break-up of the monogamous family is necessarily a bad thing because some children from broken homes are unhappy, without asking just how happy comparable children have been in stable homes; or of saying that modern society stands condemned because of the increase in the number of people asking for mental treatment, without considering whether it may not be better that many people should get mental treatment of some sort. One special but very important version of this fallacy is the 'defensive argument' which takes for granted that any attack on the values by which I have hitherto lived my life must necessarily be rebutted, without stopping to ask how really happy I have been.

3. The fallacy of arguing from hearsay without verifying facts, e.g. of arguing that religion in the past was just a great conspiracy of the privileged classes to keep the common people in order (without checking the facts of history and anthropology about the extent to which the leaders of society in religious cultures were as much bound by their belief-systems as the people they ruled); or of thinking that freer sexual morality leads to less regard for the person of women without examining how women are actually regarded in different societies.

4. The fallacy of arguing from the particular to the general, whether it be in thinking that scientific observations can disprove the possibility of miracles, or in thinking that specific religious experiences can provide grounds for believing in general theories of the universe, or in thinking that statements in the Bible about what Jesus did or said can provide grounds for believing in the authority of a particular church or way of salvation.

5. The fallacy of believing that a philosophy or system of belief necessarily promotes the practical human or religious values it claims to promote, e.g. that because Christian theologians talk a great deal about love and spiritual experience, that Christian belief necessarily promotes love or spiritual experience in people's lives to a greater extent than, say, a humanistic outlook which talks much less about these things.

6. The specific fallacy of believing that a humanistic outlook promotes materialism or is necessarily opposed to religious concerns such as interest in the transcendent, in mystical experience, or in the prospect of life beyond death.

7. The specific fallacy of trying to support a line of behaviour you approve of by calling it 'natural', or to criticise something – homosexuality, technology or anything else – by calling it 'unnatural'.

8. Most important of all, the fallacy of believing that the exposure of fallacies in people's thinking or opinions automatically disposes of feelings or experiences they have hitherto associated with those thoughts or opinions. Feelings and experiences are facts which cannot be disposed of by argument, and no one has any right to put down another person's feelings or experiences as mere delusions just because logic shows that his beliefs or opinions are false.

There is one particular area in which popular discussion today is especially bedevilled by nearly all these Eight Fatal Fallacies, which requires special mention here because it is a vexed question of enormous importance in dealing with young people just now, and that is the whole subject of the psychedelic or 'mind-opening' drugs. No adult who sets out to discuss religious questions with young people without being thoroughly briefed on this subject can hope to be taken seriously today, and it is necessary to recognise that a great many of the opinions commonly aired about it in the press or by leading public figures are nonsense and are well known to be nonsense by the young. The sheer irresponsibility of many people in public life in their utterances about this subject is quite shameful. For example, it is shocking, as well as ludicrous, for senior people in public life to say solemnly that marijuana and L.S.D. cannot give genuine religious experiences when they have never tried them, or have tried them only in conditions which would totally preclude any mystical experience. Their reasoning usually seems to be that a mere chemical cannot give a vision of the transcendent, and on this basis they are prepared to set aside the testimony of hundreds of highly responsible scholars as well as thousands of the young, notwithstanding the fact that the world's greatest mystics could have had no experience of any kind if their brains had not been supplied with 'mere chemicals' like air, food or water (to say nothing of the probability that ascetic practices like starvation, or meditational techniques like special breathing, produce their mystical effects by releasing the same chemicals into the brain as are released by hallucinogenic drugs). The 'bad trips' reported by some doctors who have carried out occasional experiments in mental hospitals on themselves or on psychiatric patients are precisely what any sensible person would expect from taking a 'mind opening' drug in such grim surroundings. The only way a parent or teacher can find out the truth about the mystical effects of these drugs is by seeking out and talking to people who have experienced them, and this is really not difficult in most western cities today if the adult is someone young people trust enough to tell him the truth.

For the psychedelic drugs are now an established part of our young people's culture, despite the draconian laws most countries have against them. The only effect these laws have is to ensure the existence of a flourishing black market in which there is a real health hazard from contaminated drugs, and when our period comes to be judged at the bar of history the people who allowed blind prejudice to produce this effect will have as much to answer for as the so-called 'drug pushers'. The young people to whom I have talked in schools have nothing but sad contempt for an Establishment that is prepared to enforce laws based on a degree of ignorance and sloppy thinking which in any other field would lead to instant dismissal from any post of responsibility. The magistrates who deliver solemn lectures to young people caught smoking marijuana, about lives being wrecked by starting down the slippery slope to hard drug addiction, should know that after the young person has put on a suitable show of contrition for the sake of appearances, he or she goes back to smoking marijuana soon afterwards and meanwhile roars with laughter at the magistrate's sheer bumbling absurdity. The theory of 'escalation' from psychedelic to hard drugs is totally discredited by all the evidence, and is able to persist only because the present laws ensure that those in authority have no idea of the millions of people, many in highly responsible positions in society, who have been experimenting regularly with psychedelic drugs for nearly a decade now with no noticeable deterioration of their ability to do serious creative work and not the slightest tendency to escalation even to larger quantities of psychedelics, let alone hard drugs. Such people – young and not so young alike – are in my experience as concerned as anyone else about the recent increase in hard drug addiction in our society, and are often doing much more in practice to try to prevent it intelligently than those who support and administer laws against drug-supply, but they know very well that the increase would be several orders of magnitude greater than it is if there were anything at all in the escalation theory. This theory rests on the same kind of reasoning as that which was used by the apocryphal naturalist who claimed to have proved that grasshoppers' ears were in their legs, because normal grasshoppers jumped at the sound of a clap, whereas those who have had their legs pulled off do not. Whatever the causes of the present increase in hard drug addiction, the one certain thing is that the potential addict is in no sense an experimenter concerned with mind-opening: he is seeking escape from the pressure and pain of life, and will try anything that is available in the hope of finding it – but his move from psychedelic to hard drugs is made precisely because they are *not* drugs of escape, and the ordinary experimenter with psychedelic drugs knows this perfectly well, since he is using them for the opposite purpose, to increase rather than decrease his sensitivity to experience generally.

The idea that ordinary people can be corrupted into becoming drug addicts against their will, by being given small doses of substances that give pleasure until they are 'hooked', is a complete myth, which has become ingrained into the minds of people whose only contact with literature about drugs has been the thrillers of a generation ago, in which the drug-smuggler was the most villainous of villains because his trade was said to rely on the slow destruction of lives. There is really no excuse for the persistence of this myth amongst people in positions of responsibility – in which category I include journalists – in the modern world, where we now have plenty of evidence both from clinical research and, alas, from the tragic lives of the increased number of addicts, that the process of becoming addicted to heroin or cocaine is really quite hard and unpleasant work, which no one would ever undertake if not driven to it by finding life intolerably painful. The claim of those who support the present panic laws against drugs, to be acting in the interests of society's health, accordingly rings some-what hollow, for although their original fears were certainly excusable, it is hard to excuse the persistent failure of people in positions of responsibility to look at up-to-date evidence. It is quite impossible to excuse anyone adopting a high moral tone about young people taking drugs 'to escape from the realities of life', when the vast majority of adults regularly do just that, not only with aspirin, sleeping pills and tranquillisers but also with drugs of addiction which have been proven beyond doubt to cause illness and death on a vast scale – tobacco, alcohol and the motor car.

The fact is, as I have said, that the psychedelic drugs are in no sense drugs of escape, but the very opposite. My conversations with many dozens of young people who have experimented with psychedelic drugs, and not a few of their elders who have done so in spite of being in highly responsible positions in society, confirm what I myself experienced some years ago during the mescalin research work, namely that although these drugs can give great pleasure, often of a highly erotic kind, the experience of taking them is an intensely serious, educative business even when it does not have religious or mystical overtones (as it often does). The people who experiment with these drugs today are in my experience more rather than less concerned than most other people with love and justice and beauty, with the great issues of the world, with morality and mortality. What they are apt to be less concerned about are matters of etiquette, convention, status-seeking, power-seeking and wealth-seeking, but it is a sad commentary on our society that this change of values should be mistaken – especially by people who claim to be upholding 'Christian standards' – for lack of seriousness about life itself.

In fact the reason why I have chosen to go into this subject in such detail in a book on religious education is that my experience in discussions with young people over the past few years has borne in on me that experimenting with psychedelic drugs has probably been responsible for the most important revival of interest in religious matters that has taken place in western civilisation for several centuries. If I were head of a Communist state dedicated to the total abolition of religion I should certainly be in favour of trying to suppress such experimentation (though I doubt if I should succeed – the experimental spirit seems to have taken root far too firmly in western civilisation for that). In societies which are supposed to hold religious values it is extraordinary that more positive interest in the phenomenon has not been aroused, and the fact that the religious authorities tend simply to reinforce the disapproving attitude of the secular ones is taken by most young people I have talked to as yet another sign that our society's supposed concern for religious values is merely hypocritical. My own diagnosis is that the strong emotions aroused by the whole subject amongst many people in positions of authority in our society is a measure of our continuing attachment, even in a so-called scientific age, to the authoritarian/traditional outlook with its deep fear of new experience. The fact that the degree of alarm is roughly the same on both sides of the Iron Curtain confirms my view that dogmatic materialism and traditional religion are not opposites at all, but merely rivals, the true opposite of both being the experimental outlook. This outlook requires both confidence and courage – courage to take risks in the interests of the enhancement of life, and confidence that if mistakes occur, we can and will cope with them as part of the price of adventure – and this seems to me to be essentially the spirit in which young people today approach the psychedelic drugs. For example, they recognise that 'bad trips' can sometimes occur even under the best conditions, but they determine to use them as means of learning more about themselves, and the general verdict seems to be that anyone who takes such trips in this spirit, especially if surrounded by helpful friends, comes out the other side enriched. But although this undoubtedly needs both courage and confidence, it seems to me absurd to suggest that the alternative approach to life advocated by the believers in traditionalist authority is in any real sense safer. It is the rivalry of the traditionalist systems, not the young people experimenting with drugs, which at the present stage of history constitutes the greatest threat to the survival of the human race, and the next greatest threat comes from the traditionalist upholding of the principle of family life dedicated to breeding, on both sides of the Iron Curtain.

I am emphatically *not* advocating the wholesale uncontrolled release of psychedelic drugs for unlimited public consumption: it would be totally unrealistic to do so even if I believed it desirable, which I do not. What I want to urge most of all is much more sanity and real honesty in the discussion of the subject, and this is another way in which I believe those engaged in religious education could spearhead a movement that would be of immense value for education as a whole and indeed for society as a whole. If parents or teachers with strong feelings against psychedelic drugs were prepared, in the interests of being taken seriously by the young in discussing religion, first of all to look as objectively as they can at the real facts (as distinct from hearsay reports), and then to engage in open encounter about their feelings with the young people themselves, I believe we might all learn something to our advantage. A saner and more balanced approach to discussion of this subject on the part of the Establishment-minded members of society would bring about an immediate narrowing of the generation gap and would reveal that a great many young people who are unrepentantly involved in experimenting with psychedelic drugs would be only too delighted to go for alternative ways of 'turning on' if these could be found: what they are not prepared to do is to accept that their desire for more abundant life is itself immoral, or even an indulgence that ought to be put aside until their elders get round to approving it. Their challenge to us, in an open encounter, would be that we should either set them free to do their own experimenting, or show ourselves serious in undertaking alternative experiments in the enhancement of life: the unacceptable alternative is for us to try to tell them they ought to be satisfied with the quality of life they inherit from us. The idea that *they* are responsible for the generation gap by rebelling wantonly for rebellion's sake is nonsense. The most striking evidence I had of this was the universal envy with which a boy in one of my groups was greeted when he announced that his sixty-year-old mother had allowed him to 'turn her on' with L.S.D. (mainly because she was interested in Aldous Huxley) with the result that hitherto impassable emotional barriers between them had disappeared. The rest of the group – including those who had never ventured on any drug experiments at all and had no intention of doing so – felt sad and lonely that none of their parents, most of whom were much younger than sixty, would be prepared even to discuss such a step.

Given a saner and more honest atmosphere, it would become obvious that whatever measures need to be taken to control the psychedelic drugs intelligently – and measures certainly *are* needed – it is unintelligent to the point of wickedness to have laws which on the one hand brand young people as criminals for wanting to explore the

possibilities of higher, richer life, and on the other prevent the carrying
out of research on just how these substances produce their remarkable
effects. For they *are* remarkable, and anyone who does not acknowledge
this is showing such culpable ignorance that it is not unreasonable to
suspect intellectual dishonesty. The attempt is often made by more
sophisticated opponents of drug experimentation to argue that we
now know, after an initial burst of enthusiasm, that the claims once
made for the psychedelic experience were largely delusory, since it
has not yielded important effects in creative art. Can those who say this
really be unaware that most leading artists admit freely in private
conversation that they have obtained much of their inspiration from
these drugs? But much more important is the fact that, even if there
were no such tangible results, great numbers of people have found the
psychedelic experience a unique personal revelation of joy, beauty and
meaningfulness: a girl in one of my school discussions said that if she
were to die tomorrow, the one event worth having lived for would
have been her acid trip. Given this kind of claim, made by many
thousands of people, it seems to me self-evident that we would have a
research topic of the highest priority even if the health hazards
associated with these drugs were a thousand times greater than they
are. As it is, the possible health hazards – certainly vastly lower than
those associated with the use of glass or electricity in homes – are
trumpeted to the skies in a fashion which clearly indicates a highly
emotional defensive reaction, while any medical evidence which seems
to count in the opposite direction is ignored to the point of suppression
of information. A saner and more honest approach would recognise
that *whatever health hazards there may be*, the challenge is to discover
safer ways of opening up the creative wellsprings of inner space, as
these drugs quite evidently do for many people. Given intensive
research on this, we might well see the total disappearance of psychedelic drugs in ten years, in favour of non-chemical methods of 'turning
on'; but it is futile, as well as unforgivable, to tell a young person who
has glimpsed the bird of paradise that it was nothing more than a piece
of criminal folly because it was associated with a drug that might
possibly have hazardous consequences for some people in some
circumstances. Many young people to whom I have talked say they
would if necessary be prepared to go to prison rather than submit to
this kind of tyranny.

I myself *never* encourage young people to experiment with drugs, but
when I find that they have already done so I will not put their experience
down in any way. My 'line', which in fact I find growing numbers of
young people are already taking on their own account, is that we should
now try to find other ways of exploring the vistas of inner space which
have been opened up for great numbers of people over the past decade

by these drugs. Many young people are already, I find, turning in this connection to eastern disciplines of yoga and meditation. Because my own religious inspiration comes mainly from the Christian tradition I very much wish I could recommend them to go to Christian sources for disciplines of this kind, but to my regret I have been quite unable to find any, though I have found plenty of open-minded clergy whose general outlook would not be uncongenial to the experimentally-minded young. The Christian tradition undoubtedly has developed its own spiritual and mystical arts, which as far as I have been able to discover (from books like the works of St John of the Cross or St Ignatius Loyola) are remarkably similar, at their best, to those of the eastern religions, but the number of clergy I have found who know anything about them in practice can be counted on the fingers of one hand. A more hopeful source of ideas in this field comes from the rapidly-growing Human Potential Movement, which draws on disciplines of yoga and meditation in a general context of emotional education through open, honest encounter in groups, bringing in also such diverse techniques as special movement exercises and the study of dreams to help people achieve what is variously described as 'mini-*satori*' or 'turning on without drugs'. The number of teachers and clergy who as yet know anything about this movement in Britain is small, and it is still relatively new even in America, but it is growing fast everywhere in the west, and I believe this is likely to be a major factor in the practical side of professional religious education in the future.

For with older children, the experimental approach to the practical side of religion must go beyond exposing them to different kinds of religious activity in the pantomime spirit, to encouraging active, interested participation – which means that schools or clubs that have religious assemblies, and churches that aim to cater for the young, will have to go well beyond any standard forms of religious service into wholly new kinds of activity. Already many British schools are experimenting with new forms of assembly in which older children are asked to organise for themselves events wherein several of them 'do their own thing', such as giving comments on items of human importance in the news, performing their own music, reading their own poems or acting out dramatic sketches. This is fine, but I think we shall need to supplement such essentially exoteric activities with others designed specifically to enable young people to explore the inner life for themselves. One of the most promising ways I have come across for ordinary people to do this without special training is through the study of dreams along the lines indicated by Ann Faraday in her book *Dreampower*, which I have already mentioned.

Dreams were, after all, regarded as of great importance in most of the world's religious traditions in the past. Now Dr Faraday uses the findings of modern dream research to show that ordinary people can use their dreams to gain enormously valuable insights about the inner conflicts that drain our spiritual energies, without any need to delve into the elaborations of professional psychoanalysis. An especially valuable approach, she argues, is for people to bring dreams for discussion to a group of friends who meet regularly on the basis of open encounter. They can try together to see how various specific dreams reflect the dreamer's problems and conflicts, either by studying the dream as a symbolic picture, or by asking the dreamer to act out a dialogue between different characters in his dream along the lines proposed by Fritz Perls. It is fascinating to see how many of the examples she quotes from her own casebook bring out problems touching on religion in various ways – problems of people haunted by a punitive conscience, problems of the tension between the mind and the body, and many others – as well as basic moral problems of love, hate, revenge, loyalty and so on. I believe dream-discussion sessions along these lines would be a most valuable basis for school assemblies, and the techniques might be extended from dreams to the direct exploration of the emotional significance of religious beliefs themselves, by the deliberate acting out of fantasies about God, Jesus and so on along the lines I have already suggested. Such explorations are highly instructive, but not merely instructive: they actually promote growth and integrity in the inner life, and as inner energies are freed from the blocks of pretence, anxiety and self-deception, they seem often to turn to opening up new levels of creative consciousness, which I believe need the language of mysticism and the supernatural to do them justice.

I see no reason why even thoroughly traditional institutions should not begin to engage in exploratory activities of this kind, for as I have said, the need for experiment, and for ecumenical openness to insights from all quarters, is now being recognised everywhere. Many of the young people to whom I have talked connect this fact with what they believe to have been the dawn, about a decade ago, of a new astrological epoch, the Age of Aquarius, the age when individuated man was traditionally supposed, in occult lore, to begin to emerge from subservience to institutions and to seek his own creative path, the age when the divine spirit was supposed to be poured forth into the hearts of men in a new way. I reserve the right to a scientist's scepticism about astrological epochs, but I am sure that no institution will survive our century which does not really embrace the experimental spirit. On the other hand if the problem of what to tell the children about religion is approached in the open fashion I have tried to advocate, I believe we may find that we are indeed living in a new era which sees the fulfilment both of humanism and of religion alike.

Notes on further reading

This is a selective guide to books dealing with the main themes of the present work. I have compiled the list under theme-headings rather than relating books to my specific chapters, because some themes overlap several chapters. I have concentrated mainly on books that can be easily understood by non-specialists, but I have included some more specialised works where I think they are of particular importance. I have starred items which I regard as essential reading.

Books concerned with the emergence of a radically new public attitude to life over the past few centuries (associated with the rise of modern experimental science and technology) and with assessing whether this represents a decline or an advance in the sanity of human society.

*AYER, A. J. (ED.): *The Humanist Outlook* (Pemberton, 1968)
    A mixed bag of essays by leading British humanists, the main burden of which is to argue that the modern world's great need is for more science and humanism rather than for any corrective.
BALTHASAR, HANS VON: *Science, Religion and Christianity* (Burns Oates, 1964)
    A Jesuit argues that the modern non-metaphysical outlook represents the fulfilment rather than the destruction of Christianity.
BERGER, PETER L.: *A Rumour of Angels* (Allen Lane, 1969)
    A sociologist's attempt to show that human experience requires belief in a supernatural order.
BUTTERFIELD, HERBERT: *The Origins of Modern Science* (George Bell, 1949)
*CLARKE, ARTHUR C.: *Profiles of the Future* (Gollancz, 1962)
    A leading science fiction writer's survey of the likely trend of future

science fact, indicating that science is already going well beyond the purely mechanistic concepts and developments at present associated with the word 'technology'.

DAVY, CHARLES: *Towards a Third Culture* (Faber, 1961)
A plea for our society to transcend its scientific outlook with a new version of the traditional outlook. It is written from the point of view of the mystical philosophy of Rudolf Steiner and contains a chapter devoted to the criticism of my own writings. Contains references to other important works in the same area, notably *Saving the Appearances* and other works by Owen Barfield.

EVANS-PRITCHARD, E. E.: *Witchcraft, Oracles and Magic Among the Azande* (Clarendon Press, 1937)
A specialist work which conveys the self-fulfilling character of magical thinking by showing it in action in a primitive community.

FOSTER, MICHAEL: *Mystery and Philosophy* (SCM Press, 1957)
Mainly a theological work, this volume reprints a famous article arguing that the experimental outlook derives directly from the revolution brought about in European thought by the Judao/Christian – as opposed to the mystical/pagan – view of God and the world.

*FROMM, ERICH: *Psychoanalysis and Religion* (Bantam Books, 1967)
An admirable short introduction to the whole subject of how modern psychological insight makes some people conclude that mankind's traditional supernaturalist outlook is a kind of neurosis. Gives references to other literature on this subject, such as the works of Freud and Jung, and also to Fromm's own earlier works, all of which are valuable, especially *Man for Himself* and *The Art of Loving*.

*GABOR, DENNIS: *Inventing the Future* (Pelican, 1964)
Innovations (Oxford University Press, 1970)
A distinguished physicist discourses on the same theme as Clarke.

GASMAN, DANIEL: *The Scientific Origins of National Socialism* (MacDonald & Co., 1971)
Shows the mystical, pseudo-scientific character of Nazism.

HALMOS, PAUL: *The Personal Service Society* (Constable, 1970)
A sociologist argues that industrialisation and technology carry a trend towards greater altruism and humanity in society.

KOESTLER ARTHUR: *The Act of Creation* (Hutchinson, 1964)
A detailed survey of the psychology of creative activity, tracing connexions with growth-processes in biology so as to argue that the materialism of the modern scientific outlook is not true to the facts of biology.

*LEACH, EDMUND: *A Runaway World?* (BBC Publications, 1968)
An anthropologist argues that mankind's greatest danger at the present time is fear of the new powers he has acquired through science and failure to take the scientific/humanist outlook really seriously.

LONERGAN, BERNARD: *Insight* (Longmans Green, 1954)
A major work by a leading Roman Catholic theologian, arguing, with minute detail and exact logic, that a proper consideration of the facts of science and of human life would lead to a return to a traditional view of the world and, more specifically, to acceptance of revealed religion.

MUMFORD, LEWIS: *The Pentagon of Power* (Secker & Warburg, 1971)
This is (at the time of compiling this list) the latest of Mumford's books analysing the ills of modern mechanical civilisation, and gives reference to his earlier works, including *The Myth of the Machine* cited in my text (Chapter 5).

PARKER, DEREK: *The Question of Astrology* (Eyre & Spottiswoode 1970)

PURVER, MARGERY: *The Royal Society; Concept and Creation* (Routledge, 1967)
A specialist historical work, but easy to read, conveying vividly the special feeling of the scientific revolution. Best read in conjunction with a more general history of seventeenth-century thought such as Basil Willey's *The Seventeenth-Century Background*, or E. M. W. Tillyard's *The Elizabethan World Picture*.

RAINE, KATHLEEN: *Blake and Tradition* (Routledge, 1969)
A massive two-volume work arguing that great art is impossible without the traditional outlook. As an account of Blake it is a classic, but in my own view falls far short of the work of Northrop Frye cited on page 220.

*ROSZAK, THEODORE: *The Making of a Counter-Culture* (Faber, 1970)
An American historian argues that the common aim underlying all the radical dissenting youth movements of our time is rebellion against the scientific outlook and a desire for return to a mystical attitude to nature.

SMYTHIES, J. R. (ED.): *Science and ESP* (Routledge, 1967)

*SNOW, C. P.: *The Two Cultures: and a Second Look* (Cambridge University Press, 1969)

TART, CHARLES (ED.): *Altered States of Consciousness* (John Wiley, 1969)
A collection of papers showing that modern psychology is beginning to take mysticism and kindred modes of experience seriously on an experimental basis.

Notes on further reading

THOMAS, KEITH: *Religion and the Decline of Magic* (Weidenfeld & Nicolson, 1971)

A massively documented history of magical thought in England from the fourteenth to the seventeenth centuries. Easy to read and full of fascinating and often amusing information.

TYRRELL, G. N. M.: *The Personality of Man* (Penguin, 1946)

A concise statement of the case that there is such good evidence for extra-sensory perception and psychic phenomena that scientific materialism is now untenable.

More specialised works on the conflict betwen religion and science.

DE SANTILLANA, GIORGIO: *The Crime of Galileo* (Mercury Books, 1961)

Although a specialised work, it is valuable in showing the social forces involved in the conflict between Galileo and the Inquisition. It adds a new concept to social thought, namely that of the 'guilt society', the kind of social order, based on dogmatic faith, in which people's loyalty is secured by their overriding feeling of a continual need to work and make sacrifices to atone for some fundamental unworthiness.

*BRECHT, BERTHOLD: *The Life of Galileo* (Methuen, 1963)

A dramatic treatment of de Santillana's theme, but lacking his perception of the oppressive character of the pre-Galilean worldview.

*WHITE, A. D.: *A History of the Warfare of Science and Theology in Christendom* (Dover Books, 1960)

Although written in the early 1890s, this has never yet been superseded by any more up-to-date history of the science-religion controversies down the ages.

*BARBOUR, I. G.: *Issues in Science and Religion* (SCM Press, 1966)

This is the most comprehensive survey I have come across of modern discussions of the 'science and religion' issue, and its many references provide a good guide to a field in which the literature is vast. Of the many other volumes written on this subject in recent years I would select as the most representative:

MASCALL, E. L.: *Christian Theology and Natural Science* (Longmans Green, 1956)

A conservative theologian's attempt to reconcile Christianity with modern science;

BIRCH, L. C.: *Nature and God* (SCM Press, 1965)
A biologist's attempt to hold modern scientific ideas and religious faith together;

JONES, BERNARD E.: *Earnest Enquirers after Truth* (Allen & Unwin, 1971)
An anthology of selections from the Gifford Lectures delivered in Scottish Universities since 1890, many of which deal with the 'science and religion' theme; and

TOWERS, BERNARD: *Concerning Teilhard, and other writings on science and religion* (Collins, 1969)
An excellent introduction to the special approach to the problem by the French Jesuit scientist Pierre Teilhard de Chardin.

Books on modern theological attempts to come to terms with the scientific/humanist outlook (with special reference to my Chapter 7, 'Humanism and the Supernatural' and my personal views expressed in Chapter 8).

BARNES, KENNETH C.: *The Involved Man; action and reflection in the life of a teacher* (Allen & Unwin, 1969)

*BUBER, MARTIN: *I and Thou* (Clark, 1960)
A famous prose-poem presenting a humanistic, experiential view of the supernatural.

FLEW, A. G. N. and MACINTYRE, A. C. (EDS.) *New Essays in Philosophical Theology* (SCM Press, 1956)
An excellent introduction to modern philosophical analysis of what religious ideas mean and the fallacies involved in much religious discussion.

*FRYE, NORTHROP: *Fearful Symmetry* (Princeton University Press, 1967)
A study of William Blake, presenting him as the exemplar of a radical humanism which embodies the supernatural without having any truck with the traditional outlook.

*GUTKIND, ERICH: *The Absolute Collective* (C. W. Daniel, 1937)
A more philosophical exposition of Buber's theme in terms of Hebrew mystical traditions.

*HAPPOLD, F. C.: *Religious Faith and Twentieth Century Man* (Penguin, 1966)

*MACMURRAY, JOHN: *The Form of the Personal* (2 vols., Faber, 1957 and 1961)
The last and most important work by a Scottish philosopher who has developed the theme of empirical, humanistic approach to religion over many decades.

*ROBINSON, J. A. T.: *Honest to God* (SCM Press, 1963)
Exploration into God (SCM Press, 1967)

Besides being important in their own right, these give full documentation of the trend which has come to be known as 'The New Theology' or 'The New Reformation', including the works of pioneer writers like Paul Tillich, Rudolf Bultmann and Dietrich Bonhoffer and also more recent writers such as Harvey Cox, Werner Pelz, Paul van Buren, and William Miller, whose anthology *The New Christianity* traces the modern movement back to Blake.

SCHARF, BETTY: *The Sociological Study of Religion* (Hutchinson, 1970)
A good recent introduction to this subject.

TOWERS, BERNARD (ED.): *Evolution, Marxism and Christianity* (Garnstone Press, 1967)
One of a number of books in the 'Teilhard de Chardin Study Library' indicating progressive trends in the Roman Catholic Church.

MOULE, C. F. G. (ED.): *Faith, Fact and Fantasy* (Fontana, 1964)

*UNWIN, GEORGE (ED.): *What I Believe* (Allen & Unwin, 1966)

MARTIN, CHRISTOPHER (ED.): *Prismatics* (Hodder & Stoughton, 1966)

MOIR, GUTHRIE (ED.): *Dialogue with Doubt* (SCM Press, 1967)

*MITCHELL, JAMES (ED.): *The God I Want* (Constable, 1967)

*DIXON, BERNARD (ED.): *Journeys in Belief* (Allen & Unwin, 1968)
These collections of essays, articles, lectures, TV discussions, etc. are useful reading because of their wide cross-section of personal views of the religious problems of modern people (mainly British). The first four contain contributions by myself. My earlier religious views, the abandonment of which is described in Chapter 6 of the present volume, are described in essays in *They Became Anglicans*, Ed. Dewi Morgan (Mowbrays, 1959) and *Essays in Anglican self-Criticism*, Ed. David Paton (SCM Press, 1958)

Further books on mysticism and religious experience (with special reference to my Chapter 8).

*AARONSON, BERNARD, and OSMOND, HUMPHREY (EDS.)
Psychedelics (Hogarth Press, 1971)
An excellent introduction to the whole thorny subject, including balanced reviews of the health hazards, the social problems associated with drugs and the relationship between drug experience and religious experience.

*COLEMAN, JOHN E.: *The Quiet Mind* (Rider, 1971)
> A young American's quest for enlightenment and final achievement of it through Buddhist techniques of transcending pain.

*HAPPOLD, F. C.: *Mysticism* (Penguin, 1963)
> An excellent introduction to the world literature, both classical and modern.

*HUXLEY, ALDOUS: *The Perennial Philosophy* (Collins, 1958)

ISHERWOOD, CHRISTOPHER (ED.): *Vedanta for the Western World* (Unwin Books, 1948)

*JAMES, WILLIAM: *The Varieties of Religious Experience* (Fontana, 1969)

*JUNG, C. G.: *Psychology and Religion, East and West* (Routledge, 1959)

* *Memories, Dreams, Reflections* (Routledge and Collins, 1963)
> The latter, a 'spiritual autobiography', is one of the great modern classics of mysticism.

*LASKI, MARGHANITA: *Ecstasy* (Cresset Press, 1961)
> An atheist's evaluation of mystical experience.

LEWIS, I. M.: *Ecstatic Religion* (Pelican, 1971)

*MARTIN, P. W.: *Experiment in Depth* (Routledge, 1955)
> Subtitled 'A study of Jung, Eliot and Toynbee', this is actually an account of ways in which ordinary people may set out to explore 'inner space' with the aid of dreams, waking fantasy, etc., and it concludes that the result will be a recovery of the experimental truth behind all religious traditions.

SUZUKI, D. T.: *Mysticism: Christian and Buddhist* (Allen & Unwin, 1957)

*TART, CHARLES (ED.): *Altered States of Consciousness* (John Wiley, 1969)

Books specially related to the ideas of the Fall, Original Sin, the tension between flesh and spirit and the problem of morality (as dealt with in my Chapter 8).

CASTLE, E. B.: *Moral Education in Christian Times* (Allen & Unwin, 1958)
> An account of the influence of the idea of original sin on punishment of children.

*COLE, W. G.: *Sex in Christianity and Psychoanalysis* (Allen & Unwin, 1956)
> An account of the essentially neurotic character of most Christian teaching abour sex.

LINDSEY, DAVID: *A Voyage to Arcturus* (Gollancz, 1946)
An astonishing early work of science fiction used to expound a
radically pessimistic view of nature as inherently evil.

ROBINSON, PAUL A.: *The Sexual Radicals* (Temple Smith, 1970)
An introduction to the group of modern writers – William Reich,
Geza Roheim, Herbert Marcuse and Norman O. Brown – who
argue that man's greatest need is liberation from sexual inhibition.

TOWERS, BERNARD, and LEWIS, JOHN (EDS.) *Naked Ape or
Homo Sapiens* (Garnstone Press, 1969)
A critique of the efforts of biological writers like Desmond Morris
and Robert Ardrey to explain human behaviour in purely evolutionary terms.

*WILLIAMS, CHARLES: *The Foregiveness of Sins* (Faber, 1950)

*WILLIAMS, N. P.: *Ideas of the Fall and Original Sin* (Longmans Green
& Co. Ltd., 1927)
A classic exposition, with full references to the literature prior to
its publication.

*WILSON, COLIN: *The Outsider* (Gollancz, 1956)
Beyond the Outsider (Barker, 1965)
Wilson's books expound the quest for religious faith as an answer
to the sense of 'existential alienation'. They provide incidently a
good guide to the literature of existentialism. *Beyond the Outsider*
rounds off the quest and contains full references to Wilson's other
works in the series.
See also my own essay 'Love's Coming-of-Age' in *Psychoanalysis
Observed*, Ed. Charles Rycroft (Constable, 1966).

Books concerned with the special claims of Christianity (as dealt with
in the final section of my Chapter 8).

ALLEGRO, JOHN: *The Sacred Mushroom and the Cross* (Hodder &
Stoughton, 1970)

MACMURRAY, JOHN: *The Clue to History* (SCM Press, 1938)

SCHONFIELD, HUGH J.: *The Passover Plot* (Hutchinson, 1965)

TILLICH, PAUL: *Christianity and the Encounter of the World Religions*
(Columbia University Press, 1963)

Books describing the 'Encounter' technique and the Human Potential
Movement.

*FARADAY, ANN: *Dream Power* (to be published by Hodder &
Stoughton, January 1972)

*GUSTAITIS, RASA: *Turning On* (Weidenfeld & Nicolson, 1969)

*HOWARD, JANE: *Please Touch: a Guided Tour of the Human Potential Movement* (McGraw-Hill, 1970)

*JOURARD, SIDNEY M.: *The Transparent Self* (van Nostrand, 1971) *Self-Disclosure* (Wiley, 1971)

LEONARD, GEORGE: *Education and Ecstasy* (Delta Books, 1968)

LOWEN, ALEXANDER: *The Betrayal of the Body* (Collier Books, 1971)

*OTTO, HERBERT A. and MANN, JOHN (EDS.) *Ways of Growth* (Viking, 1968)

*PERLS, FREDERICK: *Gestalt Therapy Verbatim* (Lafayette, California: The Real People Press, 1969) *In and Out of the Garbage Pail* (Real People Press, 1969)

*SCHUTZ, WILLIAM: *Here Comes Everybody* (Harper & Row, 1971)

General books on the problem of religious education.

*COX, EDWIN: *Changing Aims in Religious Education* (Routledge, 1966)
An excellent short introduction to the subject with a full reading list on modern research and thinking in the field.

GREELEY, ANDREW M.: *Religion in the Year 2000* (Sheed & Ward, 1969)
Some speculations about the future of religion.

*HARDING, D. E.: *Religions of the World* (Heinemann Liberal Studies Series, 1966)
A highly recommended concise guide, giving a full reading list of authoritiative works on all the particular religions and on such special subjects as yoga. Taken together with Happold's *Mysticism* it provides a good guide to the basic literature needed for teaching about religion on an ecumenical basis.

Index

Adam and Eve story, 90, 129, 133, 142, 158–65, 167, 168–71, 173, 177, 193

Agnosticism, 3

alienation, 90, 127; and sin and the Fall, 127, 130–42, 162, 164, 193; existential, 132, 135, 136–142, 153–4, 164; diverse usage of term, 138–9; and loss of openness, 168

Allegro, John, and 'sacred mushroom' theory of New Testament, 186, 193

Altered States of Consciousness research, 125

Angel-Makers, The (Taylor), 127

anti-scientific feeling, 39–46, 112

Aristotle, 10

art, symbolic function of, 17–19, 50

Assemblies in schools, 3, 201, 203–4, 214–5

astrology, 17; and the occult, 28–38

astronomy: Galileo's, 11–13, 28, 45, 56; and conflict with religious belief, 11–13, 23, 29

atheism, Comte on, 35, 71

Augustine, St, 159, 165

Azande tribe, and oracle ritual, 9–10, 12, 30, 185

Bach, J. S., 147

Back to Methuselah (Shaw), 167

Bacon, Francis; and 'experimental philosophy', 15, 20, 27, 33–4, 35, 62, 81; on 'the lonely crowd', 51; his proposed revolution, 33–4, 62, 91, 92

Beatles, 'better known than Jesus,' 185

Bhagavad-Gita, 90

Blake, William, 51; on vision of Christ, 80, 173–4; as spiritual ancestor of 'new theology', 91–93; on dualistic view of body and soul, 154–5; his Fall-doctrine, 155, 157–8; on worshipping Satan under name of God or Jesus, 174, 190; on forgiveness, 178; on the 'drop-out' Jesus, 202

Bonhoeffer, Dietrich, 85, 145, 174; and 'religionless' Christianity, 76, 77, 83–4; on humanistic outlook as mankind's coming of age, 83, 175

Brecht, Bertholt, 33, 38, 64

Brophy, Brigid, 73

Brown, Norman O., 167

Buddha, 139, 144, 182, 183, 191, 202

Buddhism, 36, 108, 191, 196, 200; and Fall-concept, 130, 132,